Pro ASP.NET SignalR

Real-Time Communication in
.NET with SignalR 2.1

Keyvan Nayyeri

Darren White

Apress®

Pro ASP.NET SignalR: Real-Time Communication in .NET with SignalR 2.1

ISBN-13 (pbk): 978-1-4302-6319-7

ISBN-13 (electronic): 978-1-4302-6320-3

Managing Director: Welmoed Spahr
Lead Editor: Gwenan Spearing
Technical Reviewer: Robert Swafford
Editorial Board: Steve Anglin, Mark Beckner, Ewan Buckingham, Gary Cornell, Louise Corrigan, Jim DeWolf, Jonathan Gennick, Robert Hutchinson, Michelle Lowman, James Markham, Matthew Moodie, Jeff Olson, Jeffrey Pepper, Douglas Pundick, Ben Renow-Clarke, Dominic Shakeshaft, Gwenan Spearing, Matt Wade, Steve Weiss
Coordinating Editor: Christine Ricketts
Copy Editor: Nancy Sixsmith
Compositor: SPi Global
Indexer: SPi Global
Artist: SPi Global
Cover Designer: Anna Ishchenko

Distributed to the book trade worldwide by Springer Science+Business Media New York, 233 Spring Street, 6th Floor, New York, NY 10013. Phone 1-800-SPRINGER, fax (201) 348-4505, e-mail orders-ny@springer-sbm.com, or visit www.springeronline.com. Apress Media, LLC is a California LLC and the sole member (owner) is Springer Science + Business Media Finance Inc (SSBM Finance Inc). SSBM Finance Inc is a Delaware corporation.

For information on translations, please e-mail rights@apress.com, or visit www.apress.com.

Apress and friends of ED books may be purchased in bulk for academic, corporate, or promotional use. eBook versions and licenses are also available for most titles. For more information, reference our Special Bulk Sales–eBook Licensing web page at www.apress.com/bulk-sales.

Any source code or other supplementary material referenced by the author in this text is available to readers at www.apress.com. For detailed information about how to locate your book's source code, go to www.apress.com/source-code/.

To my parents and sister, whom I haven't seen in years.

—Keyvan

In memory of Kae White, the greatest and most caring mother.

—Darren

Contents at a Glance

Contents

About the Authors

Keyvan Nayyeri is a software engineer with a master of science degree in computer science and a bachelor of science degree in applied mathematics. He has been an active contributor to the .NET community for more than ten years, published various articles about .NET programming, and contributed to several open-source projects.

Keyvan has authored several titles, including *Professional Community Server, Professional Visual Studio Extensibility,* and *Beginning ASP.NET MVC 1.0*. He was also a guest author and technical editor on *Professional Visual Studio 2008*.

Keyvan lives with Titan, his Siberian husky. He is a sports enthusiast and enjoys most of his spare time running and hiking outdoors or playing soccer and tennis. When he is too tired for sports, he can be found at a new restaurant trying new food or at his home reading an exotic book. You can follow him on Twitter @keyvan.

Darren White is a lead software engineer in Dallas, Texas, and has a bachelor of science in computer science from the University of Oklahoma. He is an officer in the North Dallas .NET User Group and is a local user group speaker.

Darren has been working with Microsoft technologies since Visual Basic 3. His primary technical focus is on server-side technologies using C#. In his rare moments of free time, he can be found studying new technologies, mathematics, or French. But his most important time is spent with his wife, Shazia. You can follow him on Twitter @Dowjack.

About the Technical Reviewer

Rob Swafford is a senior developer at Sonoma Partners, LLC, specializing in Microsoft Dynamics CRM and .NET web application development. He has been developing in .NET since the early days of the framework, and has been a Visual Studio user since Visual C++ 6.0. His industry experience spans nearly a decade in a wide range of companies, from small start-ups, state and local government, and multinational corporations. He currently resides in the greater Milwaukee area with his wife Jeanna and two young sons.

Acknowledgments

Writing a book is a difficult task, and at least one of us has experienced this process four times before. This difficulty comes at different levels from different aspects, and not only affects authors' lives and careers but also the people around them. So a book is not only an indicator of the authors' efforts but also of the people around them. Here we want to take a moment to mention some people who helped us finish this book.

First, we want to thank families and friends who supported us during the long writing process and put up with our absences and excuses. Thanks to Keyvan's parents and sister, who have been supporting him from a very long distance and always encouraged him to move forward with his professional life. Also, thanks to Darren's family and wife, Shazia, who supported and encouraged him to get his first book written and published.

We also have to thank our editorial team. Gwenan had a key role in coordinating this project that was faced with several challenges and tolerated our limited time and busy schedules to finally get this book done. Christine made sure that everything was clear and easy to understand and helped us follow a consistent structure. Rob, our technical editor, had a great impact on making sure that all key topics were covered in an easy-to-understand way.

A special thanks from Darren to the great friends and teachers at the University of Oklahoma. Specific thanks go to Sridhar Radhakrishnan, Moshe Gutman, Kyle Abbott, Clay Packard, and John Antonio for the solid technical foundation and growth that has lead his career.

Introduction

When we were contacted by Apress about writing a new book on ASP.NET that targets newer technologies, the first two technologies that came to mind were ASP.NET SignalR and ASP.NET Single Page Applications. We finally decided on ASP.NET SignalR because we believe that it is a great addition to the Microsoft stack of technologies and has a great future. At the same time, we noticed the lack of a good single resource for experienced ASP.NET developers to get started on using this technology, which made it even more important to write this book.

Pro ASP.NET SignalR is the outcome of the work we did in the past few months in collaboration with Apress, our editors, and others who helped us with this process. Our hope is that we have written a good resource for you and that it gives you everything you need to get started with Microsoft ASP.NET SignalR and apply it in practice.

Like any other book or training resource, this book comes with some conventions and assumptions that we had to make to adjust our content for the audience and make it most useful to those who will read it. This introduction section clarifies some of these assumptions and conventions.

Who This Book Is For

As you pick up this book, the first question is whether this is the right book for you. To answer that question, you should know what this book is about. The short answer is that this book is about Microsoft ASP.NET SignalR and serves as a unique resource to get you started with this technology to use it in practice. To achieve that goal, it assumes that you have prior knowledge in some related technologies (shown in the following section).

This book targets intermediate- or professional-level readers who are familiar with the Microsoft stack of technologies for web development as well as basic HTML and JavaScript. With such a background, we teach you how to use Microsoft ASP.NET SignalR with a pragmatic approach. We start with the basic concepts and then move on to more advanced ones, and use practical examples with explanations to make everything easier to understand.

If you want to get started with SignalR and you have the necessary background, this book is for you. If you already know about SignalR and want to advance your knowledge, this book is also for you because more than half of the book is dedicated to advanced topics that most people are not familiar with.

On the other hand, if you are not an experienced .NET developer—especially with ASP.NET, C#, HTML, and JavaScript/jQuery—you might want to start with this book before reading some background information.

Our writing experience tells us that being brief and to the point is important, especially for technical readers who have very limited time and need to keep up with several new technologies. Therefore, this book tries to be brief and cover only what you need. We avoid verbose discussions on background topics and rely on our common agreement for a basic understanding of important background information.

Prerequisites

There are two types of prerequisites you should have before reading this book: technical and tool prerequisites.

For technical prerequisites, you have to be familiar with the following technologies and concepts at a beginning to average level:

- ASP.NET (especially its fundamentals)

- Internet Information Services (IIS)

- JavaScript and jQuery library

- HTML and CSS

- Visual Studio (performing common tasks and operations in Visual Studio is basic)

- Windows Azure (having a background can help with certain chapters)

- iOS and Android programming (having a background can help with certain chapters, even though it is not essential)

For tool prerequisites, you need the following installed on your machine:

- Windows operating system (we recommend Windows 8.1, but certain versions of Windows work as long as they can support Visual Studio 2013)

- Visual Studio 2013 (we use this version, but you can use other versions if they support the features you need)

- Fiddler (a free HTTP debugging tool by Telerik used for diagnosis and tracing of applications)

- Google Chrome, Internet Explorer, or Firefox (one or more of these browsers are needed for testing the code samples)

How This Book Is Structured

Our recommendation is to read all the chapters of this book in order. We tried to keep the book short so this can be achieved in a reasonable amount of time. If you want to skip certain topics, however, the chapters are independent from each other, so you can start reading individual chapters if you have enough understanding of the topics covered.

The first two chapters of the book are introductory to get you started. The next two chapters target the most fundamental concepts needed to implement ASP.NET SignalR applications. The four chapters that come next primarily focus on a major topic about ASP.NET SignalR development. The last two chapters are two case studies to show all the concepts in two examples.

Here is a short overview of the chapters in this book:

- Chapter 1: A quick introduction to real-time web development, some general concepts, and ASP.NET SignalR's history

- Chapter 2: Getting started with ASP.NET SignalR development with some quick examples to demonstrate core concepts

- Chapter 3: Developing SignalR applications with hubs, and related concepts

- Chapter 4: Developing SignalR applications with persistent connections, and related concepts

- Chapter 5: Troubleshooting, debugging, and testing ASP.NET SignalR applications

- Chapter 6: Overview of major clients that support ASP.NET SignalR such as iOS, Android, Windows Desktop, Windows Phone, and others

- Chapter 7: Extending and customizing ASP.NET SignalR's behavior

- Chapter 8: Configuration, security, and scaling aspects of ASP.NET SignalR

- Chapter 9: Case study

- Chapter 10: Second case study

CHAPTER 1

Introduction to the Real-Time Web and ASP.NET SignalR

The Internet is one of the most important inventions in history, and it has changed our lives for the better in many ways. For social creatures such as humans, nothing could be better than a fast method of communication with the world that enables multimedia content delivery with almost no delay.

In its few decades of existence, the Internet has evolved from a basic set of network clusters with simple operations to the foundation of almost everything in our world, providing opportunities to make billions of dollars.

Our mission in this book is to walk you (and other Microsoft web developers with a good background in ASP.NET and JavaScript) through a very recent technology called ASP.NET SignalR. It enables the creation of real-time, asynchronous web applications that are the most modern type of infrastructure for building sites to deliver content from servers to clients in real time and remove any latency. Clients sit on a page on your site and receive the newest updates in real time with no need to click anything or refresh the page. For example, on Facebook when somebody leaves a comment or likes one of your photos, you do not need to refresh the page to see the notification pop up and the red counter being updated. ASP.NET SignalR provides the foundation to develop such features.

This chapter gives you some background information on SignalR and how it can help you build modern web sites. The following are the major topics covered in this chapter:

- How the Internet has evolved to where it is today

- Why client-side experience is more important than ever

- Definition of real-time web application development

- Some examples of real-time web application development

- Historical overview of ASP.NET SignalR

- Introduction to ASP.NET SignalR and some of its characteristics

- ASP.NET SignalR architecture

- Overview of different transport options in ASP.NET SignalR

- Main challenges for real-time web development

Evolution of the Internet

The Internet started as a simple set of clusters with some computers connected to perform basic operations. It quickly became a very sophisticated network of servers all around the world that serve hundreds of millions (even billions) of clients.

There have been different kinds of changes on this worldwide network in different domains. In one area, Internet connections became faster and more reliable, enabling users to download and upload larger content so that it is now possible for users to download and upload high–quality multimedia content (e.g., videos) from their mobile Internet connections. It has also opened new doors for content providers and consumers.

In another area, Internet browsers evolved to be very sophisticated, and enabled features to facilitate the creation and delivery of content in more user-friendly ways. For at least a decade, the use of Asynchronous JavaScript and XML (AJAX) technologies has given a smoother user experience to end users, for example.

In a third area, server technologies have evolved to also accommodate browser and connection advancements. New programming languages and platforms have been introduced, along with many libraries that help simplify the process of web application creation for web developers. One of these recent advancements is the support for WebSockets.

All the different trends on the Internet focused on providing a better user experience. We have moved from serving static HTML web pages to dynamic pages that can be updated based on users' actions. We can then use client-side languages (mostly JavaScript) to process certain things on the browser and reduce the need to refresh a web page to get the new content. Currently, there is a more modern approach: real-time delivery of content from servers to clients that is possible by applying server-side technologies in conjunction with JavaScript. This is the area in which SignalR comes into play.

Why the Client-Side Experience Is More Important than Ever

The concept of *user* has become the most important concept in today's Internet. Almost all businesses, regardless of their size, know how important the user experience can be. They have moved their focus to making products, technologies, and software that is intuitive and simple enough to attract almost any user regardless of age, gender, cultural background, and so on.

An important part of the user experience is the speed of delivering content. Traditionally, the Internet was a set of web pages served on servers and received by clients. These pages included many static pages that could not react dynamically to users' actions and dynamic pages that could render a dynamic content based on the inputs provided by users. Users had to send their actions to servers or request a particular Uniform Resource Locator (URL) from the server to receive HTML content. This was a very simple model and lacked the sophistication seen in modern web sites.

As the user experience became more important, web designers and developers came up with the idea of using JavaScript and XML in conjunction with partial content rendering on the servers to take advantage of the concept of AJAX. It would provide a smoother experience to users and deliver content to these users more quickly.

In the past few years, however, this approach wasn't good enough for the modern needs of the Internet. Even with AJAX, there was often a wait for users' actions to update a portion of the page and deliver the content, so the speed of content delivery was very dependent on the speed of the users' interactions.

This issue led web developers and designers to start thinking about sending the content from servers to clients as it arrives in real time, or at least invent mechanisms that simulate such a behavior. This process is called *real–time web application development*.

Real–Time Web Application Development

The term *real-time software* refers to the type of software that is subject to a soft or hard time constraint. By the nature of its business domain, this type of software must complete its processing within a particular timeframe. This time constraint can be strict to make it hard real-time software or flexible to make it soft real-time software. For example, aerospace software can be hard real-time software because it must finish its execution within a defined time interval; otherwise, operations might fail, and people's lives can be in danger. In contrast, video players can be soft real-time software because it is not mission-critical if the processing does not finish on time (although it is important to process the videos in time to display them to users).

Although real-time software and real-time computing have been around for a long time, the term *real-time web* is relatively new. This concept, which was introduced in the past few years, focuses on real-time delivery of content to clients as soon as it is available.

The real-time web is similar to soft real-time software because the delivery of content from the information source to consumers should occur in a short period of time to be considered real time (from a few milliseconds up to 1 second).

The real-time web was embraced by social networks and their need to update users with frequent status updates and content changes by friends and peers. Facebook and Twitter were among the first major sites on the Internet that pioneered in this area and implemented real-time web features.

Although the real-time web is primarily applied to soft and small updates to clients with short status updates, news headlines, and similar content, it is now also used for other purposes, such as real-time searching (more details to come in the next section). Google incorporated such features to provide real-time updates to its search results as they become available.

Examples of Real–Time Web Application Development

This section focuses on showcasing a few common examples of the real-time web to describe it and the applications it can have. One common misbelief about real–time web development technologies including SignalR is that they are designed mainly for building chat applications. The examples shown here correct this by describing different practical applications for these technologies.

Facebook

The real–time notification feature on Facebook (see Figure 1-1) is one of the best examples of the real-time web, and Facebook is a pioneer in this area. If you have a Facebook account, you have noticed the red color counter of new notifications being increased in real time while a toast appears in the bottom-left corner of new actions.

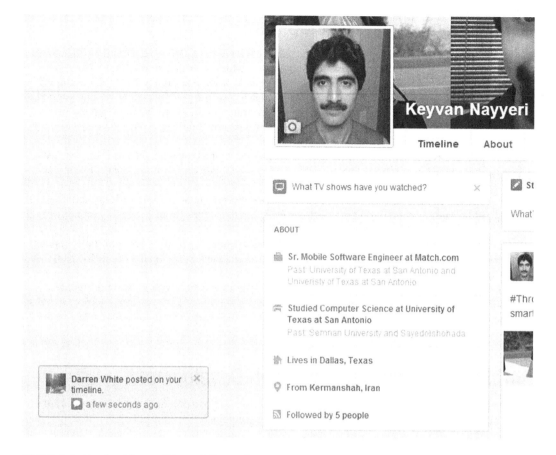

Figure 1-1. *Facebook's use of the real-time web*

Whenever there is a new like, comment, post, or other type of notification associated with your account, you see a notification toast in the bottom that appears and disappears after a few seconds. At the same time, the counter of new notifications in red is updated.

Facebook is using a combination of WebSockets and long polling to implement this feature. (These approaches are discussed in more detail later in this chapter.)

Note that Facebook uses a similar asynchronous mechanism to implement its chat system (in fact, Facebook chat and real-time notifications were rolled out together in early 2008). Facebook later enhanced its real-time features to include real-time updates to different parts of the site, such as new comments added to posts that appear in real time to users.

Such a sophisticated and reliable real–time web implementation for Facebook has an important value for its business. With the large number of users and high demand for the huge content provided by hundreds of millions of active users, the user experience is significantly improved by integrating such a real–time web ecosystem.

Technology-wise, Facebook has employed a very sophisticated custom implementation to achieve its unique business goals for the real-time web that relies on pushing the content from servers to clients. Facebook had to consider several factors, such as the large number of active publishers as well as consumers, along with keeping its data centers in sync and reducing the latency for users who are scattered throughout the world.

Twitter

Another popular social network using quick status updates is Twitter, which receives frequent updates from its users. Each user can then have many followers who want the most recent updates from that user and other users they are following. The speed of delivering these short status updates to clients is of vital importance for Twitter's business because it can improve the user experience significantly. Just imagine how frustrated Twitter users would be if they had to refresh their Twitter feed every time they wanted a new update.

Twitter employs a real-time web infrastructure to display the most recent updates to users in real time (see Figure 1-2). This implementation is Twitter's custom implementation that fits its needs. As new updates arrive in the user's feed or search results, the user interface is updated with the counter of new updates that ask the user to click the counter link to fetch the most recent updates with an AJAX call (rather than refreshing the whole page).

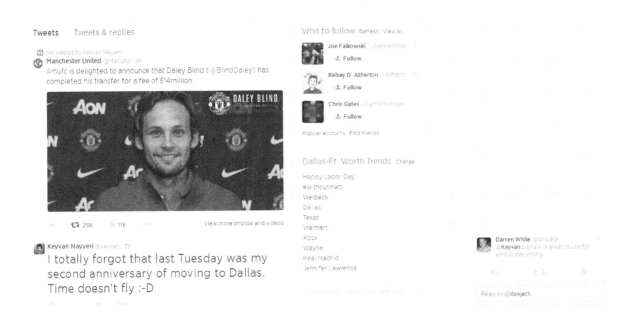

Figure 1-2. *Twitter's use of the real-time web*

Google Search

With the very fast pace of content production on the Internet, especially for trending topics, new articles and news items become available very quickly. Google uses its powerful indexing tools to capture these updates quickly. With the traditional user interface structure, after a user searched for a particular keyword, the results were presented from the original state of content repository in the Google database. To provide a better user experience, Google offered real-time search result updates in which search results were updated as new items became available, and users could see the most recent items.

Although Google was using its own real-time web implementation for real-time search results, it closed this feature in 2011 because the deal with Twitter expired for displaying the latest tweets in real time.

Google Docs

Another great example of the power of the real-time web and its impact is Google Docs, in which users have access to an online version of document-editing software for word processing, spreadsheets, and slides. Not only can users edit their own documents with the great features provided but they also can share their documents with others. The real power of the real-time web shines here: the updates made by one user are reflected in other users' displays in real time, so multiple parties from different locations are allowed to collaborate on writing and editing documents (see Figure 1-3).

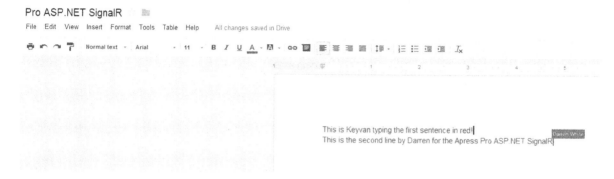

Figure 1-3. *Google Docs relies on the real-time web for its unique collaboration features*

Google Docs is a good example of how the real-time web can change the game for Internet web sites. Google Docs uses a custom and sophisticated Google implementation to achieve its goals. It treats documents as a collection of change sets instead of the traditional monolithic view. Google engineers can distribute these change sets to individual users in real time.

JabbR

Now that you have seen some famous examples of the real-time web, you should also know about some ASP.NET SignalR examples. One of the best known SignalR web sites on the Internet is JabbR (see Figure 1-4). This online chat room and discussion service is implemented by the same developers as those who founded SignalR. It has become a very prominent location for software developers to host their group chats and discuss various topics, such as live coverage of their opinions on developer conferences and similar events.

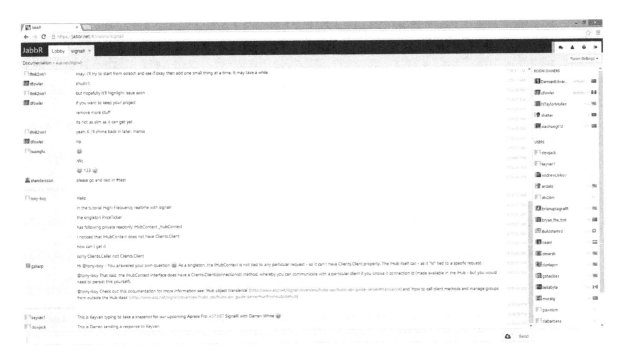

Figure 1-4. JabbR is a prominent SignalR chatroom application

JabbR, which is available at http://jabbr.net, is fully implemented with the Microsoft stack of technologies, including ASP.NET MVC and ASP.NET SignalR. The good news is that it is an open-source project, and its source code is available on GitHub at http://github.com/JabbR. Developers contribute to this project on a daily basis to make it more mature.

JabbR employs a modern and responsive web design to render well on all the desktop and mobile devices, and it can be hosted on its own or in the cloud on Windows Azure or AppHarbor.

JabbR uses SignalR to deliver the chat and related multimedia content from servers to clients in real time. The chat system's application is the most basic and common example of the real-time web that can be mistakenly treated as the only application of the real-time web. In fact, if you perform a quick search on Google or Bing for ASP.NET SignalR examples, the majority of results are chat applications. This book even uses some chat application examples because they are a good and way to illustrate the concepts of the real-time web and ASP.NET SignalR.

ShootR

We conclude our examples with another ASP.NET SignalR web site that is a little different from other examples because it is an online collaborative game. ShootR (shown in Figure 1-5) is the name of an online game available at http://shootr.signalr.net. It is an open-source project; its source code is available on GitHub as well (https://github.com/ntaylormullen/shootr).

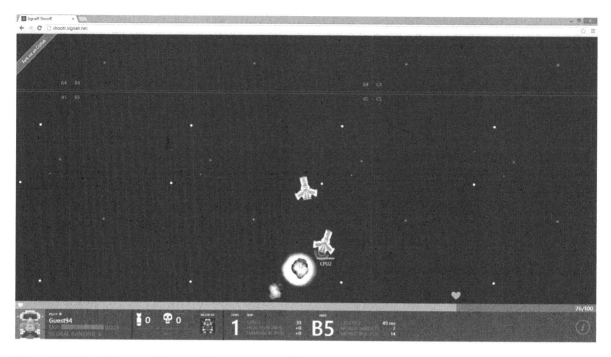

Figure 1-5. ShootR is an online spaceship game powered by ASP.NET SignalR

ShootR uses modern HTML, CSS, and JavaScript elements with ASP.NET SignalR to provide a real-time spaceship game. The role of ASP.NET SignalR is to deliver the location and status of the game canvas for the automated computer user and other human users' spaceships to the current player (and other players) in real time. Reliable delivery of content and a good experience for game players are the goals of this game.

History of ASP.NET SignalR

There was an increasing need for real-time web development features for web developers, especially Microsoft ASP.NET developers. Damian Edwards (a program manager on the Microsoft ASP.NET team) was motivated to build a solution for this common problem on Microsoft technologies. SignalR was the answer that started as an open-source project and attracted some other developers as well. Later on, David Fowler (software developer on the Microsoft ASP.NET team) took a serious role in developing this project and has continued to do so.

Although SignalR started as an open-source project, it had good community support from Microsoft, and this support was completed when Microsoft decided to bundle this open-source project as part of its ASP.NET stack and call it ASP.NET SignalR.

ASP.NET SignalR is still truly open source and is licensed under an Apache 2.0 license. You can download the source code for ASP.NET SignalR from GitHub at `http://github.com/SignalR/SignalR` and also contribute to this project. ASP.NET SignalR also has its own official home page on the Microsoft ASP.NET web site at `http://www.asp.net/signalr`. Like many other libraries and products available to Microsoft developers, ASP.NET SignalR is also available through NuGet at `http://nuget.org/packages/Microsoft.AspNet.SignalR`.

SignalR has had a very active life in its short existence, and several minor and major versions have been released. Version 2.1 is now available, and this book is based on it. ASP.NET SignalR has matured significantly in these versions and is now in a very stable and practical state.

With each release, ASP.NET SignalR has been through major and minor changes in features as well as bug fixes and better integration with latest additions to the .NET Framework, resulting in progressive integration with OWIN and a better error-handling and diagnosis mechanism. One of the most useful major changes in versions 2.x is the capability to target a particular user for sending messages to clients.

What Is ASP.NET SignalR?

So what is ASP.NET SignalR after all? Actually, it is nothing but a library on top of the .NET Framework and jQuery (or other client-side technologies). In other words, ASP.NET SignalR is work done by some developers to facilitate a job to create real-time web applications by providing application programming interfaces (APIs) that are ready to be used out of the box.

You can write your own implementation for real-time web development on top of the .NET Framework based on your needs and call it SignalR Prime, KeyvanR, or APressR, but SignalR is a mature library that is designed to address almost any common scenario in real-time web development. Therefore, it is more economical, efficient, and risk free to apply SignalR for your real-time web applications than it is to reinvent the wheel.

With SignalR, you can build real-time web applications that consist of server and client sides. ASP.NET SignalR provides both parts out of the box by offering libraries that can be integrated into your projects.

Although its name might imply that SignalR is available only in the context of web applications, you can self-host SignalR servers and consume the server data in the context of a Windows desktop application or a native mobile application (as discussed later). However, most people use SignalR in the context of web applications, and that topic is the focus of most chapters of this book. (Chapter 6 is dedicated to using SignalR outside the web context for different types of clients.) The good news is that the client-side uses of server components in ASP.NET SignalR are very similar to each other, so knowing the JavaScript concepts makes it relatively easy to adopt any other type of client.

To summarize, ASP.NET SignalR is a set of libraries for the .NET Framework, JavaScript/jQuery, iOS, and other platforms. It provides server and client implementations for building real-time web applications. SignalR simplifies real-time development by hiding implementation details and the supporting infrastructure. It is also efficient and extensible, ready to be used for a wide range of applications in industry and enterprise.

SignalR comes with three main characteristics:

- **SignalR is flexible**: It provides different layers of tools to allow developers to build their custom applications. On one hand, ASP.NET SignalR offers hubs (see Chapter 3), which are a simple and quick way to build a real-time web application and hide some of the details to facilitate the job of web developers. On the other hand, persistent connections (see Chapter 4) are a more fundamental tool for building applications that give more flexibility and power to developers, yet require more effort to handle certain things that are taken care of by hubs.

- **SignalR is extensible**: Many components in ASP.NET SignalR are designed to be easily replaced by a custom implementation if necessary. ASP.NET SignalR has integrated dependency injection into its internal structure to offer such a good level of extensibility. You usually do not need to replace these components, but it is a straightforward task if you do (see Chapter 7).

- **SignalR is scalable**: ASP.NET SignalR provides some built-in mechanisms to enable web developers to scale it up and out easily. Hosting a SignalR server application on multiple servers can introduce a set of common challenges, but these challenges are addressed by providing a set of extensible features in SignalR (see Chapter 8).

Besides these main characteristics, ASP.NET SignalR provides a set of features for common problems that might show up for any Microsoft ASP.NET developer. SignalR offers a good set of debugging and tracing features (see Chapter 5). Likewise, SignalR is easy to configure and secure to use (see Chapter 8). Cloud hosting is a hot topic in today's software, and Windows Azure is the popular option for Microsoft developers for cloud hosting (see Chapter 10).

ASP.NET SignalR Architecture

As discussed in the last section, ASP.NET SignalR is a set of different libraries for different platforms. Although the server side of SignalR is bound to the .NET Framework or Mono (the open-source Linux implementation of the .NET Framework), the client libraries are very independent and can be implemented for any platform. At a high level, ASP.NET SignalR as a technology consists of a server implementation that serves a set of various types of clients hosted on different platforms (see Figure 1-6).

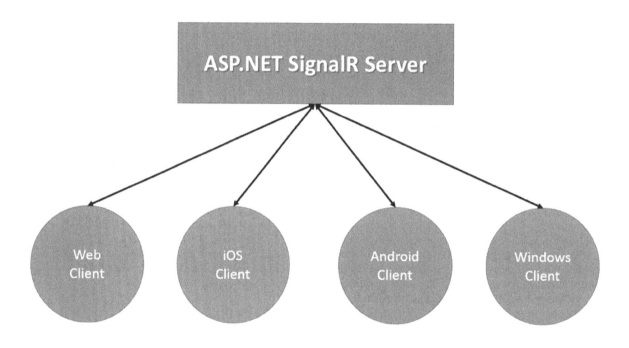

Figure 1-6. *High-level view of ASP.NET SignalR as a technology*

With this background, when we talk about *architecture*, we refer to the architecture of the server side of ASP.NET SignalR because the general high-level architecture for the whole SignalR technology is a server-client architecture. Client libraries would not have a unified architecture *per se*, although all these clients need to have some kind of support for transports to connect to the server-side transports discussed later in this chapter.

But the server side of the SignalR library consists of a stacked architecture (Figure 1-7) that uses one of the four common transport options discussed in the next section. Depending on the network infrastructure and availability, one of these four transports is used in order of priority. If hub APIs are used, they are the points of connection for clients to simplify the logic and call the underlying persistent connection APIs in SignalR. If persistent connection APIs are used directly, developers need to take care of receiving the raw data from clients and extracting metadata to respond to these requests.

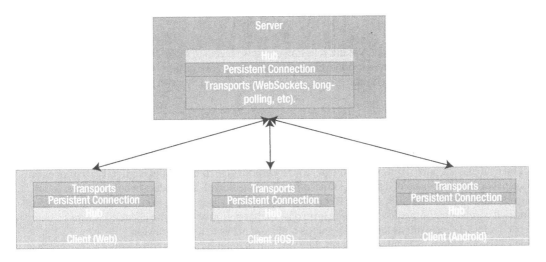

Figure 1-7. ASP.NET SignalR server architecture

Main Challenges for Real–Time Web Development

HTTP is a stateless protocol that does not provide any callback mechanism for servers and clients. This is the main challenge for real–time web development when we want to push information from servers to clients whenever it arrives. Most efforts of building real–time web development frameworks are dedicated to tackling this challenge.

To solve this problem, different techniques are used to put the content from server(s) on client(s). These techniques can be categorized into two groups:

- **Traditional approaches**: Rely mostly on using hacks and tricks to achieve this goal. These approaches are built based on the concept of long-held HTTP connections between servers and clients that are also known as *Comet*.

- **Modern approaches:** Rely on new features introduced in HTML5.

Four transport options that fall into these two categories are discussed in the next section: long polling, forever frame, server-sent events, and WebSockets.

The other related challenge for real–time web development is the resource use caused by traditional approaches (i.e., Comet) because long-held HTTP connections can drain the battery power on mobile devices and consume other resources on the client and server. Therefore, the implementations of Comet approaches are critical for maximum efficiency.

Although such a challenge exists for traditional Comet approaches, newer approaches based on HTML5 also have limitations with the current state of the Internet. For example, the use of WebSockets is dependent on hardware and software support between client and server. So the whole network infrastructure between client and server must support WebSockets, and the software infrastructure in the hosting operating system must also support them at the same time. Currently, WebSockets is a supported feature only in Windows Server 2012.

The last challenge for real–time web development is to implement hard real time. Assuming that all these challenges are resolved, content from server to client has to be delivered in a very short period of time (usually less than 1 second) to imply a real-time behavior. Such a constraint mandates developers to build lightweight and efficient implementations.

Transport Options

As discussed in the previous sections, ASP.NET SignalR relies on transport layers to make communication possible between client(s) and server(s). These four transport layers are categorized in two groups: Comet approaches and modern HTML5 approaches. Each transport option is discussed in turn, followed by a discussion of how SignalR implements these transport layers.

Long Polling

This famous Comet approach is one of the most common ways to achieve real–time web development in today's Internet. It relies on using JavaScript (or other technologies and techniques) to make a lightweight HTTP connection to a server and keep it open for a period of time (e.g., 30 seconds). In this interval, if new data becomes available on the server, it puts the data in the currently open HTTP connection and then closes it. The client receives this data and opens a new long poll connection immediately. If there is no data in that period of time, the client establishes a new long poll connection and continues this as long as the page is open and active in a web browser.

Long polling follows this simple model and reduces the overhead of opening several connections to servers that could be introduced by an interval polling approach. Interval polling is the traditional approach in which the server is checked at regular intervals (e.g., every 10 seconds) for new content. This approach is not efficient; opening and closing HTTP connections to web servers create overhead. Long polling tries to reduce this overhead.

Forever Frame

Another Comet approach that is less common than long polling is *Forever Frame* (also known as *hidden iframe*), which is an approach specific to Internet Explorer. In this approach, a hidden iframe element is attached to each web page that is kept open for the whole duration of the request (the period of time that a user stays on the page). As data becomes available on the server, it is filled with JavaScript codes in a stacked manner, and because browsers execute these scripts in order, they can provide the desired behavior needed.

Server-Sent Event

This approach is a modern HTML5 transport that enables web browsers to receive events from servers through an HTTP connection.

The main limitation of server-sent events (like any other approach based on HTML5) is browser support. Although the most recent versions of common browsers support server-sent events, Internet Explorer does not support them, which leaves a big gap for those interested in using these events for real-time web development.

WebSockets

The other HTML5 approach that has better browser support is WebSockets, which provides two-way communication channels over a TCP connection. WebSockets is not limited to HTTP, although it can also be used in that context.

The use of WebSockets is dependent on the support by the underlying operating system (among Microsoft server technologies, only Windows Server 2012 supports them, although it is also available on Windows 8 and 8.1) and the whole network infrastructure between the client and server. Of course, browser support is also needed to take advantage of WebSockets, and recent versions of most common web browsers support it.

How ASP.NET SignalR Uses Transports

The ASP.NET SignalR JavaScript library has a built-in mechanism that switches between approaches in priority based on their availability. Unless you specify one or more transport options to be used, the following order of options is considered:

1. WebSockets

2. Server-sent event

3. Forever Frame

4. Long polling

Summary

This chapter was a quick introduction to real-time web development and SignalR. You saw how SignalR fits into the big picture of rich user experience and real-time applications in general, and you had a brief look at its architecture and the challenges it faces.

In the next chapter, you get your feet wet by implementing a basic example with ASP.NET SignalR to become familiar with fundamental concepts and the development process.

CHAPTER 2

Overview of SignalR

When learning a brand-new code library, you might initially think that it is great and you will use it for every project going forward. Although sometimes the new library will work in your latest project, it is probably not the best solution. This chapter discusses the technologies on which ASP.NET SignalR is built. These are the technologies that enable SignalR to support a wide range of server and client platforms. Because you'll be eager to try SignalR, you will write your first SignalR application. After creating the first application, the focus is on when it is best to use SignalR.

To get even more out of SignalR, we go over what you can customize, extend, and scale to fit your project needs. But with all good things there are limitations, and we discuss a few of SignalR's limitations, too.

In summary, the following topics are discussed in this chapter:

- Technologies behind SignalR

- Supported server and client platforms

- Getting started with SignalR

- When to use SignalR

- Extensibility of SignalR

- Limitations of SignalR

Technologies Behind SignalR

There are a few technologies that stand out in SignalR that give it the strength and flexibility that make real-time web applications easy. These technologies help applications be flexible so they are not dependent on a specific host. They also make it easy to connect to a wide number of clients without having to worry about the client-specific transports. As well, these technologies allow your application to be highly customizable and to scale.

Open Web Interface for .NET (OWIN)

Many developers know that most ASP.NET projects are built with a dependency on the System.Web assembly that was built primarily for Internet Information Services (IIS). The first break away from the dependency to System.Web came with the release of Web API in 2012. With the System.Web dependency removed, developers could self-host Web API much more easily, which created a new issue in which there could be multiple hosted implementations (Web API, static pages, MVC, and others), all running in their own process with separate hosts. To handle this problem, web developers came up with a common interface that enables decoupling of the web applications from web servers. This common interface is OWIN, which enforces a structure and process for the HTTP requests and responses. The OWIN interface is very simple (see Listing 2-1).

Listing 2-1. OWIN Interface

```
Func<IDictionary<string, object>, Task>
```

The latest OWIN specifications can be found at http://www.owin.org/spec/owin-1.0.0.html, but the interface is the important part. The interface is a function that takes an IDictionary object that contains the environment variables and returns a task once the function is finished.

The environment variables dictionary stores information about the request, the response, and any relevant server state. There is a set of variables that is required to be populated within the dictionary during an evaluation of the function. The server is required to provide body streams and header collections for the request and response. The OWIN application is responsible for populating the response variables in the dictionary for the response data. SignalR implements the OWIN interface, allowing it to be hosted as middleware by any host that implements the OWIN interface with compatible a framework.

Connection Transports

SignalR provides four connection transports: Web Sockets, Server Sent Events, Forever Frame, and long polling. These transports provide key technology elements that make real-time or near real-time connections possible. The most desirable transport is Web Sockets, which provides real-time communication through a full-duplex socket. The other transport technologies can provide only near real-time communication because of transport limitations. Of these transports Server Sent Events is the closest to real time, followed by Forever Frame and then long polling. All the transports are part of a fallback mechanism that automatically provides the best connection by starting with the most desirable connection and falling back until an appropriate one is located.

Dependency Resolver

In SignalR there is a dependency resolver that provides a great deal of customization and flexibility. At the root of the dependency resolver is an object container with specialized logic. The container implements Inversion of Control (IoC) by the container controlling the dependencies of any object requested. This means the container has control of what dependent objects are resolved for a class instead of the class controlling its own internal dependencies. To explain how the dependency resolver works by using an IoC container, we'll go over an IoC example with dependency injection.

Inversion of Control

To understand the IoC, look at the code in Listing 2-2, which has the dependencies defined inside the class that we cannot change. This is a common pattern used by many developers that forces hard dependencies on internal classes.

Listing 2-2. Example of Code with Internal Dependencies on Other Classes

```
public class EmailAlertService
{
    public void SendAlert()
    {
        //Send Alert
    }
}

public class AlertSystem
{
    private EmailAlertService _alertService;
    public AlertSystem()
```

```
    {
        _alertService = new EmailAlertService();
    }
    public void ThresholdExceeded()
    {
        _alertService.SendAlert();
    }
}
```

If you look at the `AlertSystem` class, you see that there is a dependency on the `EmailAlertService` class that is hidden from consumers of the `AlertSystem` class. In other words, the dependency is not exposed publicly, so there is a tight coupling between `AlertSystem` and `EmailAlertService`. It might not look bad at first, but `AlertSystem` is restricted to sending only email alerts and cannot be unit tested very easily.

So for the AlertSystem class, we want to implement the IoC technique so that the control of internal dependencies is inverted to the consuming class. There are a few ways to invert control, but the most popular is by using a dependency injection pattern.

In dependency injection, a class provides a mechanism for the consuming classes to provide the internal dependencies. There are three types of dependency injection: constructor injection, property injection, and interface injection. Constructor injection is the most common and is used in SignalR.

Constructor injection has several benefits. First, any consuming class knows exactly what dependencies are needed to create the instance. Second, once the instance is created, all the required dependencies have been provided. Listing 2-3 shows an example of the constructor injection for the `AlertSystem` class.

Listing 2-3. Example of Class that Allows Constructor Dependency Injection

```
public class AlertSystem
{
    private IAlertService _alertService;
    public AlertSystem(IAlertService alertService)
    {
        _alertService = alertService;
    }
    public void ThresholdExceeded()
    {
        _alertService.SendAlert();
    }
}
```

Using IoC, we can expose internal dependencies to consuming classes. But now that we have access to internal dependencies, we need a way to control how they are used.

Inversion of Control Container

The Inversion of Control container (IoC container) controls registering, locating, and the lifetime of objects inside of it. Depending on the IoC container, it can also provide additional functionality.

To make the container aware of the objects that it is responsible for, you need to register the objects, which can be done by convention or configuration. One example of convention registration is registering any class that implements an interface with a similar name as the interface. For example, it could be a `DBAlerter` class that implements the `IAlerter` interface. Configuration registrations can generally be done in a configuration file or programmatically. An example of a programmatic registration is shown in Listing 2-4.

Listing 2-4. Configuration Registration Example

```
container.RegisterType<IAlerter,DBAlerter>();
```

Once an object has been registered in the container, there are various methods to retrieve that object. It can be retrieved by explicitly requesting (resolving) the object or by being an injected dependency of a requested object. In Listing 2-5, an object is being explicitly requested by having the container resolve that interface. Containers can also resolve objects automatically for you if they are part of a dependency chain, which typically occurs when an object is being requested that has dependencies in its constructor. If the container has those dependencies registered, it resolves them.

Listing 2-5. Resolving Objects from a Container

```
IAlerter alerter = container.Resolve<IAlerter>();
```

Every object in the container has a lifetime. The type of supported lifetimes varies depending on the container. For example, you may want the same object, such as a configuration class, to be returned on every request. To accomplish this, the object is registered as a `Singleton`. There are also times when you want a new instance of an object every time, such as a new `Controller` for a request. This type of lifetime and others can be registered on a per-object basis. When you register objects in the container, you define their lifetimes

Dependency Resolver Example

The dependency resolver allows for the replacement of most of the SignalR components. Some of the base classes such as `PersistentConnection` use the service locator pattern to resolve its dependencies.

SERVICE LOCATOR PATTERN

SignalR uses a weakly typed service locator pattern in a lot of the core classes. This pattern allows a locator object to be injected into a class via the constructor, which calls the `Resolve` method on the locator to acquire dependent objects.

As an example, in Listing 2-6 the dependency resolver is configured to use our implementation of `IJsonSerializer` for classes that derive from the `PersistentConnection` because the type is resolved from the dependency resolver.

Listing 2-6. Example of Overriding IJsonSerializer in the Dependency Resolver

```
public class MyJsonSerializer : IJsonSerializer
{
    //logic removed for simplicity
}

protected void ConfigureTypes()
{
    GlobalHost.DependencyResolver.Register(typeof(IJsonSerializer), () => new MyJsonSerializer());
}
```

This is a very powerful technology enables us to customize SignalR applications very specifically.

Task Parallel Library

The task parallel library is a set of APIs that are part of.NET Framework 4.0/4.5. These APIs help provide a simple but powerful way to add parallelism to programs, which is accomplished by abstracting the difficulties of concurrent threading into tasks controlled by a scheduler. In .NET 4.5, the Async and Await keywords were added to simplify the code even more for parallelism.

With the task parallel library, SignalR can utilize resources more efficiently. A lot of the code is written so that returns a Task; the scheduler can then optimize the code more efficiently for parallelism.

With the use of the Async and Await keywords, the SignalR code is more efficient by being able to provide more asynchronous methods. These asynchronous methods allow the scheduler to switch to other work while these methods are awaiting expensive operations such as network input/output (I/O).

These APIs provide a key functionality that allows SignalR to scale and work more efficiently.

Message Backplanes

As your application scales, you have two options: to scale up or scale out. Scaling up is when you improve or upgrade the components in a system that is running the application. This type of scaling provides only a little bit of improvement, so you also have to scale out. Scaling out is when the application is run on many computers. To scale out, the hosts need to communicate with each other, which is done with a message backplane.

A message backplane is a specialized application that is built specifically to transport messages between systems using a defined API interface. The message backplane provides a few characteristics that help applications excel in scaling out.

The first characteristic is a central routing channel for communication between all the applications. Without this central routing channel, as the number of application servers increases, the complexity of connecting all the application servers to each other increases at a quadratic rate. But this is all simplified for the application because it has to know only the address of the message backplane; the message backplane takes care of delivering the message.

The second characteristic of the message backplane is the asynchronicity of message sending. The originating application just has to send the message to the message backplane and can return back to its processing. Now that the message is in the message backplane, it is its responsibility to deliver the message to all the intended recipients.

Another characteristic of the message backplane is a common message schema. All backplane consumers have an agreed-on message schema that allows them to communicate without involving complex interface logic that is likely to change as new or updated software is used.

SignalR supports a number of backplane options and is explained in more detail later in this chapter and in Chapter 9.

Supported Server Platforms and Clients

As mentioned earlier, SignalR is very flexible, so there are numerous choices for the server and client platforms. Although the supported server platforms are generally Microsoft based, other operating systems such as Linux are available by using the Mono Framework. The clients range from current web browsers to .NET clients to iOS and Android. iOS and Android have a dependency on a customized version of the Mono Framework if using the Xamarin tools. There also is an SDK for Android that does not require the Mono Framework, but it has limited capabilities.

Server Platforms

The supported server operating systems are the following:

- Windows Server 2012 R2
- Windows Server 2012
- Windows Server 2008 R2
- Windows Server 2008
- Windows 8
- Windows 7
- Windows Azure
- Linux

▓ **Note** Again, supporting Linux requires compiling the SignalR assemblies using Mono.

Client Platforms

The number of client platforms that SignalR supports is pretty vast, thanks to the browsers that support JavaScript. The following list shows the supported clients (there may be many more that are not officially supported):

- Web browsers
  - Internet Explorer 8+
  - Google Chrome
  - Firefox
  - Safari
  - Opera
- .NET 4.5 and 4.0 clients
- Windows RT
- Windows Phone 8
- Silverlight 5
- Android
- iOS

▓ **Note** Android and iOS clients are supported by using customized versions of Mono by Xamarin.

Getting Started with SignalR

Now that we have discussed the technologies on which SignalR is built, it is time to try it. To create the sample applications, you need to have Visual Studio 2012 or later installed and be able to run the server on a platform that supports .NET 4.5. The first thing we show you is NuGet, which is used to get the needed SignalR assemblies into your solution. Next, we focus on creating a sample `PersistentConnection` server and client application.

NuGet

When incorporating third-party dependencies in the past, the usual solution involved downloading the needed assemblies and copying them into the project in a dependency directory. This solution has problems when the assemblies aren't checked in to source control properly, conflict with existing versions already on the local box, or won't be deployed correctly because of bad build setups. To resolve these problems, Visual Studio 2012 and later versions include the NuGet Package Manager.

The NuGet Package Manager allows you to add/update/delete packages that are hosted on an official NuGet feed or other feeds. These packages are then controlled on a solution and project level. NuGet packages provide versioning and dependencies, and you can specify the version that you are downloading when you install. The tool automatically pulls down any dependencies that are needed.

Package Manager Dialog Box

The Package Manager dialog box (see Figure 2-1) is a graphical interface that can be used to search, install, manage, and update packages. Here you can search for the packages that you want to add to your solution/project. Once you find the package you want to install, you can select the projects you want to install to. The Package Manager also enables you to manage packages if there is an installed package that you want to install to more projects or uninstall from projects. Finally, it allows you to update the packages that you have installed to have the latest version that is available.

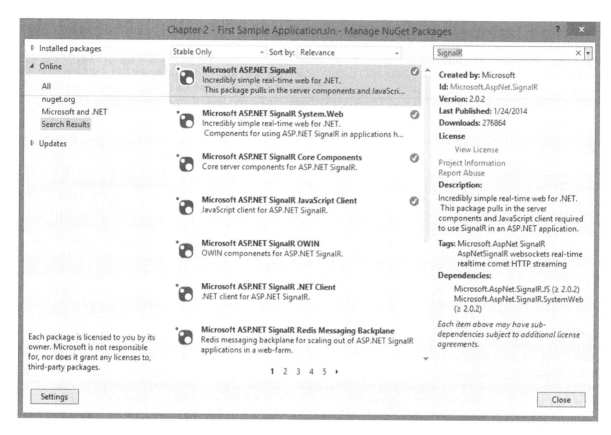

Figure 2-1. *Package Manager dialog box*

Although the Package Manager dialog box is great for simple package management, sometimes more control over packages is needed. You can use the Package Manager Console in these situations.

Package Manager Console

The Package Manager Console (see Figure 2-2) allows you to install/update/remove packages using PowerShell scripts. The level of functionality is very similar to the Package Manager dialog box, but you can be more specific with the PowerShell commands. Specific examples of using the console to gain more functionality include requesting a specific version of a package, requesting prereleased packages, and passing arguments to the package (such as the project name).

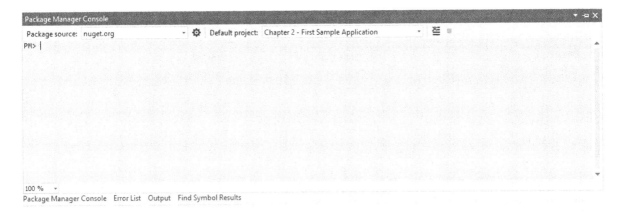

Figure 2-2. Package Manager Console

Important SignalR NuGet Packages

The following list includes some of the main packages for SignalR. The package description is listed, followed by the command to install the package using the NuGet Package Manager Console.

- Server and client package for hosting with IIS and ASP.NET and JavaScript client

```
Install-Package Microsoft.AspNet.SignalR
```

- Server package for hosting SignalR endpoints

```
Install-Package Microsoft.AspNet.SignalR.Core
```

- Client package for .NET SignalR applications

```
Install-Package Microsoft.AspNet.SignalR.Client
```

- Client package for JavaScript SignalR applications

```
Install-Package Microsoft.AspNet.SignalR.JS
```

First Sample Application

Now that you are ready to create the sample application, start Visual Studio 2012. To create a new SignalR application, follow these steps:

1. Choose File ➤ New ➤ Project, as shown in Figure 2-3.

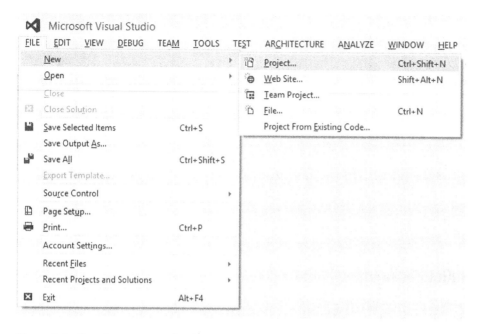

Figure 2-3. *Creating a new application project*

2. Under Installed ➤ Templates ➤ Visual C#, select ASP.NET Web Application in the New Project dialog box (see Figure 2-4).

Figure 2-4. *New Project dialog box*

3. Name the application **Chapter 2 - First Sample Application**.

4. Select OK.

5. Select the MVC template shown in Figure 2-5.

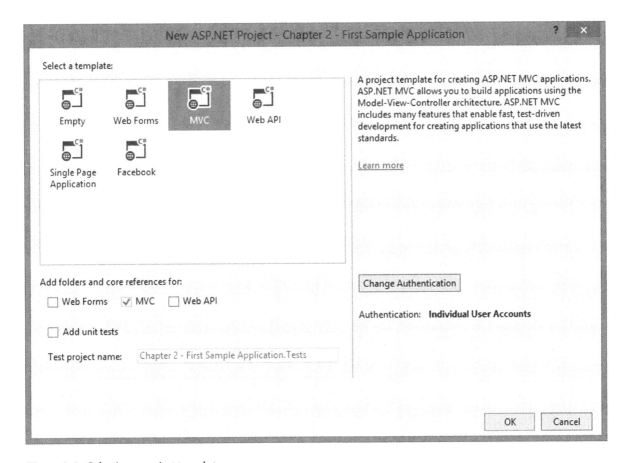

Figure 2-5. *Selecting a project template*

6. Start the Package Manager Console, which is found under Tools ➤ Library Package Manager ➤ Package Manager Console.

7. Inside the Package Manager Console, run the following command to add the SignalR assemblies to the project (see Figure 2-6):

```
Install-Package Microsoft.AspNet.SignalR
```

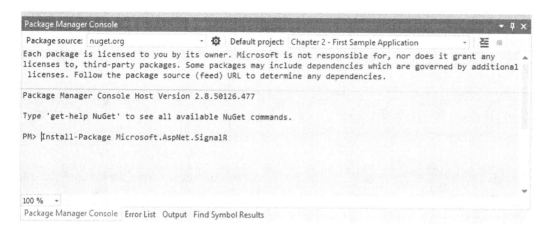

Figure 2-6. *Install of SignalR package*

You see NuGet resolving the dependencies, displaying the licenses, and adding the assemblies to the project in Figures 2-7, 2-8, and 2-9, respectively.

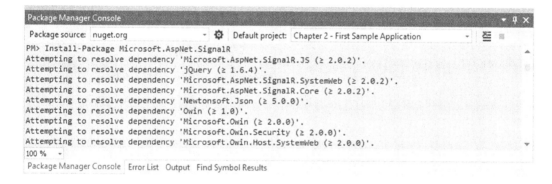

Figure 2-7. *SignalR package dependencies*

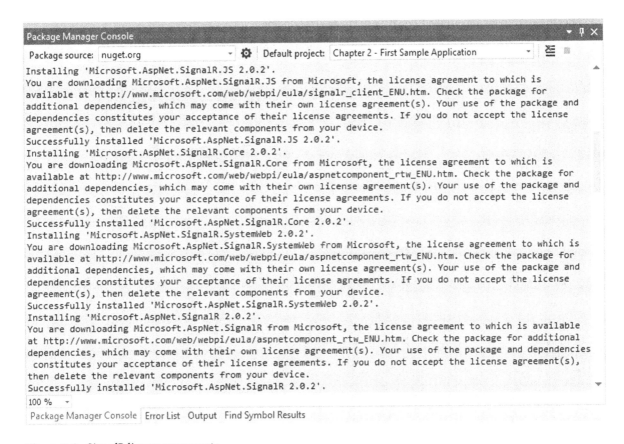

Figure 2-8. *SignalR license agreements*

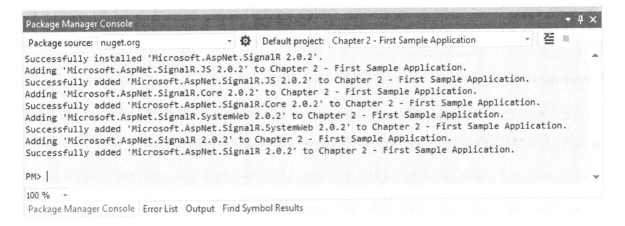

Figure 2-9. *SignalR project reference adds*

After the assemblies are installed, you have to create an endpoint.

8. Right-click on the Chapter 2 - First Sample Application project to add a folder, as shown in Figure 2-10.

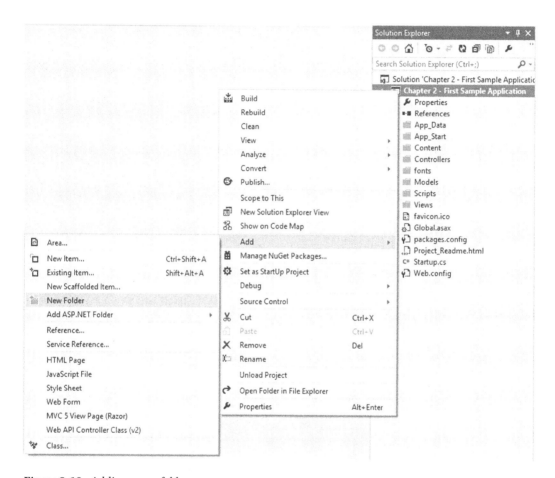

Figure 2-10. *Adding a new folder*

9. Name the new folder `PersistentConnections`.

10. Right-click the `PersistentConnections` folder and add a class, as shown in Figure 2-11.

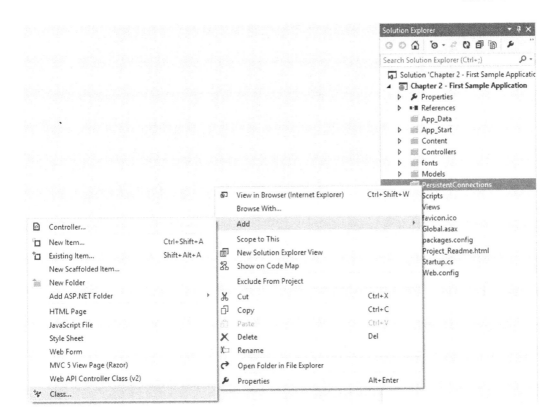

Figure 2-11. *Adding a class*

11. Name this class `SamplePersistentConnection`, as shown in Figure 2-12.

Figure 2-12. *SamplePersistentConnection class name dialog box*

12. Update the SamplePersistentConnection class to what is shown in Listing 2-7. Resolve any missing using statements.

Listing 2-7. SamplePersistentConnection Class

```
public class SamplePersistentConnection : PersistentConnection
{
    protected override Task OnReceived(IRequest request, string connectionId, string data)
    {
        return Connection.Broadcast(data);
    }
}
```

13. Update the `StartUp.cs` class to what is shown in Listing 2-8.

Listing 2-8. StartUp.cs Class

```
public partial class Startup
{
    public void Configuration(IAppBuilder app)
    {
        app.MapSignalR<SamplePersistentConnection>("SamplePC");
        ConfigureAuth(app);
    }
}
```

14. Right-click on the Chapter 2 - First Sample Application project and add an HTML page, as shown in Figure 2-13.

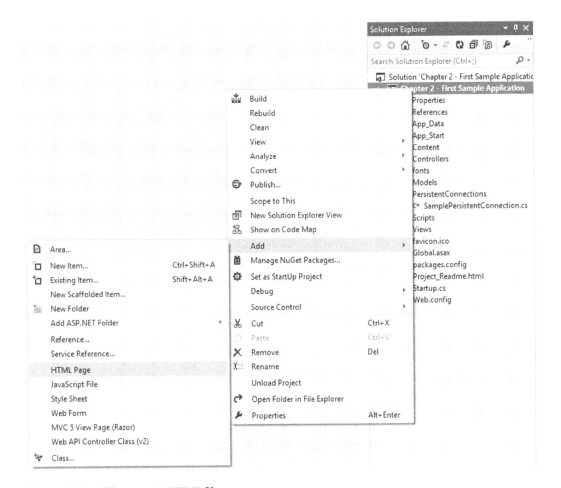

Figure 2-13. *Adding a static HTML file*

15.   Name the HTML file Index (see Figure 2-14).

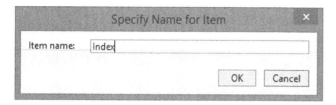

Figure 2-14. *Specifying a name*

16.   Add the scripts in Listing 2-9 to the head section of Index.html with the correct versions
in your project.

Listing 2-9. JavaScript for SignalR Client Application

```
<script src="/scripts/jquery-1.8.2.js" type="text/javascript"></script>
<script src="/scripts/jquery.signalR-1.1.2.js" type="text/javascript"></script>

<script>
    $(function () {
        var connection = $.connection('/SamplePC');

        connection.received(function (data) {
            $('#messages').append('<li>' + data + '</li>');
        });

        connection.start().done(function () {
            $("#send").click(function () {
                connection.send($('#name').val() + ': ' +$('#message').val());
            });
        });

    });
</script>
```

17.   Add the HTML content in Listing 2-10 to the body section of Index.html.

Listing 2-10. HTML for SignalR client Application

```
<label>Name: </label>
<input id="name" /><br />
<input id="message" />
<button id="send" >Send</button>        <ul id="messages"></ul>
```

18.   Press F5 to start the server.

■ **Note** If you get a missing reference to `Microsoft.Owin` or `Microsoft.Owin.Security` when you run the project, your MVC template may be out of date. You can correct these errors by running `Install-Package Microsoft.Owin` and `Install-Package Microsoft.Owin.Security`, respectively, in the Package Manager Console.

---

19. Go to `http://localhost:####/Index.html`, where #### is the assigned port name.

20. Open up a second browser and enter the URL from step 19.

21. Type a message; it should appear on both browsers (see Figure 2-15).

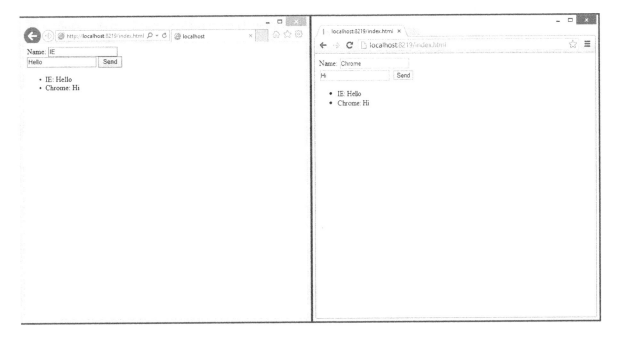

Figure 2-15. *Two sample client applications communicating*

That's all that you have to do to have a fully functioning SignalR application. The next section shows you when SignalR should be used.

When to Use SignalR

Although we can build pages in a web server, these pages are static, and the user has to manually refresh the page to see whether there is new content. This experience can be improved by refreshing at set intervals or updating page content using Ajax calls in response to user actions.

But even this improved experience still feels disconnected, especially when actions or content delivery is delayed by the nature of the implementation. SignalR provides an enhanced experience that allows content to be pushed from the server when it is available and actions to be executed immediately on the server. This functionality is provided by having a connection persisted between the server and client.

Understanding the User Experience

To understand the experience, start by looking at a personal blog. The blog content is generally authored by one person and it is usually updated about once per day (if the user is a frequent blogger). Even the visible comments are not updated frequently because they are not visible until approved by a moderator. So it is common for the user to have to manually refresh the web site to check for updated content.

A more interactive experience involves an e-commerce site. When using this type of site, it is expected that interactions such as adding items to the cart occur on the current page without the need to refresh the page or post back. The content has the potential to change during a user's session so there is usually a timer or an expiration on the pages to ensure that the latest content is displayed.

For a fully interactive site, many examples that are used every day include live news stories, chat rooms, games, and stock tickers. These sites demand that the latest content is pushed and the actions are performed as soon as possible. Using games as an example, you want to know your opponent's position as soon as it is available so that you can react and quickly take action.

General Categories of SignalR Applications

Even though the same technology is used by SignalR applications, they provide different experiences. These experiences generally fall into the following categories.

- Real-time notification
- Peer-to-peer collaboration
- Real-time content delivery

The real-time notification category contains applications that receive a notification to the application that an event from the server has occurred. The notification is pushed from the server in real time to the client. The notification can provide information or notify the user or client that an action is available.

Here is an example of a real-time notification: you are on an e-mail client, and the inbox count increases in response to a command from the server. The command from the server does not provide any detail of the new inbox items, just the information that the count increased.

The peer-to-peer collaboration category is for applications that allow two or more clients to communicate interactively. These applications work on a shared set of data that is delivered and acted on in real time. Google Docs is a great example of how shared content is updated among two or more authors in real time.

With real-time content delivery, applications are fed content in real time. This content can be displayed to the user or consumed by the application. In a breaking news feed site, the content displays directly to the user as it is pushed from the server. In a game, however, the content delivery can be the current game state with no information displayed to the user.

When Not to Use SignalR

As great as SignalR is, there are times when you should not use it. In general, if the content is updated very infrequently or the client connection is unreliable, SignalR should not be used.

The previous example of a personal blog can be used to describe why SignalR should not be used with content that is infrequently updated. In this scenario, a persistent connection is made every time a user visits the site. Because the odds are that the content is not being updated while a visitor is visiting the site, no content is delivered using the persistent connection that was created. As with many personal blogs, there are very few interactions that a visitor is allowed to do, and the impact of the action does not need to be in real time. The benefits that SignalR provides are not used, so overhead is created for every visitor by creating a persistent connection.

It is also not a good idea to use SignalR in your applications when the client connection is known to be unreliable. Even if it would be great to use SignalR to provide real-time functionality to clients, there is an overhead to keep the persistent connection alive, and SignalR doesn't provide a robust delivery mechanism. If the unreliable connection is a cell phone, the application has to use more battery power to keep up the persistent connection. The other issue with unreliable connections is that the delivery mechanisms were not built to be robust. So if the connection were to fail in the middle of message, logic would have to be added to both the client and the server to provide fail-proof mechanisms.

Extensibility of SignalR

SignalR is very extensible, thanks to the technologies behind it. The extensibility is possible because of the forethought to make it support OWIN, IoC containers, and message backplanes. Summaries of these technologies are provided in the following paragraphs.

OWIN Components

With the support of OWIN, SignalR allows you to host your application on any operating system in which the assemblies are executable and the OWIN middleware interface is provided. This means that you can run your applications on a current version Windows server that is running IIS or on a Linux box that is running Mono. It also enables your application to run with other OWIN middleware such as Web API.

IoC Containers

As discussed previously, it is very easy to customize SignalR by using IoC containers. With SignalR, you can register types with the default implementation or provide your own IoC container. There are many examples of people successfully using containers such as Unity, Structure Map, and Ninject.

Scaling Out with Message Backplanes

You learned earlier in the chapter that message backplanes can be used to scale out SignalR. The SignalR assemblies provide message backplane support for SQL Server, Windows Azure Service Bus, and Redis. (We go into more detail about message backplanes in Chapter 9 and 10.)

SQL Server

The message backplane can be used with SQL Server, with Service Broker enabled or disabled for that database server. The messages are persisted into tables that are managed by SignalR. The SQL Server implementation of message backplane performance is much better with Service Broker enabled. Service Broker is the database's internal queuing mechanism. This NuGet package can be installed with the `Install-Package Microsoft.AspNet.SignalR.SqlServer` command in the Package Manager Console.

Windows Azure Service Bus

The Windows Azure Service Bus allows you to create a message backplane that is managed in Windows Azure by Microsoft. This implementation of the service bus uses topics to send messages. The cost for using this cloud service is not very expensive; at the time of this writing, sending 1,000,000 messages and having 744 relay hours (about a month) costs less than $2.00. (This NuGet package can be installed with the `Install-Package Microsoft.AspNet.SignalR.ServiceBus` command in the Package Manager Console.) The Windows Azure Service Bus implementation is fairly easy to set up and provides good throughput, but it is hosted in Azure, which might add significant overhead and delay for on-premise applications.

Redis

Redis is an open source, advanced key-value store that is stored in memory. It supports a publisher/subscriber model used by SignalR to send the messages. (This NuGet package can be installed with the `Install-Package Microsoft.AspNet.SignalR.Redis` command in the Package Manager Console.) This implementation can be scaled to have great throughput, but it is the most complex message backplane.

Limitations of SignalR

When developing with SignalR, you might be affected by SignalR's limitations. The power and extensibility of SignalR can be reduced, depending on the operating system and host on which you deploy it. Clients can have limitations as well. Depending on the type of application, the scale of an application can also be affected. Finally, there are limitations that are outside of your controllable environment that can limit your applications.

Server Platform Limitations

The server platform must support the .NET 4.5 runtime because the server code uses the `Async` and `Await` keywords extensively. When IIS is run on client OSs such as Windows 7 or Windows 8, there is a limitation of up to ten concurrent connections, whereas the server OSs are generally limited only by the amount of server resources.

Use of the Web Sockets protocol is limited by a few factors. The first factor is that in IIS-hosted applications, the Web Sockets protocol is supported only on IIS 8, IIS 8 express, or later versions of IIS that require the use of Windows Server 2012 or later.

Client Platform Limitations

Clients that are web browser–based may see limitations on how many connections can be made to the server from a web browser. These are internal rules that are set to keep the web browser stable.

Message Backplane Limitations

In scenarios in which the number of messages grows proportionally to the number of users or when there are high-frequency real-time collaborations, the message backplane can be a limiting factor. As the number of messages going through the message backplane increases, a bottleneck can occur.

External Limitations

Web Sockets are limited by the fact that every hop from server to client and back must support Web Sockets; otherwise, parts of the connection might be downgraded, or the protocol might not be supported at all.

Summary

This chapter provided an overview of SignalR. We started by discussing its core technologies: OWIN, connection transports, dependency resolvers, the task parallel library, and message backplanes. You saw that SignalR is supported on a wide range of servers and clients from Windows to iOS. We showed you how very little is needed to get started with SignalR development. You learned how SignalR can be customized, scaled, and extended through the core technologies. Finally, you saw that even great frameworks can have limitations, depending on the type of application.

CHAPTER 3

■ ■ ■

Developing SignalR Applications Using Hubs

Chapter 1 provided some background information about real-time web development and ASP.NET SignalR that is necessary for understanding the content of this book. In Chapter 2, we went through some basic information about ASP.NET SignalR to get you started with this technology. In this chapter and Chapter 4, you get your feet wet with some technical details about ASP.NET SignalR that can actually help you develop real-world SignalR applications. This chapter is about hubs, and Chapter 4 is about persistent connections.

Hubs are discussed in detail in this chapter, but as a quick starter, hubs are an abstraction on top of persistent connections that enable ease of access to a set of APIs for the .NET Framework, jQuery, or other client types that allow web developers to build real-time web applications.

By nature, hubs are a high-level abstraction offered for those who want to build real-time web applications faster and easier and do not need to worry about extensibility and other professional aspects of their applications. Hubs are very dependent on persistent connections (see Chapter 4), and the same principles for persistent connections apply to hubs as well. Hubs are discussed before persistent connections because they are easier to learn and can prepare you to understand persistent connections better. Thanks to the good abstraction and independence of components in ASP.NET SignalR, hubs can be learned totally independently from persistent connections; you do not need to know persistent connections to build real-world ASP.NET SignalR applications. Understanding hubs suffices for most common scenarios, whereas persistent connections can be used for more-advanced cases.

This chapter discusses the following topics:

- The concept of hubs and how they work in general

- How to configure routing to use hubs

- How to implement hubs

- Client-side implementation of hubs

- The concept of groups and how to use them

- How the JavaScript proxy for hubs is generated and works

- Connection lifetime and how to control it

- State management between server and client with hubs

- The foundation of the hubs ecosystem and how `HubDispatcher` and `HubPipelineModule` work.

Overview of Hubs

Building a real-time web development platform from scratch can be an intimidating task, especially if you plan to build a thorough framework. ASP.NET SignalR is built to provide a complete set of APIs for web developers to simplify this task. ASP.NET SignalR provides these APIs in a very clean and layered structure, so you have a set of easy-to-use, high-level APIs as well as a set of lower-level extensible ones. Those high-level APIs appear under the name *hubs* and provide an abstraction on top of the lower-level APIs called persistent connections (see Chapter 4).

Hubs provide a set of two groups of libraries that expose easy-to-use APIs for programmers:

- **Server-side libraries:** These ASP.NET libraries provide a mechanism to implement server-side methods that can be called by clients as well as mechanisms to call some methods defined on the clients from the server side.

- **Client-side libraries:** These libraries (written in JavaScript, .NET, Objective-C, Java, and other platforms) provide a mechanism to implement client-side methods that can be called by server as well as mechanisms to call server-side methods.

■ **Note** As discussed in Chapter 1, an ASP.NET SignalR application usually has a single server component (although this software component can be distributed among several physical servers), and there can be various clients connecting to this server component. The server-side component is implemented in the .NET Framework (or Mono), but the client(s) can be implemented in various languages and technologies. The most common client-side implementations are with JavaScript, but there are .NET desktop clients as well as iOS, Android, and Windows Phone implementations.

The basis of the hubs ecosystem on server and client is the *remote procedure call (RPC)*, which has a wide meaning in computer science. In general, an RPC is a mechanism that enables methods on a system/computer/component to be called by an external or independent system/computer/component. In the case of ASP.NET SignalR, because the architecture is a client-server architecture, and these two sides are independent, RPCs are made from one of these two components to the other one.

The previous description of hubs is depicted in Figure 3-1 with a visual representation. A single-server software component can serve multiple clients and receive RPCs from them or make such calls to individual clients to trigger particular actions.

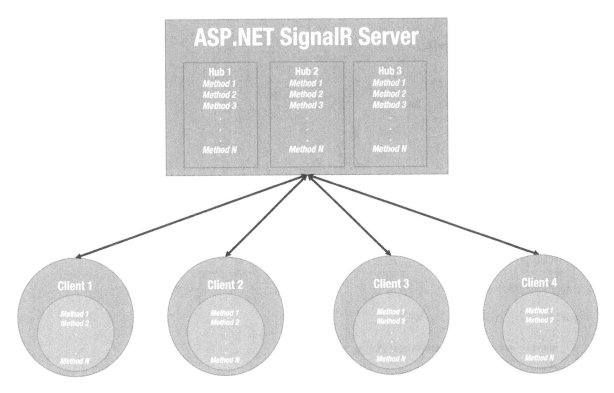

Figure 3-1. *General hub structure*

How does it work in general? This question is critical: making calls from the client(s) to server is a fairly common task, but making calls from the server to a particular client (or all clients) is not.

ASP.NET SignalR employs the concept of a persistent HTTP connection that is in contrast with the traditional HTTP connections that can be disconnected. Persistent HTTP connections remain open for a long time, which enables the ASP.NET SignalR server component to push any content that it wants to the client using this persistent connection.

The hubs ecosystem in ASP.NET SignalR applies the concept of hub proxies to simplify the process of working with server-side methods on the client as well as the process of working with client-side methods from the server. Hub proxies (discussed later in this chapter) are a set of JavaScript libraries automatically generated on the fly by the ASP.NET SignalR server based on the code implemented on the server to simplify the previously mentioned process.

To discuss this in more detail, we have to know that whenever server code calls a client-side method, the persistent connection is used to pass a set of data to the client with the name of the client-side method to be called, along with the parameters. Objects passed as parameters are serialized as JavaScript Object Notation (JSON), and if a method name is matched on the client side, the parameters (metadata) are deserialized and used to execute that particular method.

Getting Started with Hubs

Let's get started with some code. The first point about implementing hubs in ASP.NET SignalR is to know that a hub is nothing but a C# class that derives from the Microsoft.Aspnet.Signalr.Hub base class and implements a set of methods. These methods can take primitive .NET types or your custom types as their parameter(s) and return them as well.

The code in Listing 3-1 shows the basic implementation of a hub called Chapter3Hub that derives from the Hub base class.

Listing 3-1. Basic Hub Implementation

```
using Microsoft.AspNet.SignalR;

namespace Chapter3.Code
{
    public class Chapter3Hub : Hub
    {
    }
}
```

Let's take it a step farther and convert this basic implementation to a more realistic one. We can add a single method to this hub that receives a message and broadcasts it to all clients by calling a method on them. Listing 3-2 shows this code.

Listing 3-2. More Realistic Server-Side Hub Implementation

```
using Microsoft.AspNet.SignalR;

namespace Chapter3.Code
{
    public class Chapter3Hub : Hub
    {
        public void BroadcastMessage(string text)
        {
            Clients.All.displayText(text);
        }
    }
}
```

Do not worry about the details because we will discuss them later in this chapter, but for now you need to know that we have defined a public method in our hub called BroadcastMessage that gets a string parameter. It then uses the Clients object provided by ASP.NET SignalR that refers to the clients connecting to the server. Using the All property that refers to all clients (in contrast with a particular one or a group of them), it calls a client-side method called displayText by passing the text parameter. We will implement this client-side method in a moment.

Listing 3-3 shows the client-side implementation of this simple broadcasting system. This code is embedded within a simple HTML page and does not even need to be inside any ASP.NET web form or ASP.NET model-view-controller (MVC) view.

Listing 3-3. Client-Side Implementation

```
<!DOCTYPE html>

<html xmlns="http://www.w3.org/1999/xhtml">
<head runat="server">
    <title>Chapter 3 - Getting Started with Hub Implementation</title>
</head>
<body>
    <script src="Scripts/jquery-1.6.4.js"></script>
    <script src="Scripts/jquery.signalR-2.0.0-beta2.js"></script>
    <script src="/signalr/hubs" type="text/javascript"></script>
```

```
<script type="text/javascript">
    $(function () {
        var broadcaster = $.connection.chapter3Hub;

        broadcaster.client.displayText = function (text) {
            $('#messages').append('<li>' + text + '</li>');
        };

        $.connection.hub.start().done(function () {
            $("#broadcast").click(function () {
                broadcaster.server.broadcastMessage($('#msg').val());
            });
        });
    });
</script>

<div>
    <input type="text" id="msg" />
    <input type="button" id="broadcast" value="Broadcast" />

    <ul id="messages">
    </ul>
</div>
</body>
</html>
```

There are few important features of this code. First, there are three JavaScript references to the SignalR jQuery library and dynamic hubs proxy generated by SignalR. The first two are straightforward references that are typically done in any web application. The version of jQuery depends on the version of ASP.NET SignalR being used, even though there are some proxy libraries that create backward compatibility for ASP.NET SignalR for older versions of jQuery. You can find these proxy implementations by searching on the Internet, or you can easily implement your own.

The third JavaScript reference to /signalr/hubs is a reference to a library generated dynamically when the ASP.NET application loads. As discussed later, ASP.NET SignalR looks at your hubs implementation and generates a JavaScript library that can be accessed at this URL by default. We will discuss how to customize the location of this library and how it is generated later on.

There are also a few lines of JavaScript implementation with jQuery that connect the pieces of the user interface to the previously mentioned JavaScript libraries. First, we create a connection to the particular hub class by calling $.connection.chapter3Hub. We use this connection to get access to the client part and define our client-side method called displayText (already used to call on the client). This method adds a text message to a list of messages. After that, we use the hub object of the connection to start a connection and use its callback to handle any click event to a button. Inside this event, we use the server object of the connection to call the server-side method called broadcastMessage by passing the entered message.

▪ **Note** A common fact about ASP.NET SignalR happens to be a source of issues for newcomers as well. ASP.NET SignalR translates the Pascal naming of method names on the server side (e.g., *MethodName*) to a camel case (e.g., *methodName*). If you forget to apply such a change in your client-side code, your application will not function correctly.

At this point, we have all the elements we need to run this application and test it, but if we do, we will not get the expected result. Figure 3-2 shows the application window. Pressing the Broadcast button has no visible effect.

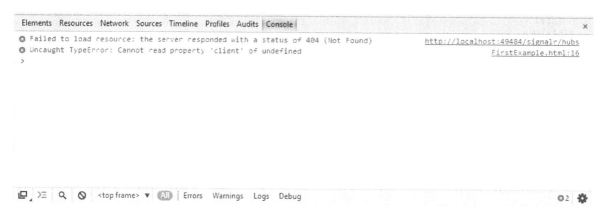

Figure 3-2. The code does not function correctly, and the message is not broadcast

By debugging the client-side execution of this application using Google Chrome Developer Tools (or any other client-side debugger such as Firebug), you see that there is a JavaScript error: the application cannot find any resource at the dynamic hub proxy location (see Figure 3-3).

Figure 3-3. The hub proxy library cannot be found

This problem is caused because we are missing one vital step in any ASP.NET SignalR application development: we need to map the hubs during application startup. To do this, we need to create a class called Startup in our application. This class must be available in the form of AssemblyName.Startup, where *assembly name* is the name of the assembly we assign to the project that executes the ASP.NET SignalR application. Inside this class, we must implement a method called Configuration. Listing 3-4 shows such an implementation. You often need to use the same code and change the namespace only to reflect your assembly name.

Listing 3-4. Mapping Hubs at Startup

```
using Owin;

// This needs to be AssemblyName.Startup or it will fail to load
namespace Chapter3
{
    public class Startup
    {
        // The name *MUST* be Configuration
        public void Configuration(IAppBuilder app)
        {
            app.MapHubs();
        }
    }
}
```

■ **Note**   We host our SignalR applications in this chapter using OWIN. We will discuss this in detail, along with alternatives, in Chapter 8. As a quick background for starters, OWIN stands for Open Web Interface for .NET and is a set of standards defined for communications between a .NET server and web application. There can be different implementations of this standard to host a web application on different types of servers, such as Internet Information Services (IIS), among others. For now, let's ignore the details and postpone the rest of the discussion to Chapter 8.

Now we are ready to run our application and get the result shown in Figure 3-4.

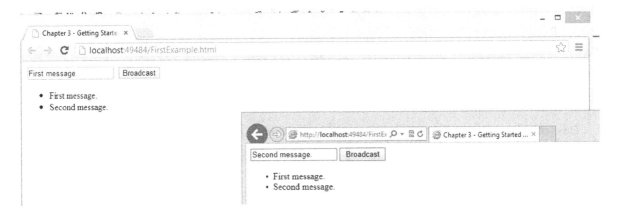

Figure 3-4. *Simple broadcasting application*

This was a quick start to the main steps and points needed to use hubs in ASP.NET SignalR. In the rest of this chapter, we discuss more details about each step and some related notes that would come in handy when developing ASP.NET SignalR applications using hubs.

Route Configuration

A vital step of the functioning of any ASP.NET SignalR application using hubs is to have the hubs mapped in routing, which was done in the Startup class and within the Configuration method (refer to Listing 3-4). This particular class name is called at the startup time of any ASP.NET SignalR application to map the routes for hubs.

You can modify this URL however you want, and we show you how in a moment. By default, ASP.NET SignalR is configured to serve requests in the same domain meaning that it assumes that you are calling the ASP.NET SignalR server component from the same client-side domain in which the server-side component is hosted. This might not be the case in the real world, however, so we need to enable cross-domain calls, which is another topic related to route configuration that we discuss here.

Customize the Hubs Proxy Location

As mentioned in the previous section, the hubs proxy is configured to be available at /signalr (this is different from /signalr/hubs, which is where you access your hubs). There might be some particular circumstances under which you have to change this default URL to something else. For example, you might have a folder with the name signalr in your project that has a conflict with this name. This part is easily configurable, both on the server side and on the client side.

On the server side, all you need to do is to modify the `Configuration` method in the `Startup` class to use an alternative overload of the `MapHubs` method to specify this new URL (see Listing 3-5).

Listing 3-5. Specifying an Alternative Location for the Hubs Proxy at Startup

```
using Owin;

// This needs to be AssemblyName.Startup or it will fail to load
namespace Chapter3
{
    public class Startup
    {
        // The name *MUST* be Configuration
        public void Configuration(IAppBuilder app)
        {
            app.MapHubs("/chapter3signalr", new Microsoft.AspNet.SignalR.HubConfiguration());
        }
    }
}
```

This particular overload requires the string value of the new location along with an instance of the `Microsoft.AspNet.SignalR.HubConfiguration` object.

On the client side, we can change the location of the JavaScript reference to the dynamic hubs proxy to use this new URL (see Listing 3-6).

Listing 3-6. Changing the JavaScript Reference Location for the Hubs Proxy

```
<!DOCTYPE html>

<html xmlns="http://www.w3.org/1999/xhtml">
<head runat="server">
    <title>Chapter 3 - Getting Started with Hub Implementation</title>
</head>
<body>
    <script src="Scripts/jquery-1.6.4.js"></script>
    <script src="Scripts/jquery.signalR-2.0.0-beta2.js"></script>
    <script src="/chapter3signalr/hubs" type="text/javascript"></script>

    <script type="text/javascript">
        $(function () {
            var broadcaster = $.connection.chapter3Hub;

            broadcaster.client.displayText = function (text) {
                $('#messages').append('<li>' + text + '</li>');
            };

            $.connection.hub.start().done(function () {
                $("#broadcast").click(function () {
                    broadcaster.server.broadcastMessage($('#msg').val());
                });
            });
        });
    </script>
```

```
<div>
    <input type="text" id="msg" />
    <input type="button" id="broadcast" value="Broadcast" />

    <ul id="messages">
    </ul>
</div>
</body>
</html>
```

Cross-Domain Connections

By default, ASP.NET SignalR assumes that your clients are connecting to your server component on the same domain as the execution location. For example, if you have a web site such as apress.com, your application is running on the same domain as the ASP.NET SignalR domain. In reality, it might not be the case for bigger-scale applications. You might want to host your ASP.NET SignalR server independently from your main application on a separate domain and probably on separate servers.

In this case, you can run your application on apress.com, but run the ASP.NET SignalR server on signalr.apress.com. You have to enable cross-domain connections in ASP.NET SignalR that are disabled by default. To enable these cross-domain connections in your application, go to the Startup class and its Configuration method again to modify the construction and initiation of routes to handle cross-domain connections.

After constructing your own HubConfiguration object, you can set its EnableCrossDomain property to true and then pass this custom HubConfiguration object to the MapHubs method. Listing 3-7 shows this and applies the default hub proxy location (i.e., /signalr).

Listing 3-7. Enabling Cross-Domain Connections on a Server

```
using Microsoft.AspNet.SignalR;
using Owin;

// This needs to be AssemblyName.Startup or it will fail to load
namespace Chapter3
{
    public class Startup
    {
        // The name *MUST* be Configuration
        public void Configuration(IAppBuilder app)
        {
            HubConfiguration configuration = new HubConfiguration();
            configuration.EnableCrossDomain = true;
            app.MapHubs(configuration);
        }
    }
}
```

Note   Different versions of browsers handle cross-domain connections differently, so it is recommended that you research these differences before implementing a real ASP.NET SignalR application. As a common example, IE10 considers anything on the local host as the same domain and does not treat it as a cross-domain connection. Remember that you cannot set `jQuery.support.cors` to `true` because it makes ASP.NET SignalR assume that the browser supports CORS and disables JSONP.

On the client side, you can reference your JavaScript library from the external domain, as is shown in Listing 3-8.

Listing 3-8. Cross-Domain Connections on the Client

```html
<!DOCTYPE html>

<html xmlns="http://www.w3.org/1999/xhtml">
<head runat="server">
    <title>Chapter 3 - Getting Started with Hub Implementation</title>
</head>
<body>
    <script src="Scripts/jquery-1.6.4.js"></script>
    <script src="Scripts/jquery.signalR-2.0.0-beta2.js"></script>
    <script src="http://signalr.apress.com/signalr/hubs" type="text/javascript"></script>

    <script type="text/javascript">
        $(function () {
            var broadcaster = $.connection.chapter3Hub;

            broadcaster.client.displayText = function (text) {
                $('#messages').append('<li>' + text + '</li>');
            };

            $.connection.hub.start().done(function () {
                $("#broadcast").click(function () {
                    broadcaster.server.broadcastMessage($('#msg').val());
                });
            });
        });
    </script>

    <div>
        <input type="text" id="msg" />
        <input type="button" id="broadcast" value="Broadcast" />

        <ul id="messages">
        </ul>
    </div>
</body>
</html>
```

Now let's take a deeper look at the server-side elements of ASP.NET SignalR hubs. There are few main elements:

- Declaration of multiple hubs on the server
- Use of custom hub names and methods
- How to use complex types as parameters and return the types of method
- How to access and deal with particular clients
- Asynchronous execution of hub methods

Multiple Hub Declaration

In practice, you need to create a modular ASP.NET SignalR program that needs to deal with smaller units of the business domain. For example, you might have a system that manages the online status of users to show when they come online or leave, as well as an online chat system. This requirement might impose the need to separate your hub's logic into different hubs that serve different areas of your application.

This is certainly possible in ASP.NET SignalR, and it is as easy as implementing different hub classes. For example, assume that you want to add the functionality to the existing broadcaster application to not only broadcast the message but also to send it to all the clients except the one sending it. For the sake of this example, also assume that this functionality better fits into a separate hub. Listing 3-9 shows the source code for the new hub that we define here.

Listing 3-9. Declaring a Second Hub on the Server

```
using Microsoft.AspNet.SignalR;

namespace Chapter3.Code
{
    public class Chapter3SecondHub : Hub
    {
        public void SendMessage(string text)
        {
            Clients.Others.displayText(text);
        }
    }
}
```

This is very similar to the first hub. It only has a different class name and a different internal logic to use the Others property rather than All to refer to all the clients except the caller.

Declaring multiple hubs on the server side does not need any special action on the hubs proxy generation because they are added to the same hubs proxy and work fine out of the box. There is no performance penalty associated with declaring multiple hubs, either, so feel free to use them to create a good level of abstraction in your program and make it easier to maintain.

The client side of code is also very simple and is shown in Listing 3-10. The JavaScript implementation can be refactored to be simpler, but for education purposes we keep it as is for now.

Listing 3-10. Consuming Multiple Hubs on the Client Side

```html
<!DOCTYPE html>

<html xmlns="http://www.w3.org/1999/xhtml">
<head runat="server">
    <title>Chapter 3 - Getting Started with Hub Implementation</title>
</head>
<body>
    <script src="Scripts/jquery-1.6.4.js"></script>
    <script src="Scripts/jquery.signalR-2.0.0-beta2.js"></script>
    <script src="/signalr/hubs" type="text/javascript"></script>

    <script type="text/javascript">
        $(function () {
            var broadcaster = $.connection.chapter3Hub;

            broadcaster.client.displayText = function (text) {
                $('#messages').append('<li>' + text + '</li>');
            };

            var sender = $.connection.chapter3SecondHub;

            sender.client.displayText = function (text) {
                $('#messages').append('<li>' + text + '</li>');
            };

            $.connection.hub.start().done(function () {
                $("#broadcast").click(function () {
                    broadcaster.server.broadcastMessage($('#msg').val());
                });
                $("#send").click(function () {
                    sender.server.sendMessage($('#msg').val());
                });
            });
        });
    </script>

    <div>
        <input type="text" id="msg" />
        <input type="button" id="broadcast" value="Broadcast" />
        <input type="button" id="send" value="Send" />

        <ul id="messages">
        </ul>
    </div>
</body>
</html>
```

Here we add a new button to the user interface that sends the message to all clients except the caller. Inside the JavaScript code, we create a connection to chapter3SecondHub and we add our client method implementation, similar to the first hub.

■ **Note** Multiple hubs do not affect the way you need to map your hubs in the Startup class, so you can leave them as they are.

Figure 3-5 shows the output of this application with the new hub in action.

Figure 3-5. *Testing multiple hubs in action*

Custom Hub Names

ASP.NET SignalR takes the declared class names in hubs and applies camel casing to them to generate the hubs proxy. Sometimes you might need to customize this behavior to use your own custom names, which you can do by applying a HubName attribute to your hub classes (see Listings 3-11 and 3-12).

Listing 3-11. Applying a Custom Hub Name to the First Hub Class

```
using Microsoft.AspNet.SignalR;
using Microsoft.AspNet.SignalR.Hubs;

namespace Chapter3.Code
{
    [HubName("FirstHub")]
    public class Chapter3Hub : Hub
    {
        public void BroadcastMessage(string text)
        {
            Clients.All.displayText(text);
        }
    }
}
```

Listing 3-12. Applying a Custom Hub Name to the Second Hub Class

```
using Microsoft.AspNet.SignalR;
using Microsoft.AspNet.SignalR.Hubs;

namespace Chapter3.Code
{
    [HubName("SecondHub")]
    public class Chapter3SecondHub : Hub
    {
        public void SendMessage(string text)
        {
            Clients.Others.displayText(text);
        }
    }
}
```

The client-side code is very straightforward and only needs to apply the new hub names (see Listing 3-13).

Listing 3-13. Using Custom Hub Names on the Client Side

```
<!DOCTYPE html>

<html xmlns="http://www.w3.org/1999/xhtml">
<head runat="server">
    <title>Chapter 3 - Getting Started with Hub Implementation</title>
</head>
<body>
    <script src="Scripts/jquery-1.6.4.js"></script>
    <script src="Scripts/jquery.signalR-2.0.0-beta2.js"></script>
    <script src="/signalr/hubs" type="text/javascript"></script>

    <script type="text/javascript">
        $(function () {
            var broadcaster = $.connection.FirstHub;

            broadcaster.client.displayText = function (text) {
                $('#messages').append('<li>' + text + '</li>');
            };

            var sender = $.connection.SecondHub;

            sender.client.displayText = function (text) {
                $('#messages').append('<li>' + text + '</li>');
            };

            $.connection.hub.start().done (function () {
                $("#broadcast").click(function () {
                    broadcaster.server.broadcastMessage($('#msg').val());
                });
```

```
                $("#send").click(function () {
                    sender.server.sendMessage($('#msg').val());
                });
            });
        });
    </script>

    <div>
        <input type="text" id="msg" />
        <input type="button" id="broadcast" value="Broadcast" />
        <input type="button" id="send" value="Send" />

        <ul id="messages">
        </ul>
    </div>
</body>
</html>
```

■ **Note** With the custom hub names, no camel casing convention is done in the hubs proxy; we had to use the original custom hub name on the client side in the Pascal naming convention. We took this approach to clarify it, but it is recommended to use a camel casing convention for custom hub names to be consistent with JavaScript coding styles.

Custom Types

So far, we applied only the string type in the .NET Framework as a parameter to our methods and consumed them. However, you might have more complex entities in your business domain that require you to declare custom complex types that employ a set of these primitive types. For example, you might need to pass around user information, including username, e-mail address, user ID, and last login time to and from your hubs. In this case, it is much easier to create a compound type to handle it.

The good news is that ASP.NET SignalR provides an easy way to use your own custom types in action just by defining them and using them in your hub declarations. ASP.NET SignalR uses its JSON serializer to automatically serialize and deserialize these objects out of the box. You only need to make sure that your custom types are serializable.

Let's modify our original broadcaster application to take advantage of this. We want to alter the functionality so it displays the name of the sender along with the message sent. To do this, we declare a custom type called Person (shown in Listing 3-14) that has two string properties for this purpose.

Listing 3-14. Custom Person Type

```
namespace Chapter3.Code
{
    public class Person
    {
        public string Name { get; set; }

        public string Message { get; set; }
    }
}
```

Now we can modify the hub class to get an instance of this object and then use these two properties to call a new version of the client-side method (see Listing 3-15).

Listing 3-15. Using Custom Types with Hubs on the Server

```
using Microsoft.AspNet.SignalR;
using Microsoft.AspNet.SignalR.Hubs;

namespace Chapter3.Code
{
    [HubName("firstHub")]
    public class Chapter3Hub : Hub
    {
        public void BroadcastMessage (Person person)
        {
            Clients.All.displayText(person.Name, person.Message);
        }
    }
}
```

We get an instance of the Person object as a parameter and then call the client-side displayText method by passing the Name and Message properties as its parameters.

On the client side, we have to make some modifications to pass an instance of this custom Person type with the additional data needed and then customize the client-side displayText method to accept an additional parameter and display it (see Listing 3-16).

Listing 3-16. Consuming Custom Types on the Client

```
<!DOCTYPE html>

<html xmlns="http://www.w3.org/1999/xhtml">
<head runat="server">
    <title>Chapter 3 - Getting Started with Hub Implementation</title>
</head>
<body>
    <script src="Scripts/jquery-1.6.4.js"></script>
    <script src="Scripts/jquery.signalR-2.0.0-beta2.js"></script>
    <script src="/signalr/hubs" type="text/javascript"></script>

    <script type="text/javascript">
        $(function () {
            var broadcaster = $.connection.firstHub;

            broadcaster.client.displayText = function (name, message) {
                $('#messages').append('<li>' + name + ' said: ' + message + '</li>');
            };
```

```
            $.connection.hub.start().done(function () {
                $("#broadcast").click(function () {
                    broadcaster.server.broadcastMessage({ Name: $('#name').val(),
                    Message: $('#message').val() });
                });
            });
        });
    </script>

    <div>
        <input type="text" id="name" />
        <input type="text" id="message" />
        <input type="button" id="broadcast" value="Broadcast" />

        <ul id="messages">
        </ul>
    </div>
</body>
</html>
```

Here we customize the displayText method to receive two parameters from the server and display them appropriately. We also modify the click handle for the Broadcast button to construct the custom Person type by passing its properties to the server. Pretty simple, right?

Now we test this application and get the desired result shown in Figure 3-6.

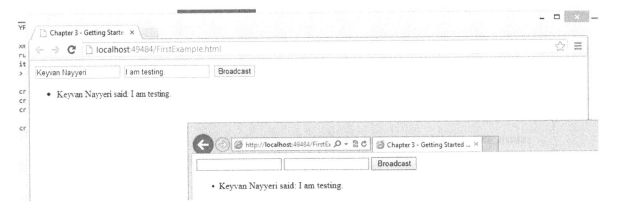

Figure 3-6. *Testing custom types in an application*

Groups

Under several different circumstances, you might need to deal with a particular set of clients in your application. One good example is a chat room in which particular clients want to connect and discuss things related to a particular topic. In such a case, you need to deliver messages from a server only to these clients.

ASP.NET SignalR provides the concept of groups along with an easy-to-use set of APIs for this purpose. These facilities are provided in the Groups class, and all you need to do is join and leave clients to particular groups as you want.

Let's modify the broadcaster example to include a new option to put users in groups and broadcast messages only within a particular group. First, we modify the Person class to also have a Group property (see Listing 3-17).

Listing 3-17. Modify the Person Class to Include a Group Property

```
namespace Chapter3.Code
{
    public class Person
    {
        public string Name { get; set; }

        public string Message { get; set; }

        public string Group { get; set; }
    }
}
```

The server-side hub is modified to allow clients to join and leave groups and also send a message to the groups that the user is a member of (see Listing 3-18).

Listing 3-18. Declare Groups on the Server

```
using Microsoft.AspNet.SignalR;
using Microsoft.AspNet.SignalR.Hubs;
using System.Threading.Tasks;

namespace Chapter3.Code
{
    [HubName("firstHub")]
    public class Chapter3Hub : Hub
    {
        public void BroadcastMessage(Person person)
        {
            Clients.Group(person.Group).displayText(person.Name, person.Message);
        }

        public Task Join(string groupName)
        {
            return Groups.Add(Context.ConnectionId, groupName);
        }

        public Task Leave(string groupName)
        {
            return Groups.Remove(Context.ConnectionId, groupName);
        }
    }
}
```

Here we use the Group property of Clients to broadcast the message to only a particular group name rather than everyone. Inside the Join and Leave methods, we use the Groups class to add and remove the current client (identified by Context.ConnectionId) to a particular group name passed in.

On the client side, we need to introduce a new text box to enter a group name and then adjust everything to take advantage of the groups. We also have to ensure that the client is joined to the particular group before broadcasting and leaves that groups afterward (see Listing 3-19).

Listing 3-19. Use Groups on the Client Side

```
<!DOCTYPE html>

<html xmlns="http://www.w3.org/1999/xhtml">
<head runat="server">
    <title>Chapter 3 - Getting Started with Hub Implementation</title>
</head>
<body>
    <script src="Scripts/jquery-1.6.4.js"></script>
    <script src="Scripts/jquery.signalR-2.0.0-beta2.js"></script>
    <script src="/signalr/hubs" type="text/javascript"></script>

    <script type="text/javascript">
        $(function () {
            var broadcaster = $.connection.firstHub;

            broadcaster.client.displayText = function (name, message) {
                $('#messages').append('<li>' + name + ' said: ' + message + '</li>');
            };

            $.connection.hub.start().done(function () {
                $("#broadcast").click(function () {
                    broadcaster.server.join($('#groupName').val());
                    broadcaster.server.broadcastMessage({ Name: $('#name').val(),
                    Message: $('#message').val(), Group: $('#groupName').val() });
                    broadcaster.server.leave($('#groupName').val());
                });
            });
        });
    </script>

    <div>
        <input type="text" id="groupName" />
        <input type="text" id="name" />
        <input type="text" id="message" />
        <input type="button" id="broadcast" value="Broadcast" />

        <ul id="messages">
        </ul>
    </div>
</body>
</html>
```

These changes are straightforward. The only point to note is the use of the broadcaster.server.join and broadcaster.server.leave methods that are similar to other hub method calls on the server that you have seen before. They make the client join and leave a group.

After running this code, we get the result shown in Figure 3-7.

Figure 3-7. *Groups in action*

Accessing Particular Clients

So far, we have mainly relied on a broadcasting scenario in which the server calls a method on all the clients. This is not always true, however. Sometimes we need to target a particular set of clients as a group, sometimes we need to exclude some clients, and there are many other scenarios that depend on our business needs. ASP.NET SignalR provides a good set of APIs to support such scenarios.

The first case that we already used several times is to broadcast a message to all the clients. We use `Clients.All` for this purpose (see Listing 3-20).

Listing 3-20. Using Clients.All to Broadcast to All Clients

```
public void BroadcastMessage(Person person)
{
    Clients.All.displayText(person.Name, person.Message);
}
```

Sometimes we want to send a message to all clients except the current client that is calling the server. We can apply `Clients.Others` in this case (see Listing 3-21).

Listing 3-21. Using Clients.Others to Broadcast to Other Clients

```
public void BroadcastMessage(Person person)
{
    Clients.Others.displayText(person.Name, person.Message);
}
```

The other case is when we want to send a message only to the particular client that is calling the server. We use `Clients.Caller` for this purpose (see Listing 3-22).

Listing 3-22. Using Clients.Caller to Broadcast to the Caller Client

```
public void BroadcastMessage(Person person)
{
    Clients.Caller.displayText(person.Name, person.Message);
}
```

One way to identify clients is to apply the connection ID. Each client in ASP.NET SignalR is assigned a unique connection ID in globally unique identifier (GUID) format. We can direct messages to particular clients by using their client IDs. For example, we can send a message to the caller client by using `Context.ConnectId` in conjunction with `Clients.Client`. This process is identical to using `Clients.Caller` (see Listing 3-23).

Listing 3-23. Using a Connection ID to Access a Particular Client

```
public void BroadcastMessage(Person person)
{
    Clients.Client(Context.ConnectionId).displayText(person.Name, person.Message);
}
```

We can also exclude one or more particular connection IDs from a message by calling `Clients.AllExcept` and passing one or more connection IDs. The following code excludes the caller to simulate a behavior identical to `Clients.Others` (see Listing 3-24).

Listing 3-24. Using Clients.AllExcept to Exclude a Particular Client

```
public void BroadcastMessage(Person person)
{
    Clients.AllExcept(Context.ConnectionId).displayText(person.Name, person.Message);
}
```

The same operations can be extended to the context of a group. We can send a message to all other clients (except the caller) in a group by using `Clients.OthersInGroup` (see Listing 3-25).

Listing 3-25. Using Clients.OthersInGroup to Access All Other Clients in a Group

```
public void BroadcastMessage(Person person)
{
    Clients.OthersInGroup(person.Group).displayText(person.Name, person.Message);
}
```

Last but not least, we can exclude particular clients by connection ID from receiving a message in a group. All we need to do is to use `Clients.Group` and pass the list of connection IDs as secondary parameters (see Listing 3-26).

Listing 3-26. Using Clients.Group to Exclude Particular Clients in a Group

```
public void BroadcastMessage(Person person)
{
    Clients.Group(person.Group, Context.ConnectionId).displayText(person.Name, person.Message);
}
```

Connection Lifetime Management

Persistent connections (see Chapter 4) are the basis of the hubs ecosystem. Connections play the key role in ASP.NET SignalR, hence hubs. Whenever you open a new page and navigate away from one, you close a connection and open a new one. There are three main connection events in ASP.NET SignalR:

- Connected: Occurs whenever a new connection is established between a client and the server. For example, in a chat application, it can be used to update the status of the user as online.

- Disconnected: Occurs whenever the connection from a client to the server is closed. For example, in a chat application, it can be used to update the status of the user to offline.

- Reconnected: Occurs whenever the connection is reestablished from a client to the server due to various reasons such as an inactive connection. For example, in a chat application, it can be used to update the status of the user to offline after a period of inactivity.

ASP.NET SignalR offers three events: OnConnected, OnDisconnected, and OnReconnected in the Hub base class that corresponds to these three events in order. You can override these events and implement them in your hubs to add your own business logic (see Listing 3-27).

Listing 3-27. Connection Lifetime Events

```
using Microsoft.AspNet.SignalR;
using Microsoft.AspNet.SignalR.Hubs;
using System.Threading.Tasks;

namespace Chapter3.Code
{
    [HubName("firstHub")]
    public class Chapter3Hub : Hub
    {
        public void BroadcastMessage(Person person)
        {
            Clients.Group(person.Group, Context.ConnectionId).displayText(person.Name, person.Message);
        }

        public Task Join(string groupName)
        {
            return Groups.Add(Context.ConnectionId, groupName);
        }

        public Task Leave(string groupName)
        {
            return Groups.Remove(Context.ConnectionId, groupName);
        }

        public override Task OnConnected()
        {
            return base.OnConnected();
        }
```

```
    public override Task OnDisconnected(bool stopCalled)
    {
        return base.OnDisconnected(stopCalled);
    }

    public override Task OnReconnected()
    {
        return base.OnReconnected();
    }
    }
}
```

■ **Note**   Similar to many other operations in ASP.NET SignalR, these events are asynchronous. ASP.NET SignalR is built to be an asynchronous technology. For more on asynchronous programming in .NET, you can read Apress Pro Asynchronous Programming in .NET (ISBN 978-1430259206).

The only possible sequences of these events are OnConnected -> OnReconnected -> OnDisconnected or OnConnected -> OnDisconnected, and it is impossible to have OnConnected -> OnDisconnected -> OnReconnected for a client. Note that under particular circumstances, OnDisconnected might not be called—when the application is recycled, for example.

Context

ASP.NET SignalR needs to offer some information about the context of application execution (similar to the HttpContext object in ASP.NET). It can be done via the Context property of the Hub base class.

The most common use of the Context property was to use ConnectionId to find the connection ID for the caller client. But you can also use the Headers property to have access to HTTP headers of the request or the QueryString property to retrieve query string parameters. You can also use the Request and RequestCookies properties, respectively, to access the request and its cookies. There is also a User property that allows you to find information about the authenticated user.

Listing 3-28 shows how the Headers property of Context is used to write the value of the Date header to the debugger.

Listing 3-28. Use Context.Headers to Access HTTP Headers

```
using Microsoft.AspNet.SignalR;
using Microsoft.AspNet.SignalR.Hubs;
using System.Diagnostics;
using System.Threading.Tasks;

namespace Chapter3.Code
{
    [HubName("firstHub")]
    public class Chapter3Hub : Hub
    {
        public void BroadcastMessage(Person person)
        {
            Debug.WriteLine(Context.Headers["Date"]);
            Clients.Group(person.Group, Context.ConnectionId).displayText(person.Name, person.Message);
        }
```

```
        public Task Join(string groupName)
        {
            return Groups.Add(Context.ConnectionId, groupName);
        }

        public Task Leave(string groupName)
        {
            return Groups.Remove(Context.ConnectionId, groupName);
        }
    }
}
```

State Management

By default, ASP.NET SignalR is built on top of the stateless HTTP protocol, so it is not easy to persist and communicate data between client(s) and the server. The hubs proxy provides a mechanism to facilitate this using the state property of the client and Clients.Caller on the server. By using these two tools, you can easily pass data from the client to the server or from the server to the client.

■ **Caution**   It is extremely important to know that the data passed between client(s) and the server in ASP.NET SignalR is added to each request that travels between them. Therefore, these mechanisms are intended to be used for smaller sizes of data, not bigger data sets. If used inappropriately, these mechanisms can have a huge performance impact on your application.

Let's go back and modify the group example to remove the Group property from the Person class and instead pass the name of the group using this mechanism. Listing 3-29 shows the new code for the Person class.

Listing 3-29. The Person Class with No Group Property

```
namespace Chapter3.Code
{
    public class Person
    {
        public string Name { get; set; }

        public string Message { get; set; }
    }
}
```

Now we modify the client code to pass the group name using the state property of the client proxy object (see Listing 3-30).

Listing 3-30. Client Code to Pass the State

```
<!DOCTYPE html>

<html xmlns="http://www.w3.org/1999/xhtml">
<head runat="server">
    <title>Chapter 3 - Getting Started with Hub Implementation</title>
</head>
<body>
    <script src="Scripts/jquery-1.6.4.js"></script>
    <script src="Scripts/jquery.signalR-2.0.0-beta2.js"></script>
    <script src="/signalr/hubs" type="text/javascript"></script>

    <script type="text/javascript">
        $(function () {
            var broadcaster = $.connection.firstHub;

            broadcaster.client.displayText = function (name, message) {
                $('#messages').append('<li>' + name + ' said: ' + message + '</li>');
            };

            $.connection.hub.start().done(function () {
                $("#broadcast").click(function () {
                    broadcaster.server.join($('#groupName').val());
                    broadcaster.state.GroupName = $('#groupName').val();
                    broadcaster.server.broadcastMessage({ Name: $('#name').val(),
                    Message: $('#message').val() });
                    broadcaster.server.leave($('#groupName').val());
                });
            });
        });
    </script>

    <div>
        <input type="text" id="groupName" />
        <input type="text" id="name" />
        <input type="text" id="message" />
        <input type="button" id="broadcast" value="Broadcast" />

        <ul id="messages">
        </ul>
    </div>
</body>
</html>
```

Here we use the `broadcaster.state.GroupName` property to pass the state value for the group name to the server. The server-side hub implementation is also very simple (see Listing 3-31).

Listing 3-31. Hub Implementation to Use the State Values

```
using Microsoft.AspNet.SignalR;
using Microsoft.AspNet.SignalR.Hubs;
using System.Threading.Tasks;

namespace Chapter3.Code
{
    [HubName("firstHub")]
    public class Chapter3Hub : Hub
    {
        public void BroadcastMessage(Person person)
        {
            Clients.Group(Clients.Caller.GroupName).displayText(person.Name, person.Message);
        }

        public Task Join(string groupName)
        {
            return Groups.Add(Context.ConnectionId, groupName);
        }

        public Task Leave(string groupName)
        {
            return Groups.Remove(Context.ConnectionId, groupName);
        }
    }
}
```

Here, `Clients.Caller.GroupName` is the same value passed from the client for this state.
Running this application results in the desired output (see Figure 3-8).

Figure 3-8. *Output of state management application*

Tracing

Tracing an ASP.NET SignalR application can become an important task to find out about the issues in your application. Just like ASP.NET, which provides some tracing mechanisms by configuration, ASP.NET SignalR offers a built-in set of tools that enables you to trace the execution of your program.

All you need to do is to modify the Web.Config file to include some new elements that take advantage of these tools. Listing 3-32 shows the code needed for this purpose.

Listing 3-32. Enabling Tracing in ASP.NET SignalR Applications

```xml
<?xml version="1.0"?>

<configuration>
  <system.web>
    <compilation debug="true" targetFramework="4.5" />
    <httpRuntime targetFramework="4.5" />
  </system.web>
  <system.diagnostics>
    <sources>
      <source name="SignalR.SqlMessageBus">
        <listeners>
          <add name="SignalR-Bus" />
        </listeners>
      </source>
      <source name="SignalR.ServiceBusMessageBus">
        <listeners>
          <add name="SignalR-Bus" />
        </listeners>
      </source>
      <source name="SignalR.ScaleoutMessageBus">
        <listeners>
          <add name="SignalR-Bus" />
        </listeners>
      </source>
      <source name="SignalR.Transports.WebSocketTransport">
        <listeners>
          <add name="SignalR-Transports" />
        </listeners>
      </source>
      <source name="SignalR.Transports.ServerSentEventsTransport">
        <listeners>
          <add name="SignalR-Transports" />
        </listeners>
      </source>
      <source name="SignalR.Transports.ForeverFrameTransport">
        <listeners>
          <add name="SignalR-Transports" />
        </listeners>
      </source>
```

```xml
    <source name="SignalR.Transports.LongPollingTransport">
      <listeners>
        <add name="SignalR-Transports" />
      </listeners>
    </source>
    <source name="SignalR.Transports.TransportHeartBeat">
      <listeners>
        <add name="SignalR-Transports" />
      </listeners>
    </source>
  </sources>
  <switches>
    <add name="SignalRSwitch" value="Verbose" />
  </switches>
  <sharedListeners>
    <add name="SignalR-Transports"
        type="System.Diagnostics.TextWriterTraceListener"
        initializeData="transports.log.txt" />
    <add name="SignalR-Bus"
        type="System.Diagnostics.TextWriterTraceListener"
        initializeData="bus.log.txt" />
  </sharedListeners>
  <trace autoflush="true" />
</system.diagnostics>
</configuration>
```

By running the ASP.NET SignalR application with tracing, you can monitor different information about your application execution in the Output window (see Figure 3-9).

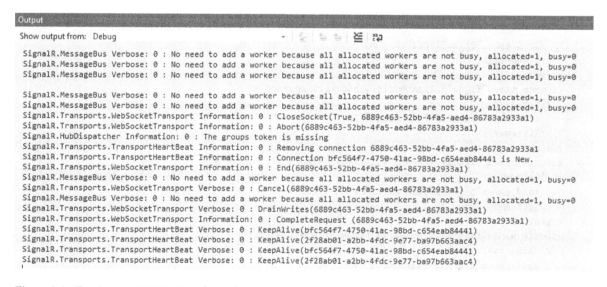

Figure 3-9. *Tracing an ASP.NET SignalR application*

This was a brief introduction to tracing in ASP.NET SignalR although it pretty much covers the main uses of tracing. Later in this book in Chapter 5 we come back to tracing again when we discuss troubleshooting and monitoring ASP.NET SignaslR applications.

HubDispatcher

We talked a lot about hubs in this chapter and how they simplify the task of building an ASP.NET SignalR application. We also mentioned that hubs are nothing but an abstraction on top of the persistent connection that we will discuss in chapter 4. However, it would be a good idea to have a brief discussion on how hubs achieve this goal.

Hubs apply a persistent connection in their core to communication with the clients and take care of serialization and serialization of data and complex types. In order to achieve this goal, they apply a class called HubDispatcher which is derived from PersistentConnection class. In fact, this means that HubDispatcher is nothing but a derivation of a persistent connection that overrides the key methods and properties on this class and adds some extra functionality to manage certain scnearios that we already discussed in this chapter.

For example, HubDispatcher override ProcessRequest method from PersistentConnection with its own logic shown in Listing 3-33. As you see, this code simply adds certain functionality to handle the hubs JavaScript.

Listing 3-33. ProcessRequest implementation in HubDispatcher

```
public override Task ProcessRequest(HostContext context)
{
    if (context == null)
    {
        throw new ArgumentNullException("context");
    }

    // Trim any trailing slashes
    string normalized = context.Request.LocalPath.TrimEnd('/');

    int suffixLength = -1;
    if (normalized.EndsWith(HubsSuffix, StringComparison.OrdinalIgnoreCase))
    {
        suffixLength = HubsSuffix.Length;
    }
    else if (normalized.EndsWith(JsSuffix, StringComparison.OrdinalIgnoreCase))
    {
        suffixLength = JsSuffix.Length;
    }

    if (suffixLength != -1)
    {
        // Generate the proper JS proxy url
        string hubUrl = normalized.Substring(0, normalized.Length - suffixLength);

        // Generate the proxy
        context.Response.ContentType = JsonUtility.JavaScriptMimeType;
        return context.Response.End(_proxyGenerator.GenerateProxy(hubUrl));
    }

    _isDebuggingEnabled = context.Environment.IsDebugEnabled();

    return base.ProcessRequest(context);
}
```

HubPipelineModule

Another fundamental concept about how hubs work in ASP.NET SignalR that we would like to briefly touch before wrapping up this chapter is around IHubPipelineModule and its common base class, HubPipelineModule.

Different instances of HubPipelineModule implement the IHubPipelineModule and can be added to an ASP.NET SignalR application to handle different stages of processing requests to hubs such as connecting, reconnecting, disconnecting, and others. Such modules need to be added to the IHubPipeline which allows another interface called IHubPipelineInvoker to invoke them in order.

There are different cases where you would need to apply your own HubPipelineModule implementations to customize the handling of various actions on your hubs. One example would be around exception handling and what you want to do with an incoming error. In this case, you can observe any incoming exception from hubs by implementing OnIncomingError method in your module.

Summary

This chapter was dedicated to hubs in ASP.NET SignalR. Hubs are the high-level set of APIs available for web developers to build ASP.NET SignalR applications quickly and easily without worrying about the underlying complexities of persistent connections.

You learned about the basics of hubs and how route configuration, cross-domain connections, multiple hub declarations, and custom types work.

You also learned how groups work to send messages to particular clients or a set of clients, along with connection lifetime management, context property, and state management. The next chapter focuses on the persistent connections that underlie hubs and how to work with them directly.

CHAPTER 4

Developing SignalR Applications Using Persistent Connections

This chapter shows you how to develop applications using persistent connections. We define a persistent connection is and show you how it can be configured. The next step is to see the communication and event signaling that occurs between the server and client. You will explore this communication with a persistent connection example with the JavaScript client. Finally, we discuss groups and how they can be used with persistent connections.

Here is a brief list of the topics covered in this chapter:

- How to configure persistent connections
- Server communication to clients over persistent connections
- Signaling between server and clients
- Example using the JavaScript client
- Groups

What Is a Persistent Connection?

A *persistent connection* is a communication channel between a server and a client that is kept open to facilitate secure, robust, low-latency, and full-duplex communication. The channel is identified by a unique connection ID. The channel is provided by one of a variety of transports that have logic to give the illusion that the connection is always persisted.

Properties of a Persistent Connection

There are four key properties that make persistent connections ideal for many implementations. These properties are the following:

- Robust connection
- Full-duplex communication
- Low latency
- Secure communication (optional)

The following sections discuss each property and the benefits it provides.

The first property is the *robust connection*, which ensures that a connected connection stays connected. If it is disconnected, it raises an event so that corrective action may be taken. The mechanisms that a persistent connection has to keep it robust are keep-alive packets, disconnect timeout and connection timeout monitors, reconnect logic, and connection state event notification. The *keep-alive packets* keep the channel "warm," which prevents routers and switches from prematurely closing a connection because of lack of data movement. The keep-alive packets also provide a heartbeat for the connection. This heartbeat updates the last update time, which is used to check for *disconnect timeouts*, which are used to detect connections that were terminated but have not signaled that they were disconnecting. Once the disconnected timeout has occurred, the connection has logic to reconnect. The reconnect logic attempts to reconnect with the same connection ID that returns the connection to the state before it disconnected. The *connection timeout* is used to provide new connections for the *long polling* transport because it does not receive keep-alive packets.

The second property is *full-duplex communication*, which allows communication to occur bidirectionally and asynchronously. Each connection has the capability to send and receive data. Depending on the transport, there may be one or two channels to provide full-duplex communication. The Web Sockets transport allows one channel to be created for full-duplex operation. The other transports require two channels, one for sending and one that receives.

The third property is *low latency*, which allows the connection to be real time or near real time. The low-latency property is ideal for applications that need to be responsive without having to deal with connection handshaking. The latency is different for most of the transports, and the transport with the lowest latency in both directions is Web Sockets. This transport keeps one channel open to communicate both ways so it does not need to complete a connection handshake after it has been connected. The ServerSendEvents and ForeverFrame transports have to complete the receive handshake only once and keep the receive channel open. However, the send channel has to be re-created for every message sent, which adds latency to every send for the connection handshake. Long polling, which has the worst latency, has to do a connection handshake every *connection timeout* interval, after receiving data from the server, or any time it needs to send data upstream to the server.

The final property, *secure communication*, enables safe and trusted communication over the connection. This property is optional, depending on the implementation chosen. Secure communication for a persistent connection may be provided by being encrypted by SSL and/or secured by using encrypted tokens for the connection and group IDs. Any time a connection or group token is transmitted to the user, it is encrypted by the server. The server encrypts the token based on the authenticated user. These secure tokens prevent attackers from forging requests for a connection ID or joining groups that it does not have permission to join.

How Persistent Connection Works

To the user, a persisted connection always seems connected, but SignalR has logic in place for the multiple phases of a connection: connecting, maintaining, and disconnecting. For a persistent connection, the connection phase consists of the following steps:

1. The client sends a negotiation request.

2. The server responds to the negotiation request with a payload of negotiation properties.

3. The client uses the payload to negotiate the best transport option.

4. The client sends a connect request with the negotiated transport.

5. Once the server has accepted the connect request, the persistent connection is made.

After the connection is made, the following steps are taken simultaneously to keep maintaining the connection:

- Retrieve any data that is on the server

- Send any data that is pending to be sent to the server

- Retrieve and acknowledge keep-alive packets or reconnect after polling timeout

Finally, when a connection is no longer needed and goes into the disconnecting phase, there is separate logic on the client and server. For the client, it sends an abort command and then closes the connection. If the server receives the abort command, it cleans up the connection. If the server does not receive the abort command, there is a timeout that fires to clean up any connections in which the abort message was missed. Later in the chapter, you will learn more about the way various aspects of the persistent connection work.

Using a Persistent Connection Instead of a Hub

When determining whether to use a persistent connection or a hub, keep the following few factors in mind:

- Message format
- Communication model
- SignalR customization

Depending on the application, these factors can have varying degrees of impact on the decision. To demonstrate the differences, we show partial examples of persistent connection and hub. The examples can request the time or broadcast a message. Although the implementations are slightly different, they demonstrate the differences well.

The persistent connection example is shown first, with the server shown in Listing 4-1 and the client shown in Listing 4-2.

Listing 4-1. Persistent Connection Server Example

```
public class TestPersistentConnection : PersistentConnection
{
    protected override Task OnReceived(IRequest request, string connectionId, string data)
    {
        return (data.StartsWith("GetTime")) ? Connection.Send(connectionId, "Time:" +
        DateTime.Now.ToString()) : Connection.Broadcast(data);
    }
}
```

Listing 4-2. Persistent Connection Client Example

```
var connection = $.connection('/TestPC');
connection.received(function (data) {
    var messageData = '';
    if (data.indexOf('Time:') > -1) { messageData = 'The time is: ' + data.substring(5); }
    else { messageData = data;}
    $('#messages').append('<li>' + messageData + '</li>');
});

connection.start().done(function () {
    $("#send").click(function () {
        connection.send($('#data').val());
    });
    $("#getTime").click(function () {
        connection.send('GetTime');
    });
});
```

Next is the hub example, with the server shown in Listing 4-3 and the client shown in Listing 4-4.

Listing 4-3. Hub Server Example

```
public class TestHub : Hub
{
    public void BroadcastMessage(string message)
    {
        Clients.All.SendMessage(message);
    }
    public void GetTime()
    {
        Clients.Caller.SendTime(DateTime.Now.ToString());
    }
}
```

Listing 4-4. Hub Client Example

```
var connection = $.hubConnection();
var hubProxy = connection.createHubProxy('TestHub');
hubProxy.on('SendMessage', function (data) {
    $('#messages').append('<li>' + data + '</li>');
});
hubProxy.on('SendTime', function (data) {
    $('#messages').append('<li>' + 'The time is: ' + data + '</li>');
});
connection.start().done(function () {
    $('#send').click(function () { hubProxy.invoke('BroadcastMessage', $('#data').val()); });
    $('#getTime').click(function () { hubProxy.invoke('GetTime'); });
});
```

The first area to look at (with no focus on importance) is the message format. In persistent connections, you are responsible for parsing and tokenizing the data that goes back and forth; in hubs, this message format is already handled. As shown in Listing 4-5, the data payload for a persistent connection is very simple, but it may be complicated to parse on the server. On the other hand, looking at the data payload in Listings 4-6 and 4-7 for hubs, the message is in a format that the hub logic parses automatically into static types on the server.

Listing 4-5. Request Body of a Persistent Connection with the Data "Hello"

```
data=Hello
```

Listing 4-6. Request Body of a Hub BroadcastMessage function with the "Hello" Parameter

```
data=%7B%22H%22%3A%22testhub%22%2C%22M%22%3A%22BroadcastMessage%22%2C%22A%22%3A%5B%22Hello%22%5D%2C
%22I%22%3A1%7D
```

Listing 4-7. Decoding of Listing 4-6

```
Data= {"H":"testhub","M":"BroadcastMessage","A":["Hello"],"I":1}
```

Another aspect of the message format is the size of the message. If the size is very important to the application, the persistent connection has the advantage of having smaller payloads. You can see in Listings 4-5 and 4-8 for persistent connections that the data payloads are considerably smaller than the hubs in Listings 4-7 and 4-9.

Listing 4-8. Persistent Connection Response to the GetTime Function

```
{"C":"d-4E3C7594-B,4|L,2|M,0","M":["Time:4/26/2014 2:00:00 AM"]}
```

Listing 4-9. Hub Response to the GetTime function with a call to the SendTime function

```
{"C":"d-2CF99ADA-E,0|I,1|J,1|K,0","M":[{"H":"TestHub","M":"SendTime","A":["4/26/2014 2:00:00 AM"]}]}
```

Next is the communication model of each of the APIs. For persistent connections, this model closely resembles the *connection model*, which usually has one function for sending and one function for receiving on each end of the connection. A hub abstracts this model and presents a *remote procedure call (RPC) model*, which provides many functions with unique function signatures on either the client or server. Look at the examples provided earlier in the chapter to see how they fit into their respective models.

In the persistent connection server example shown in Listing 4-1, there is only one function that receives requests: OnReceived. And for sending data to the client, there is only one function: Send. Even though the Broadcast function is shown in the example, it calls the Send function internally.

The persistent connection client example shown in Listing 4-2 also provides only one function to send and one function to receive. The received function calls the callback function, which has logic to determine what to do with the payload that is received. The Send function is called with different input data, depending on what type of request is being made to the server.

For a hub example, look at Listing 4-3, in which there are two functions provided by the server: BroadcastMessage and GetTime. These functions take one and zero parameters, respectively, and make calls to unique functions on the clients.

The hub client example in Listing 4-4 shows the RPC model with different functions that are callable from the server and has logic to invoke different functions on the server. Look at the invoking calls: the BroadcastMessage function takes one parameter, and the GetTime function takes zero parameters. The client also provides two functions (SendMessage and SendTime) that are for receiving message data and the time, respectively.

Finally, depending on the customization that is to be done to the SignalR classes, it is easier to extend and customize persistent connection classes. Hubs are built on top of the persistent connection APIs, so they are more rigid and present more challenges to customize. Many of the components of persistent connections and hubs are swappable using the dependency resolver. Although these components are changeable, the hub classes have shared hub classes that you might want to change (for example, creating a customized encrypted data parser for incoming data for specific endpoints). For persistent connections, you can override the OnReceived method with your custom encryption for that connection. It is much more difficult for hubs, considering that they have logic to bind to static types to which modifying could affect all the hubs.

How to Configure Persistent Connections

Depending on the type of application that you are writing, sometimes you need to configure the persistent connection to be tailored to your application. There are many options available to configure the persistent connection. The first required configuration is the route configuration, so that your persistent connection is registered to the correct endpoint. Another critical piece that can be configured is the supported transports. Other properties can be configured using the OWIN properties that a connection uses. If the configuration does not provide everything you need, the persistent connection can be extended with custom classes. (Extending with custom classes is discussed in Chapter 7).

Persistent Connection Route Configuration

To create a persistent connection class, derive it from the `PersistentConnection` class, as demonstrated in Listing 4-10.

Listing 4-10. The PersistentConnection Class Deriving from a PersistentConnection

```
public class TestPersistentConnection : PersistentConnection
```

Although you have created the persistent connection class to access it, you must configure the binding to a route. Under IIS and self-host applications, you create this mapping in the `Startup.cs` file.

Mapping Routes in Startup.cs

Mapping routes should occur in the `Startup.cs` file. If the file doesn't exist, you can add it by adding a file of type OWIN startup class. Once you have the file, you configure the mapping in the `Configuration` function using the `IAppBuilder` interface. You can use the `IAppBuilder` to register all your OWIN middleware components, including the `PersistentConnection` and `Hub` classes.

The easiest way to map a connection is to use an extension method provided by SignalR (see Listing 4-11). The example maps the `TestPersistentConnection` class shown in Listing 4-10 to the path TestPC. So if your host were `http://localhost`, you could access the `TestPersistentConnection` at `http://localhost/TestPC`.

Listing 4-11. Example of Mapping a Route in Startup.cs

```
public void Configuration(IAppBuilder app)
{
    app.MapSignalR<TestPersistentConnection>("/TestPC");
}
```

Note that the order in which routes are added is the order used in matching a route. Beyond route configuration, there are other areas of a persistent connection that can be configured, such as the connection timeouts and Web Sockets support discussed in the next couple of sections.

Global Timeout and Keep-Alive Configurations

The `GlobalHost` class provides a static property that exposes an `IConfigurationManager` interface that can be used to set the connection timeout, disconnect timeout and keep-alive interval settings.

The `ConnectionTimeout` property is the amount of time that a connection remains open without receiving data. After this timeout, the connection is closed, and another connection is opened. The default `ConnectionTimeout` is 110 seconds; this property is used only by the long polling transport.

The `DisconnectTimeout` property is the amount of time to wait after a connection goes away before raising the disconnect event. The default `DisconnectTimeout` is 30 seconds whenever the `DisconnectTimeout` is set; the `KeepAlive` property is set to 1/3 of the value set.

The `KeepAlive` property is the amount of time between the sending of keep-alive messages. This property is set to 1/3 the value of the `DisconnectTimeout` property by default, except for the long polling transport, for which it is set to `null`. If the value is set to `null`, the `KeepAlive` property is disabled; if it is set to a value, the minimum value must be at least 2 seconds, and the maximum value is 1/3 of the `DisconnectTimeout`.

■ **Note** To configure the `DisconnectTimeout` and `KeepAlive` settings, you must set the `DisconnectTimeout` first, or else an invalid operation exception will be thrown.

HostContext Configuration

The HostContext is created for every request that comes into a persistent connection. The configuration can be updated using HostContext and overriding the Initialize method in the PersistentConnection derived class.

SupportsWebSockets

This property provides a flag to the clients to tell them whether a connection supports Web Sockets. The property can be set by setting the key HostConstants.SupportsWebSockets in the HostContext Items collection (see Listing 4-12). Set the value of true to flag for the client to attempt to use Web Sockets or to false to skip the attempt to use the Web Sockets transport.

Listing 4-12. Example of Setting SupportsWebSockets

```
public override void Initialize(IDependencyResolver resolver, HostContext context)
{
    context.Items[HostConstants.SupportsWebSockets] = true;
    base.Initialize(resolver, context);
}
```

> ■ **Note** The expected object type for this value is a Boolean. If SupportsWebSockets were to be set using true as a value, the code would throw an exception.

WebSocketServerUrl

The WebSocketServerUrl property provides the client with an override server URL to call for Web Sockets connections. This property can be set by setting the key HostConstants.WebSocketServerUrl in the HostContext Items collection to set the value of the WebSocketsServerUrl (see Listing 4-13).

Listing 4-13. Example of Setting WebSocketServerUrl

```
public override void Initialize(IDependencyResolver resolver, HostContext context)
{
    context.Items[HostConstants.WebSocketServerUrl] = "ws://localhost:8219";
    base.Initialize(resolver, context);
}
```

Server Communication to Clients Over Persistent Connections

Persistent connections have a set of communications that occurs between the client and server to initialize and maintain the connection, and to send and receive data. The communications start with a negotiate request to determine which transports are available on the server. There is a set of logic that each client has to determine which transport is the best. Once the transport has been agreed on, the connect communication sets up an upgraded socket for Web Sockets or a receiving channel for the other transports. When data needs to be sent to the server, and the transport is not Web Sockets, the send communication is used to send data.

Because the long polling transport is not as reliable, it has two communication methods. The first is the ping method, which determines whether the server is available; the second is the poll method, which is used to keep an open receive channel. Finally, for any transports that want to close their connection, there is an abort communication that terminates the connection.

Negotiation

The negotiation is the first SignalR-based communication that occurs between the server and client. In this first phase, the server receives a request ending in */negotiate*. In the processing of this negotiate request, the server generates the ConnectionId and ConnectionToken for that connection. This process also returns a payload of server properties, which are returned as a JSON payload. If the negotiation is a JSONP request, the payload is returned with a callback.

Negotiation Properties

The negotiation properties are returned in the payload from the negotiate request (see Listing 4-14). Let's take a look at each property and see what they are used for.

Listing 4-14. Example of Negotiation Properties Payload

```
{"Url":"/SamplePC","ConnectionToken":
"Udy6quBS2y3yQpElIQKg3memfXI56A4tdBqzwTNLB2jQNDOz2YYVFGwpFJKxjCrF81t+
pOIItZKoOuqcU7ZlWNwLnPJfod7E9fuBK1gEIb6UTfNhFiFSEt4dTEfDi1Z0",
"ConnectionId":"6a246327-fd16-4a90-8a76-e87ef5d14642","KeepAliveTimeout":20.0,
"DisconnectTimeout":30.0,"TryWebSockets":true,"ProtocolVersion":"1.3",
"TransportConnectTimeout":5.0}
```

URL

The URL property is the relative URL to the persistent connection endpoint. It is used only by the JavaScript SignalR client library.

ConnectionId

The ConnectionId property is generated by the .NET Framework Guid.NewGuid() function, formatted with dashes. ConnectionId is a critical key that is used to identify the connection.

ConnectionToken

The ConnectionToken property is generated by appending together ConnectionId, a colon, and the user identity. The user identity is the current request's username provided by the .NET Framework or an empty string. This token is then encrypted before being sent to the user.

KeepAliveTimeout

The KeepAliveTimeout property is the value specified in the IConfigurationManager for KeepAlive. (More information about KeepAlive was discussed previously in the section called "Global Timeout and Keep-Alive Configurations.")

DisconnectTimeout

The `DisconnectTimeout` property is the value specified in the `IConfigurationManager` for `DisconnectTimeout`. (More information about `DisconnectTimeout` was discussed previously in the section called "Global Timeout and Keep-Alive Configurations.")

TryWebSockets

The `TryWebSockets` property value is returned `true` if the `TransportManager` supports Web Sockets, the `ServerRequest` is of type `IWebSocketRequest`, and the OWIN `SupportsWebSockets` environment variable is true. The `TransportManager` check is true if the transport name *webSockets* is present in the collection of transport names. If the SignalR library is built with .NET 4.5, the `ServerRequest` object derives from `IWebSocketRequest`; otherwise, it derives from the `IRequest` class. The third check, which is a little more complex, checks `HostContext` for the `supportsWebSockets` entry that is determined in the Invoke method of the call handler. It is based on the `websocket.Version` key being present in the `server.Capabilities` environment variable passed into the OWIN Invoke function.

WebSocketsServerUrl

By default, this property is `null`. The property value is determined from the `HostConstants.WebSocketServerUrl` property in the `HostContext Items` collection.

ProtocolVersion

`ProtocolVersion` is the current version of SignalR, which is provided so that the clients can maintain compatibility. As of the time of this writing, the current version is 1.3.

TransportConnectTimeout

`TransportConnectTimeout` is the amount of time in seconds that a client should allow before trying another transport or failing.

Client Negotiation

Once the negotiation payload has been processed, the client has enough information to determine which transport it can use to connect to the server. The client first looks at its list of supported clients; if the list contains Web Sockets, it evaluates the `TryWebSockets` parameter of the negotiate payload to see whether the server supports Web Sockets.

If it is not supported, the next two transports that a client has in its list of transports are usually ServerSendEvents and ForeverFrame, respectively. The client checks its compatibility with each transport to see whether it is supported. If not satisfactory, the last transport tried is the long polling transport, which is usually the last supported transport in the clients list. Because there are no other transport options left to check, the client then throws an error, and no connection is made.

Ping

The ping request is one of the simplest client-server communications. This request is initiated only by the long polling transport when using the JavaScript client. The request does a simple get-to-the-base URL with */ping* appended. The response from the server is a very basic JSON data payload. The JSON object is a single variable "Response" with a value of "pong" that is verified by the client (see Listing 4-15).

Listing 4-15. Example of a Response from a Ping Request

```
{"Response":"pong"}
```

Connect

Once the client has found the most appropriate transport, it sends a connect response. For Web Sockets, the request is a transport of "websockets" and the `connection token` provided in the negotiation. The Web Sockets connection is returned with an HTTP status of 101, which means that the response has been upgraded. For all other transports, the connection include the transport and the connection token.

The transport signifies which type of transport it is sending for (ServerSendEvents, ForeverFrame, or long polling). The connection token is the encrypted token for the connection. For the non–Web Sockets transports, this connection is the listening channel until the connection is reconnected for a timeout or poll.

Send

The send request is a post for all the transports besides Web Sockets, which the send occurs on the channel so a new request is not created. The send command contains the transport and connection token in the header, and data in the body. The transport signifies which type of transport it is sending for (ServerSendEvents, ForeverFrame, and long polling). The connection token is the encrypted token for the connection. The data section of the body is the value of the object that was sent. In Listing 4-16, the data sent is `User A:Hello`.

Listing 4-16. Example of Sending Hello from User A

```
data=User+A%3A+Hello
```

Poll

Poll is a get request that is used only when the transport is long polling. The parameters of the get request are transport, connection token, message ID, and the optional group token. The transport signifies which type of transport it is sending for, but for this request only long polling is supported. The connection token is the encrypted token for the current connection. The optional group token is present when the connection is a member of one or more groups and contains the keys to those groups. The message ID is simply the message ID of the current poll request.

The data that is returned from the poll is from a class called `PersistentResponse`. This class contains several properties that affect the connection:

- `Messages`: An array of messages being sent to the client.

- `Disconnect`: An indicator that the connection has received a disconnect command.

- `TimedOut`: An indicator that the connection timed out.

- `GroupsToken`: An encrypted token of the list of groups the connection is a member of. `GroupsToken` is `null` if the connection is not part of a group.

- `LongPollDelay`: The length of time the client should wait before reconnecting if no data was received. `LongPollDelay` is `null` for any transport other than long polling.

- `Cursors`: A special data set that contains a string of the minified event keys and IDs in a hexadecimal format. The cursors represent the message ID, but are encoded by converting the values to numbers.

The JSON representation of `PersistentResponse` is written in the format *key: value* with a comma separating the key value pairs. If the `Disconnect`, `TimedOut`, `GroupsToken`, or `LongPollDelay` properties do not have a value or are `false`, they are not included in the JSON response. Table 4-1 is a map from key to property in the JSON response.

Table 4-1. *Relation Table of Key to Property PersistentResponse JSON Object*

Key	Property
C	Cursors
D	Disconnect
T	TimedOut
G	GroupsToken
L	LongPollDelay
M	Messages

The response of the poll is JSON data returned from the `PersistentResponse` class. An example of the response is shown in Listing 4-17. This data is evaluated by the client to determine the connection's current state. If the transport is long polling, it inspects this data for the L key to see whether it contains a numeric value for a new polling delay. If the D key is present, the client interprets it as a disconnect signal from the server and issues a stop locally. If the C key is present, clients set their message ID to the cursor data provided. When the G key is present, the client updates its list of groups. Finally, the client goes through each message provided under the M key. For each message, it triggers the client `OnReceived` command if appropriate.

Listing 4-17. Example of the Persistent Response Received on a Poll

```
{"C":"d-C16EF02C-B,1|C,1|D,0","M":["User A: Hello"]}
```

Abort

The abort request is sent when the connection is being terminated by the client. Whenever the stop method is issued on the connection or (with a JavaScript client) the web page is navigated away from, the abort command is issued. The abort request is posted for all transports besides Web Sockets, in which the abort occurs on the channel so a new request is not created. The abort command contains transport and connection token in the header. The transport signifies which type of transport it is sending for (Web Sockets, ServerSendEvents, ForeverFrame, or long polling). The connection token is the encrypted token for the current connection.

Signaling Between Server and Clients

Throughout the life cycle of a persistent connection, signals occur on the server and client that represent events affecting the connection. Although the signals for the server and client are similar, they are usually used differently. These events signal the state of a connection, removing the need to poll each connection to determine its current connection state.

Server-side Events

Server-side events are events raised on the server that can be generated by any connection or the server if it realizes that a connection is no longer available.

OnReceived

The OnReceived event, which is one of the most important, occurs when data is received from a persistent connection. On this event, the message is decoded, and the choice of data distribution occurs. Depending on the application, you can choose to broadcast, send to a group, or consume the data without redistributing.

OnConnected

The OnConnected event occurs when a new connection is made. On this event, the logic to add a user to a group can be added. Logic can also be added to maintain a user presence of being logged in. Depending on the type of transport, the connection can be logged in very frequently. So instead of directly displaying whether the user is currently logged in, displaying a last-logged-in time might provide a better experience.

OnDisconnected

The OnDisconnected event occurs when a connection disconnects, either through sending an abort command or the server realizes that the connection is no longer available. On this event, the logic to remove users from groups is added. Logic can also be added here to complement the logic added to the OnConnected event to maintain the user state by knowing when the user is disconnected. Depending on the transport used, updating the user state based on the connect and disconnect state might provide a bad experience, so maybe OnConnected should be used only to determine the last-logged-in time.

OnReconnected

When a connection is reconnected after a timeout using the same connection ID, the OnReconnected event is raised. On this event, logic can be added to see whether the client is in the correct state because of missing data during the timeout.

OnRejoiningGroups

The OnRejoiningGroups event occurs when a connection reconnects after a timeout to determine which groups should be rejoined automatically. On this event, you might have additional logic check to see whether the connection should be added back to a group instead of automatically adding to the groups that it had before the connection timed out.

AuthorizeRequest

The AuthorizeRequest event occurs before every request to authorize the user. On this event, you can add customized logic that returns a Boolean value whether the client is authorized to use the persistent connection and/or requested resource that is specified in the request object.

Client-side Events

Client-side events are events that are raised on the client for the persistent connection. These events signal how the connection has changed or data has arrived from the server. These events signal that a connection is starting, reconnecting, or closed. They also signal when there is an error, when new data is available from the server to the connection, when connection has slowed, or when it is changing connection state.

Received

The Received event, which is one of the most important, is raised when the connection has received data from the server. The event is called with one parameter that contains the data that the server has sent.

Error

The Error event occurs when the connection has encountered an error; generally this returns for errors in creating the connection. The event is called with one parameter that might not have data on the reason why the error was generated.

Closed/Disconnected

The Closed/Disconnected event occurs when the connection is stopped. The event name is dependent on the client that is being used.

Reconnecting

The Reconnecting event occurs when the connection starts reconnecting after a connection interruption. While the connection is reconnecting, the connection is unavailable for use.

Reconnected

Once a connection has been reestablished after a timeout, the Reconnected event signals that the connection is available for use again.

StateChanged

This event occurs when the connection state changes. There are four connection states: connecting, connected, reconnecting, and disconnected. There are seven possible state transitions (see Figure 4-1).

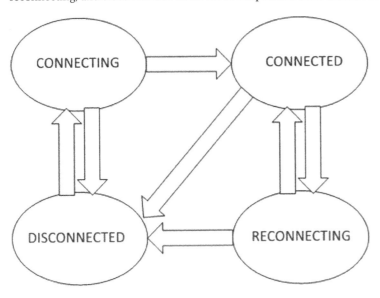

Figure 4-1. *ConnectionState state diagram*

ConnectionSlow

This event occurs when the connection has crossed more than two-thirds of the disconnect timeout without a keep-alive message being received. Once the event has been fired, it fires again only if a keep-alive message is received before the connection times out.

OnStart

Used by all the transports, but are exposed as events only in the SignalR JavaScript library. This event occurs once the Start function has been called by the client.

OnStarting

Used by all the transports, but are exposed as events only in the SignalR JavaScript library. This event occurs after a successful negotiate request is made.

Communication and Signaling Example Using a JavaScript Client

To demonstrate the communication and signaling that occurs between a server and client, we show a JavaScript example. This example focuses heavily on the signaling that occurs on the client when events are raised. Some of these events, such as the connection state, are exposed on the client UI to get a visual feel of what is going on in the application.

Server Code for Client Example

We reuse the persistent connection server example from Chapter 2. It is a brief overview; if more detail is needed, please revisit Chapter 2.

1. Create a new ASP.NET web application using the model-view-controller (MVC) template.

2. Run the following command in the Package Manager Console to install the necessary SignalR files: Install-Package Microsoft.AspNet.SignalR.

3. Create a PersistentConnections folder.

4. Add a new class to the PersistentConnections folder called SamplePersistentConnection.

5. Update the new class to look like Listing 4-18. Add any missing using statements.

   Listing 4-18. PersistentConnection Sample Code

```
public class SamplePersistentConnection : PersistentConnection
{
    protected override Task OnReceived(IRequest request, string connectionId, string data)
    {
        return Connection.Broadcast(data);
    }
}
```

6. Add the code in Listing 4-19 to `Startup.cs` after the `ConfigureAuth` statement to register the `PersistentConnection`. Add any missing using statements.

Listing 4-19. Registering PersistentConnection Route

```
app.MapSignalR<SamplePersistentConnection>("/SamplePC");
```

Now that the server is created, the next step is to create the client, which is discussed in the next section.

JavaScript Client Example

Chapter 2 showed an example of JavaScript-based persistent connections; here, we expand the sample to show the client-side events in action. As was done before, an HTML page should be added to the project.

1. Add the scripts shown in Listing 4-20 to the head section of the HTML page.

Listing 4-20. Javascript Sample Client Script Code

```javascript
<script src="/scripts/jquery-1.10.2.js" type="text/javascript"></script>
    <script src="/scripts/jquery.signalR-2.0.3.js" type="text/javascript"></script>

    <script>
        $(function () {
            var connection = $.connection('http://localhost:####/samplepc');

            connection.received(function (data) {
                $('#messages').append('<li>' + data + '</li>');
            });

            connection.connectionSlow(function () {
                $('#connectionStatus').html('Connection slowed');
            });
            connection.disconnected(function () {
                disableChat();
            });
            connection.error(function (errorData) {
                console.log(errorData);
            });
            connection.reconnected(function () {
                enableChat();
            });
            connection.reconnecting(function () {
                disableChat();
            });

            connection.stateChanged(function (states) {
                var oldState = states.oldState;
                var newState = states.newState;
                var connectionStatus = '';
```

```javascript
                switch (newState) {
                    case $.connection.connectionState.connected:
                        connectionStatus = 'Connected';
                        enableChat();
                        break;
                    case $.connection.connectionState.connecting:
                        connectionStatus = 'Connecting';
                        break;
                    case $.connection.connectionState.reconnecting:
                        connectionStatus = 'Reconnecting';
                        break;
                    case $.connection.connectionState.disconnected:
                        connectionStatus = 'Disconnected';
                        break;
                }
                $('#connectionStatus').html(connectionStatus);
            });

            connection.starting(function () {
                console.log('Successful negotiation request');
            });

            $("#btnSend").click(function () {
                connection.send($('#name').val() + ': ' + $('#message').val());
            });

            $("#btnConnect").click(function () {
                connection.start();
            });

            $("#btnDisconnect").click(function () {
                connection.stop();
            });

            function enableChat() {
                $("#btnSend").removeAttr("disabled");
                $("#btnDisconnect").removeAttr("disabled");
                $("#btnConnect").attr("disabled", "disabled");
            }

            function disableChat() {
                $("#btnSend").attr("disabled", "disabled");
                $("#btnDisconnect").attr("disabled", "disabled");
                $("#btnConnect").removeAttr("disabled");
            }
        });
    </script>
```

▓ **Note** The JQuery and SignalR library references might need to be updated in the script to the current version supplied by the NuGet package installation. The port that the server is running on needs to be replaced in the script where the #### are.

2. Add the code in Listing 4-21 to the body section of the HTML page.

Listing 4-21. JavaScript Sample Client HTML

```
<button id="btnConnect" >Connect</button>
    <button id="btnDisconnect" disabled="disabled">Disconnect</button>
    <label id="connectionStatus">Disconnected</label>
    <ul id="messages" style="border: 1px solid black; height: 250px; width: 450px;
     overflow:scroll; list-style:none;"></ul>
    <label>Name: </label>
    <input id="name" value="User A" />
    <label>Message: </label>
    <input id="message" />
    <button id="btnSend" disabled="disabled">Send</button>
```

Once the example is complete, you should see something similar to Figure 4-2.

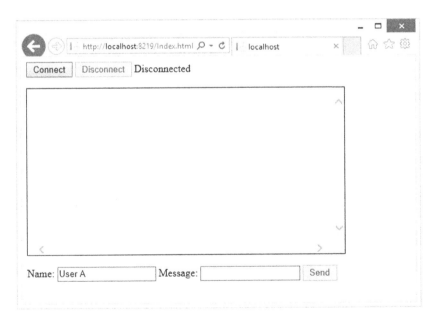

Figure 4-2. JavaScript SignalR client interface

This example showed you the various connection states of a persistent connection. The next section discusses groups, which provide the grouping of connections based on a common factor.

Connection Grouping

When your application needs more than one concurrent persistent connection per user or communication, it has to go out to a group of people. You can use groups to accomplish this. The group management and membership can be controlled by simple interfaces provided in the `PersistentConnection` class. Depending on where the group data is persisted, the group information may be only on the server for the lifetime of the application or it may be stored in an out-of-process store that will live beyond the lifetime of the application.

GroupManager

`GroupManager` provides group management for the persistent connection. The `GroupManager` provides three functions: `Send`, `Add`, and `Remove`. These functions provide the base functionality to communicate and manage the group.

Send Function

The group `Send` function sends the data locally to any connection IDs that are connected to the local server and then publishes a message bus to send the message to groups that may exist on other servers that are connected via a message bus.

Add Function

The group `Add` function is responsible for adding a user to a group. It also creates the group if it does not exist and publishes an add command to the other servers that are connected via a message bus.

Remove Function

The group `Remove` function is responsible for removing a user from the group. It also removes the group if there are no more connections remaining and publishes a remove command to the other servers that are connected via a message bus.

Group Membership

Group membership follows a subscriber/publisher pattern. The membership for groups can be any combination of connections. The lifetime of a group is handled internally by SignalR, including the creation and removal of the group. The membership of the group can be single-user or multiple-user.

Group Subscription

When users join a group, they do so in a subscriber/publisher pattern. SignalR does not expose any methods to return information about subscribers to a group. So if the members of a group need to be known, customized logic needs to be added to capture the group's subscribers and to expose this list.

Group Life Cycle

A group life cycle begins the first time a connection is added to a group that does not exist. SignalR creates the new group and enrolls that connection in the group. The group membership is updated as connections are added or removed from a group via `GroupManager`. When all the connections have been removed from a group, SignalR cleans up the group and removes it from memory.

Single-user Group

A single-user group contains the connection ID of only a single user. The group is used to message the user who might have persistent connections open over multiple tabs or moving around a site, so the user's connection ID regenerates every time a new page is visited.

Listing 4-22 is an example of the logic for a single-user group. The logic requires that the user be authenticated so that the Identity object is populated with the user's name.

Listing 4-22. Example of Logic to Add/Remove Connections from a Single-user Group

```
protected override Task OnConnected(IRequest request, string connectionId)
{
    string groupName = request.User.Identity.Name;
    if (!string.IsNullOrWhiteSpace(groupName))
      this.Groups.Add(connectionId, groupName);
    return base.OnConnected(request, connectionId);
}

protected override Task OnDisconnected(IRequest request, string connectionId, bool stopCalled)
{
    string groupName = request.User.Identity.Name;
    if (!string.IsNullOrWhiteSpace(groupName))
      this.Groups.Remove(connectionId, groupName);
    return base.OnDisconnected(request, connectionId, stopCalled);
}
```

■ **Note**   This sample relies on the User.Identity.Name having a valid value by using an authentication method other than anonymous authentication.

Multiple-user Group

A multiple-user group contains multiple users with one or more connection IDs. These groups can be used to target connection subgroups.

Suppose that you run a forum and want to have a chat room associated with the major forum topics. In this example, for every page that the user is under a different major forum topic, we provide a chat window centered on the major forum topic. To accomplish this, we can group the connection from that page to that major topic. With SignalR, this process is very easy: adding group name logic to the client and adding the grouping methods to the server.

Modifying the client is very easy; we use a connection constructor that allows us to pass the query string values, as shown in Listing 4-23.

Listing 4-23. Example of Client Update to Provide Query String Values During Request

```
var roomName = getRoomName();
var connection = $.connection('http://localhost:8219/chat', 'roomName=' + roomName, false);
```

■ **Note**   The getRoomName() function is a custom function to return the group or, in this example, the chat room to be part of.

In the example, the first line determines what group to be in from custom logic in the getRoomName function. In the second line, the constructor that allows query string values is used. The first parameter is the SignalR endpoint URL, the second is the query string parameters that should be appended as-is, and the third determines whether logging should be on.

For the server, to determine which chat room the user is viewing, we need to add the logic to add or remove from the group based on the query string value that we are using. Logic also needs to be added so that messages can be sent to the group specified by the query string, similar to Listing 4-24.

Listing 4-24. Example of Server Update to Use Query String Values to Determine Group Name

```
protected override Task OnReceived(IRequest request, string connectionId, string data)
{
    string groupName = request.QueryString["roomName"];
    return this.Groups.Send(groupName, data, connectionId);
}

protected override Task OnConnected(IRequest request, string connectionId)
{
    string groupName = request.QueryString["roomName"];
    if (!string.IsNullOrWhiteSpace(groupName))
     this.Groups.Add(connectionId, groupName);
    return base.OnConnected(request, connectionId);
}

protected override Task OnDisconnected(IRequest request, string connectionId, bool stopCalled)
{
    string groupName = request.QueryString["roomName"];
    if (!string.IsNullOrWhiteSpace(groupName))
     this.Groups.Remove(connectionId, groupName);
    return base.OnDisconnected(request, connectionId, stopCalled);
}
```

The first method we modify is OnReceived. In this method, we look at the query string value to determine the group name. We then use this name and send the data sent from the client to the group, excluding our own connection ID. The second and third methods we modify are the OnConnected and OnDisconnect functions. In these functions, the first thing to do is to determine the group name from the query string. Once we have the group name and we determine that the group name is valid, we call GroupManager to add or remove the function, respectively.

Group Persistence

Persisting a group can be done either in-memory or to a long-term storage medium such as a database or a caching tier. The persistence mediums have trade-offs such as speed, durability, and scalability.

Let's first take a look at the in-memory group solution, which is very fast because a request does not have to go out of process to obtain group information. The downside of this solution is that it cannot scale beyond the server on which it is running, and the group information is lost if the application is restarted. This solution works well for applications that run on only one server, do not need to have group communication across servers, and can tolerate losing the group data with a restart.

Another solution is to use a database or a caching tier to store group information. The group information can then be shared with many servers and persisted across server restarts. The problem is that to access this group information, every request has to go out of process to get the group data, which is generally multiple times slower than in-memory access. So even if the application can scale, there is a performance penalty for using an external storage medium, plus the added complexity of guaranteeing that the external storage medium is accessible and is synchronized with all the other servers.

To determine which solution is best to use depends on whether you are running on multiple servers and whether the group data needs to be synchronized and/or persisted. If you need to persist group data between restarts, or if you have multiple servers and need the group data synchronized, you should store the group information in an external storage medium, as described in the second solution. If that is not the case, an in-memory solution provides the best benefit. (More information about message buses and scaling using the message buses is provided in Chapters 9 and 10).

Summary

In this chapter, we described a persistent connection. We explained the communication and signaling that occurs between the server and client. A JavaScript sample of persistent connections was shown to explain the communication and signaling that occurs. Finally, we discussed how to use groups in the context of a persistent connection.

CHAPTER 5

Troubleshooting ASP.NET SignalR Applications

Chapter 1 gave you some background information about real-time web and SignalR. Chapter 2 was a quick start to ASP.NET SignalR, and in Chapters 3 and 4 you discovered two important methods for building ASP.NET SignalR applications: hubs and persistent connections.

These two concepts are sufficient to get most of the common jobs done with ASP.NET SignalR, but that's in a perfect world. In practice, we often face issues when we write programs, and there are several other topics that we encounter for scaling up and out, and for deploying to different environments. In the current chapter and the rest of this book, we focus on topics that target different aspects of such problems to give you more practical knowledge about building real ASP.NET SignalR applications.

This chapter is all about one of the main phases of developing any type of software: troubleshooting—in other words, debugging and testing. You need to debug and test almost any program that you write, regardless of its size. This process can be easier for smaller programs that run on a single environment such as console applications because you can easily see the output and can use many debugging features such as breakpoints.

However, the world is not always that simple, and there are often more difficult cases to deal with. One example is the case for client-server applications such as those we build with ASP.NET SignalR. The whole program execution is distributed among two independent components that execute in two different contexts (and most likely different environments or machines): server and client. Debugging such programs requires more efforts and needs better tooling support.

This chapter goes through common techniques and tools for debugging the server and client components of ASP.NET SignalR and discusses the common issues that you might face during the development of an ASP.NET SignalR application.

Here is a brief list of the major topics covered in Chapter 5:

- General process of troubleshooting an ASP.NET SignalR application

- How to use Chrome Developer Tools to debug the client-side execution of an application and JavaScript or jQuery issues

- How to use Fiddler to troubleshoot client-to-server (and server-to-client) communications

- How to troubleshoot the server-side execution of an application

- How to enable tracing in ASP.NET SignalR

- Common issues with ASP.NET SignalR applications

ASP.NET SignalR Troubleshooting Overview

There is no silver bullet for troubleshooting an ASP.NET SignalR application (or any server-client application for that matter) because there are different independent pieces that are working together, executing in different contexts, and even running on different machines to debug. Therefore, the whole idea of troubleshooting a SignalR application requires some experience and following general guidelines.

Here we outline a general list of areas to be checked in order to troubleshoot an ASP.NET SignalR application (although you might want to look only into a subset of these items and not necessarily follow them in order):

- JavaScript errors on the client (using debugging tools such as Chrome Developer Tools or others)

- Communication issues from the client to the server or vice versa (using HTTP debugging tools such as Fiddler)

- Server-side issues (using Visual Studio debugging features)

- Trace logs for any invisible or silent problem (using the tracing mechanisms provided in ASP.NET SignalR and Visual Studio outputs)

These steps might need to be followed in conjunction with each other. For example, if server-side debugging is needed, there is a high probability that corresponding JavaScript debugging and client-side actions are also needed.

The rest of the chapter discusses more details about each of these items.

■ **Note**   Although we try to cover the common troubleshooting process and development tools for .NET developers such as Google Chrome Developer Tools, Fiddler, and Visual Studio, there are alternative tools available to use for the same purposes. The functionality and features of such tools are often very similar to tools discussed here (we chose the most popular and common tools for discussion), so it is worth reading this chapter to know how to use other tools.

Using Chrome Developer Tools for Client-Side Debugging

Common issues with ASP.NET SignalR applications are generated on the client side because of the lack of data coming from the server blowing up the JavaScript functionality, incorrect data coming from the server, or even a logic problem in the client JavaScript code.

In any case, we need to debug the JavaScript code to find out what is wrong in order to take the correct action. With the fast-growing and common uses of JavaScript in software development, there have been many tools developed to simplify JavaScript debugging. Historically, it has been tricky and sometimes challenging to debug JavaScript code. These obstacles come from the nature of this language, which is different from other programming languages (although it also runs in a browser).

Regardless, quite a few tools are used by developers to debug JavaScript; it has been a need that has led browser builders to integrate very rich JavaScript debugging tools with the recent versions of all the major browsers such as Google Chrome, Mozilla Firefox (it comes as an extension), and Microsoft Internet Explorer.

Not only do these browsers come with a good JavaScript debugger but they also support other tracing capabilities such as network access to resources, HTML and CSS code viewing, and profiling, among others. These tools allow you to view, test, and debug your HTML, CSS, and JavaScript for different browser versions to ensure that your application renders correctly on all the major browsers for all the recent versions.

Chrome Developer Tools (see Figure 5-1), Firefox Firebug (see Figure 5-2), and Internet Explorer Developer Tools (see Figure 5-3) are mentioned here. In this chapter, we focus on using Google Chrome Developer Tools because it is more popular among web developers and also provides a slightly richer set of debugging features that are easier to use. The use of other tools is very similar.

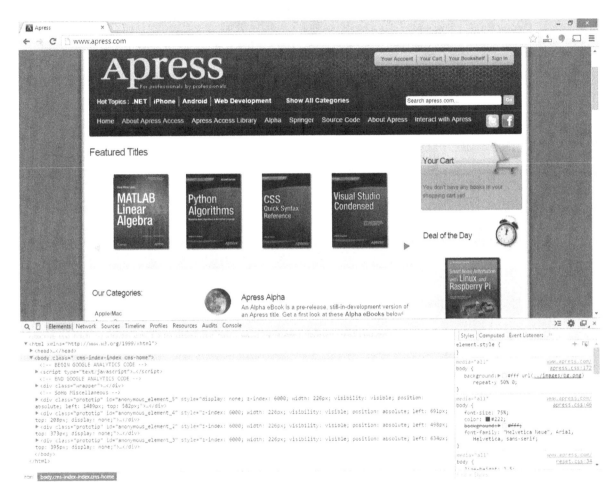

Figure 5-1. Example of Google Chrome Developer Tools

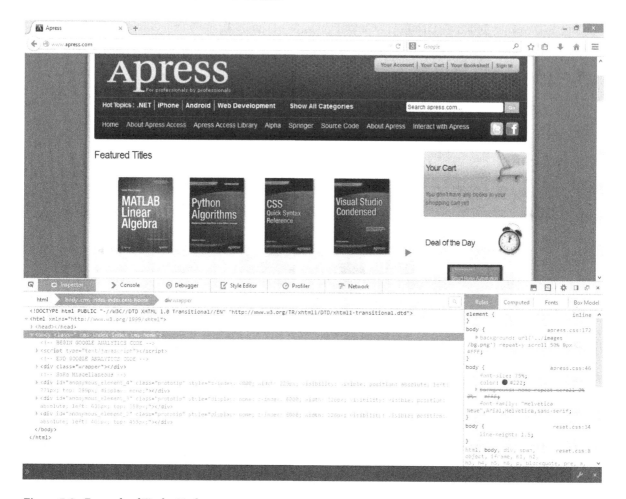

Figure 5-2. *Example of Firefox Firebug*

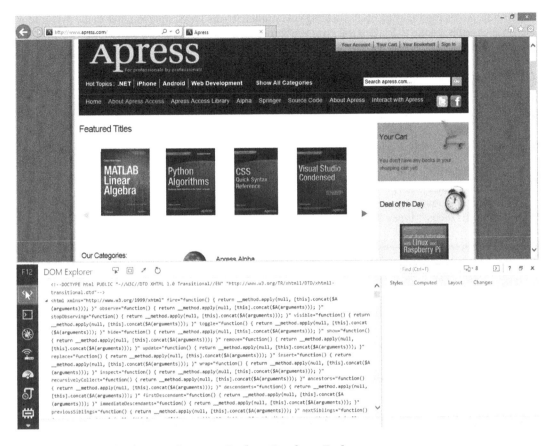

Figure 5-3. *Example of Microsoft Internet Explorer Developer Tools*

In this section, we focus on Google Chrome Developer Tools and give you a quick overview of how to use it to debug possible client-side JavaScript errors in ASP.NET SignalR.

First, we create a simple ASP.NET SignalR application with hubs. It is a very basic message-broadcasting application that shows some common scenarios. (We described the details about developing such an application in Chapter 3.) The code for the BroadcastHub class implementation is shown in Listing 5-1.

Listing 5-1. Broadcast Hub Implementation

```
using Microsoft.AspNet.SignalR;

namespace Chapter5.Controllers
{
    public class BroadcastHub : Hub
    {
        public void BroadcastMessage(string message)
        {
            Clients.All.sendMessage(message);
        }
    }
}
```

For this application, we avoided starting up the hosting environment so the JavaScript reference to the dynamic hubs proxy failed to access this resource. A JavaScript error was introduced that we can detect and debug. But first, we have to write the client-side code presented in Listing 5-2.

Listing 5-2. Client-Side Implementation of the Broadcast Application

```
<!DOCTYPE html>
<html xmlns="http://www.w3.org/1999/xhtml">
<head>
    <title></title>
</head>
<body>
    <script src="Scripts/jquery-1.6.4.js"></script>
    <script src="Scripts/jquery.signalR-2.0.0-rc1.js"></script>
    <script src="/signalr/hubs" type="text/javascript"></script>

    <script type="text/javascript">
        $(function () {
            var broadcaster = $.connection.broadcastHub;

            broadcaster.client.displayText = function (text) {
                $('#messages').append('<li>' + text + '</li>');
            };

            $.connection.hub.start().done(function () {
                $("#broadcast").click(function () {
                    broadcaster.server.broadcastMessage($('#msg').val());
                });
            });
        });
    </script>

    <div>
        <input type="text" id="msg" />
        <input type="button" id="broadcast" value="Broadcast" />

        <ul id="messages">
        </ul>
    </div>
</body>
</html>
```

If we run this application in Google Chrome, we don't get the expected behavior. At this point, if we open Google Chrome Developer Tools and navigate to the Console tab, the JavaScript errors can be seen (see Figure 5-4).

Figure 5-4. JavaScript error for dynamic hub proxy

As shown in the figure, the top error suggests that the JavaScript reference to the dynamic hubs proxy is throwing a 500 HTTP status error, which suggests a server error because the hosting is not set correctly. The second error is a side effect of the first one, and because the dynamic proxy is not loaded correctly, the client property of that proxy cannot be loaded, either.

You can find the name of the resource file and line number on the right side of each error line where that error is happening. By clicking this link, you are navigated to the actual source code at the location in which it is happening in the Sources tab (see Figure 5-5). This tab has more information about the error to help you debug the problem.

Figure 5-5. Source of JavaScript errors in Google Chrome Developer Tools

Now let's focus on another scenario in which we want to actually see the values being communicated between client and server, and vice versa. This scenario requires the use of breakpoints in JavaScript, and Google Chrome Developer Tools comes with a handy set of features to simplify it.

Let's assume that we want to debug the existing code and find out what message is sent from the server to clients with broadcasting. To detect it, we need to insert a breakpoint inside the displayText function callback in JavaScript (see Listing 5-3).

Listing 5-3. Code to Insert a JavaScript Breakpoint

```
broadcaster.client.displayText = function (text) {
    $('#messages').append('<li>' + text + '</li>');
};
```

By running the application and going to Google Chrome Developer Tools and then to the Sources tab, we can find the JavaScript code in the HTML file. By clicking the left column next to the line of code, we can insert a breakpoint (see Figure 5-6). This mechanism is very similar to the breakpoint system in Visual Studio.

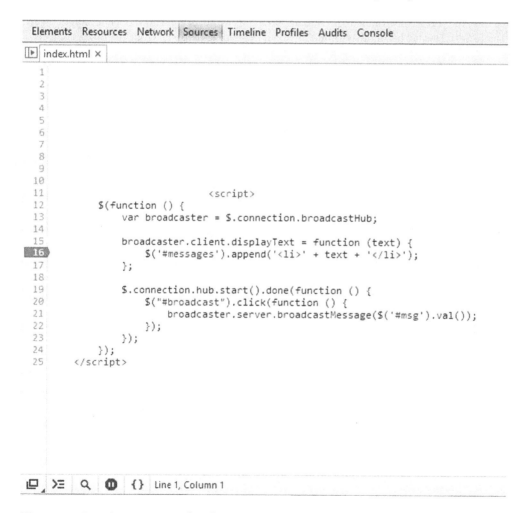

Figure 5-6. *Inserting a JavaScript breakpoint in Google Chrome Developers Tools*

After executing the code and entering a message to broadcast, the code stops at this line and enables us to view the value of a variable by moving the cursor over the variable name (see Figure 5-7).

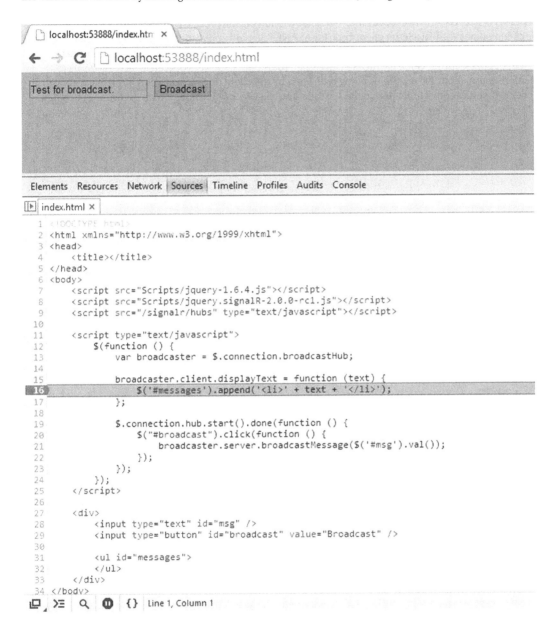

Figure 5-7. *Debugging variable values in Google Chrome Developers Tools*

As shown in the figure, it is easy to pause and continue the execution, add variables to a watch list, and check the call stack on the right column of Google Chrome Developer Tools.

This set of features (along with many more that can be discovered by reading the documentation available at https://developers.google.com/chrome-developer-tools and following the process) can be used to troubleshoot any problematic circumstance with JavaScript client code for ASP.NET SignalR applications. If other client types are used (such as iOS, Android, or Windows Desktop), similar troubleshooting features exist to assist you with diagnosing them.

Besides the debugging features, Google Chrome Developer Tools offers the Network tab, which allows us to retrieve helpful information about the resources being requested by the client during execution. (You learn about debugging the client-to-server communication in the next section.) Figure 5-8 shows a general overview of this tab.

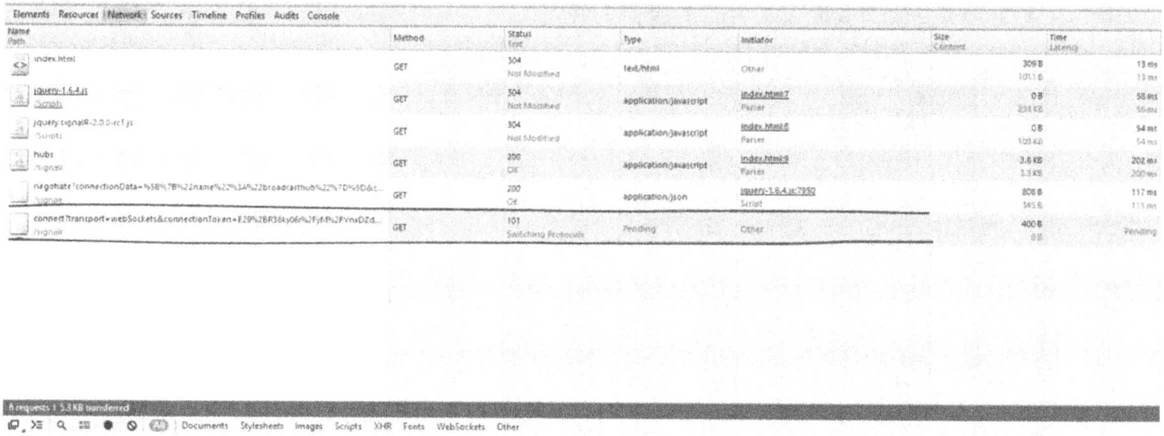

Figure 5-8. *Networks tab in Google Chrome Developer Tools*

The figure shows all the network requests made by the client (including any long-polling connections). The requests made by the ASP.NET SignalR library are highlighted, and there is an initiator column that shows which part of the code each resource is requesting. There are also some reporting numbers about the time that it takes for a resource to be retrieved as well as an HTTP status code that helps to determine and diagnose the application's health.

Using Fiddler for Client-to-Server Communication Debugging

The other aspect of any server-client application, including SignalR applications, is the communication between client to server and server to client that is a very critical point of the whole architecture (everything fails if this communication hub is broken).

There are several tools and methods that can be used to debug and trace this communication for ASP.NET SignalR. Generally speaking, any HTTP debugging tool can assist us in this area, but most .NET developers agree that the most popular tool in the Microsoft (and even non-Microsoft) communities is Fiddler (http://fiddler2.com).

Fiddler was developed as a pet project by Eric Lawrence when he was working at Microsoft. It was acquired by Telerik, and Eric was hired to dedicate his time to advancing the tool features. Telerik Fiddler, which has been a very handy tool for developers for many years, enables you to easily test and trace communication requests on different protocols on your machine.

Although we focus on Fiddler, there are many other tools available for achieving the same goal. All browser debuggers (such as Google Chrome Developer Tools) provide some kind of features for this purpose. Charles is a good example of a similar tool for the Apple community.

Let's take a look at the Fiddler output when we run our example from the previous section and enter a text to broadcast (see Figure 5-9).

#	Result	Protocol	Host	URL	Body	Caching	Content-Type	Process	Comments	Custom
1	304	HTTP	localhost:53888	/index.html	0			chrome...		
3	304	HTTP	localhost:53888	/Scripts/jquery-1.6.4.js	0			chrome...		
4	304	HTTP	localhost:53888	/Scripts/jquery.signalR-2....	0			chrome...		
5	200	HTTP	localhost:53888	/signalr/hubs	3,429	no-cac...	application/...	chrome...		
6	200	HTTP	localhost:53888	/signalr/negotiate?connec...	357	no-cac...	application/...	chrome...		
7	200	HTTP	Tunnel to	localhost:53888	0			chrome...		
8	101	HTTP	localhost:53888	/signalr/connect?transpor...	0			chrome...		
9	200	HTTP	localhost:53888	/signalr/connect?transpor...	325	no-cac...	text/event-...	chrome...		
10	200	HTTP	localhost:53888	/signalr/send?transport=s...	19	no-cac...	application/...	chrome...		
26	200	HTTP	localhost:53888	/signalr/abort?transport=...	0	no-cac...		chrome...		

Figure 5-9. *Fiddler output for the example program*

In the left pane, you see a list of resources requested by the application, including the request to the static HTML page, jQuery file, and dynamic ASP.NET SignalR hub proxy library.

After these requests comes the negotiation call, which is followed by connect, send, and abort steps that are necessary for ASP.NET SignalR to work (discussed later). The abortion step comes when we close the browser or move away from the page and try to end the connection with the server.

On this page you see information about these requests, including the result status code, protocol used, hostname, URL, body size, content type, and other valuable information. The right pane is for details about each of these requests. For example, the Statistics tab shown in Figure 5-10 displays the details for one of the connect steps.

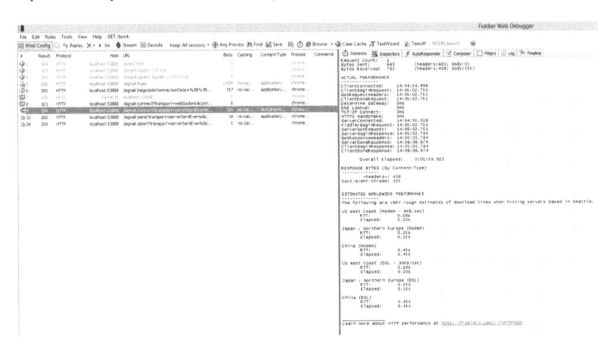

Figure 5-10. *Fiddler request details*

The details pane is split into a few tabs categorized by the type of information needed for each request. Some of these tabs are split into two horizontal panes as well to let you view more details. The Statistics tab gives general statistics about the request and response such as the protocol used, the execution time, size, and so on.

The handiest tab for troubleshooting ASP.NET SignalR applications is the Inspectors tab, which enables you to view the actual request and response headers and data in several formats.

Figure 5-11 shows the request and response for the connect request discussed previously.

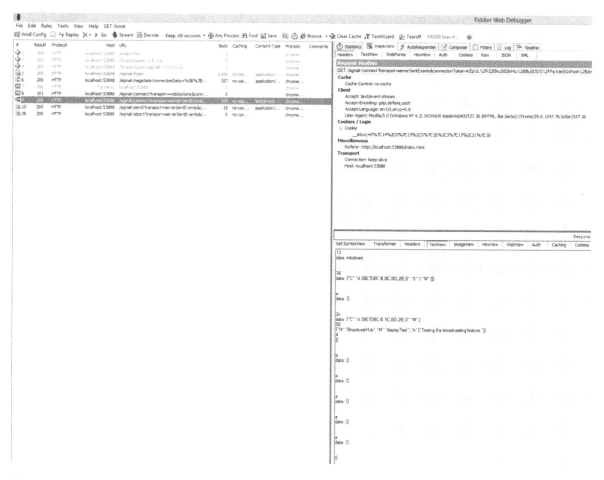

Figure 5-11. *Request and response details*

This pane has some valuable details about the request and response. One interesting part of this data is the URL requested with a GET verb that shows some of the details about the request, such as the type of transport used. It is very helpful to see the actual data being communicated between server and client to find where the communication failed.

Debugging the Server-Side Execution

The server component of ASP.NET SignalR is very similar to a typical ASP.NET application, in which you can set up breakpoint in Visual Studio and use other debugging features to test program execution. It can be used in conjunction with the previous approaches used to debug the client–side JavaScript code as well as in client-to-server communication.

> ■ **Note** For further information on how to debug an ASP.NET application, see *Pro ASP.NET 4 in C# 2010*, by Matthew MacDonald and Adam Freeman (Apress 2010), or any similar title on ASP.NET or C# development and debugging.

We don't want to repeat what you already know about Visual Studio debugging, so we don't go into more detail. We assume that you are already familiar with debugging features and techniques in Visual Studio.

Tracing Features

One great feature available in ASP.NET SignalR is the capability to trace many things on the server side to know what is exactly going on with clients. As discussed in Chapter 3, you can enable tracing features in ASP.NET SignalR by adding certain elements to your Web.Config file or editing your application configuration in IIS.

Here we discuss tracing features in ASP.NET SignalR because they assist in debugging applications much more easily, especially by looking at what is happening on the server side for each and every client. The bold code in Listing 5-4 is all the code needed to enable the tracing capabilities on a server in an ASP.NET SignalR application. (Although this code enables the whole tracing functionality, you usually don't need all the elements.)

Listing 5-4. Enable Tracing in ASP.NET SignalR

```xml
<?xml version="1.0" encoding="utf-8"?>
<!--
  For more information on how to configure your ASP.NET application, please visit
  http://go.microsoft.com/fwlink/?LinkId=169433
  -->
<configuration>
  <appSettings>
    <add key="webpages:Version" value="2.0.0.0" />
    <add key="webpages:Enabled" value="false" />
    <add key="PreserveLoginUrl" value="true" />
    <add key="ClientValidationEnabled" value="true" />
    <add key="UnobtrusiveJavaScriptEnabled" value="true" />
  </appSettings>
  <system.web>
    <httpRuntime targetFramework="4.5" />
    <compilation debug="true" targetFramework="4.5" />
    <pages>
      <namespaces>
        <add namespace="System.Web.Helpers" />
        <add namespace="System.Web.Mvc" />
        <add namespace="System.Web.Mvc.Ajax" />
        <add namespace="System.Web.Mvc.Html" />
        <add namespace="System.Web.Routing" />
        <add namespace="System.Web.WebPages" />
      </namespaces>
    </pages>
  </system.web>
```

```xml
<system.webServer>
  <validation validateIntegratedModeConfiguration="false" />
  <handlers>
    <remove name="ExtensionlessUrlHandler-ISAPI-4.0_32bit" />
    <remove name="ExtensionlessUrlHandler-ISAPI-4.0_64bit" />
    <remove name="ExtensionlessUrlHandler-Integrated-4.0" />
    <add name="ExtensionlessUrlHandler-ISAPI-4.0_32bit" path="*." verb="GET,HEAD,POST,DEBUG,
      PUT,DELETE,PATCH,OPTIONS" modules="IsapiModule" scriptProcessor="%windir%\Microsoft.NET\
      Framework\v4.0.30319\aspnet_isapi.dll" preCondition="classicMode,runtimeVersionv4.0,
      bitness32" responseBufferLimit="0" />
    <add name="ExtensionlessUrlHandler-ISAPI-4.0_64bit" path="*." verb="GET,HEAD,POST,DEBUG,
      PUT,DELETE,PATCH,OPTIONS" modules="IsapiModule" scriptProcessor="%windir%\Microsoft.NET\
      Framework64\v4.0.30319\aspnet_isapi.dll" preCondition="classicMode,runtimeVersionv4.0,
      bitness64" responseBufferLimit="0" />
    <add name="ExtensionlessUrlHandler-Integrated-4.0" path="*." verb="GET,HEAD,POST,DEBUG,
      PUT,DELETE,PATCH,OPTIONS" type="System.Web.Handlers.TransferRequestHandler"
      preCondition="integratedMode,runtimeVersionv4.0" />
  </handlers>
</system.webServer>
<system.diagnostics>
  <trace autoflush="true" indentsize="4">
    <listeners>
      <add name="default_traces" type="System.Diagnostics.TextWriterTraceListener"
        initializeData="default_traces.txt" />
    </listeners>
  </trace>
  <switches>
    <add name="SignalRSwitch" value="All" />
  </switches>
  <sources>
    <source name="Application" switchValue="All">
      <listeners>
        <add name="traces" />
      </listeners>
    </source>
    <source name="Microsoft.Owin.Host.SystemWeb" switchValue="All">
      <listeners>
        <add name="traces" />
      </listeners>
    </source>
    <source name="SignalR.Connection">
      <listeners>
        <add name="traces" />
      </listeners>
    </source>
    <source name="SignalR.PersistentConnection">
      <listeners>
        <add name="traces" />
      </listeners>
    </source>
```

```xml
    <source name="SignalR.HubDispatcher">
      <listeners>
        <add name="traces" />
      </listeners>
    </source>
    <source name="SignalR.Transports.WebSocketTransport">
      <listeners>
        <add name="traces" />
      </listeners>
    </source>
    <source name="SignalR.Transports.ServerSentEventsTransport">
      <listeners>
        <add name="traces" />
      </listeners>
    </source>
    <source name="SignalR.Transports.ForeverFrameTransport">
      <listeners>
        <add name="traces" />
      </listeners>
    </source>
    <source name="SignalR.Transports.LongPollingTransport">
      <listeners>
        <add name="traces" />
      </listeners>
    </source>
  </sources>
  <sharedListeners>
    <add name="traces" type="System.Diagnostics.TextWriterTraceListener"
      initializeData="server_traces.txt" />
  </sharedListeners>
  </system.diagnostics>
</configuration>
```

This code consists of some switches, listeners, and sources that help you trace different sources of information in an application. These are some concepts in the .NET Framework for the diagnostics features. If you're not familiar with them, take a look at MSDN documentation and other online sources to understand what they do.

ASP.NET SignalR has implemented these sources by default and has simplified the process for developers to enable tracing to diagnose application problems.

Here is a brief list of different sources that are self-explanatory by name:

- `Application`

- `Microsoft.Owin.Host.SystemWeb`

- `SignalR.Connection`

- `SignalR.PersistentConnection`

- `SignalR.HubDispatcher`

- `SignalR.Transports.WebSocketTransport`

- SignalR.Transports.ServerSentEventsTransport

- SignalR.Transports.ForeverFrameTransport

- SignalR.Transports.LongPollingTransport

Figure 5-12 shows the output when we run our example on two browsers to broadcast messages.

```
Output
Show output from: Debug                                        ▼  ↕  ↕↕  ↕  ⬚  ₐᵇ⊐
'iisexpress.exe' (Managed (v4.0.30319)): Loaded 'C:\Windows\Microsoft.Net\assembly\GAC_MSIL\System.Dynamic\v4.0_
SignalR.Transports.TransportHeartBeat Verbose: 0 : KeepAlive(e4f0be21-936f-4bd5-a6dc-a3fc992c71b3)
SignalR.Transports.TransportHeartBeat Verbose: 0 : KeepAlive(caee0072-465f-41c8-91a5-579dbdca44c1)
SignalR.HubDispatcher Information: 0 : The groups token is missing
SignalR.Transports.WebSocketTransport Information: 0 : Abort(caee0072-465f-41c8-91a5-579dbdca44c1)
SignalR.Transports.TransportHeartBeat Information: 0 : Removing connection caee0072-465f-41c8-91a5-579dbdca44c1
SignalR.HubDispatcher Information: 0 : The groups token is missing
SignalR.Transports.WebSocketTransport Information: 0 : End(caee0072-465f-41c8-91a5-579dbdca44c1)
SignalR.Transports.TransportHeartBeat Information: 0 : Connection 4c08a891-bc8f-4b55-942a-23b654e5a5e8 is New.
SignalR.Transports.WebSocketTransport Verbose: 0 : DrainWrites(caee0072-465f-41c8-91a5-579dbdca44c1)
SignalR.Transports.WebSocketTransport Information: 0 : CompleteRequest (caee0072-465f-41c8-91a5-579dbdca44c1)
SignalR.HubDispatcher Information: 0 : The groups token is missing
SignalR.Transports.WebSocketTransport Information: 0 : Abort(e4f0be21-936f-4bd5-a6dc-a3fc992c71b3)
SignalR.Transports.TransportHeartBeat Information: 0 : Removing connection e4f0be21-936f-4bd5-a6dc-a3fc992c71b3
SignalR.Transports.WebSocketTransport Information: 0 : End(e4f0be21-936f-4bd5-a6dc-a3fc992c71b3)
SignalR.Transports.WebSocketTransport Verbose: 0 : DrainWrites(e4f0be21-936f-4bd5-a6dc-a3fc992c71b3)
SignalR.Transports.WebSocketTransport Information: 0 : CompleteRequest (e4f0be21-936f-4bd5-a6dc-a3fc992c71b3)
SignalR.HubDispatcher Information: 0 : The groups token is missing
SignalR.Transports.TransportHeartBeat Information: 0 : Connection ed9e0ca5-b698-4c1f-9e73-4e19ecd37871 is New.
SignalR.Transports.TransportHeartBeat Verbose: 0 : KeepAlive(4c08a891-bc8f-4b55-942a-23b654e5a5e8)
SignalR.Transports.TransportHeartBeat Verbose: 0 : KeepAlive(ed9e0ca5-b698-4c1f-9e73-4e19ecd37871)
SignalR.Transports.TransportHeartBeat Verbose: 0 : KeepAlive(4c08a891-bc8f-4b55-942a-23b654e5a5e8)
SignalR.Transports.TransportHeartBeat Verbose: 0 : KeepAlive(ed9e0ca5-b698-4c1f-9e73-4e19ecd37871)
SignalR.Transports.TransportHeartBeat Verbose: 0 : KeepAlive(4c08a891-bc8f-4b55-942a-23b654e5a5e8)
SignalR.Transports.TransportHeartBeat Verbose: 0 : KeepAlive(ed9e0ca5-b698-4c1f-9e73-4e19ecd37871)
The thread '<No Name>' (0x48) has exited with code 0 (0x0).
```

Figure 5-12. *Tracing output*

As shown in the figure, there are two connections established from two different browsers, and the previous connections are dropped. On the left side of each tracing line, you see the name of the source that is generating the output.

If a request by a client gets to the server but fails to be processed, and you cannot find any appropriate exception using your debugging features, the good news is that such an exception should show up with details in the Output window.

Summary

This chapter discussed the important topic of debugging and tracing ASP.NET SignalR applications. These are essential steps of developing any SignalR application and can be complicated due to the server-client nature of ASP.NET SignalR.

We discussed the client-side JavaScript debugging of applications using browser tools, especially Google Chrome Developers Tools; then discussed the debugging of the communication bridge between client(s) and server using HTTP debugging tools, particularly Telerik Fiddler. Next was a brief discussion on debugging the server-side execution of applications.

You saw the helpful feature in ASP.NET SignalR that traces the server-side execution, and the chapter concluded with a discussion of the custom performance counters bundled with ASP.NET SignalR to monitor its performance.

Some common principles, tools, and techniques for debugging and tracing were discussed, and it is important to note that these tasks vary significantly by circumstance. Depending on your situation, you have to use your experience, skills, and these principles to take the appropriate actions.

CHAPTER 6

An Overview of the Clients that Support SignalR

This chapter discusses clients that are supported in SignalR and the details that separate individual clients. First, we show clients' configuration and how they can be adjusted for your application. The next section shows the communication that occurs between the client and server, which is followed by connection lifetime events that occur that can affect the client's connection. Finally, we go over a sample server and individual clients with details about clients' differences.

For you to get a good understanding of the clients, we discuss the supported clients and their interactions with the server. The clients are all very similar in terms of configuration, communication, and connection lifetime events. To demonstrate the interaction with the server, we furnish an example server code that can be used with all the clients of the particular type of persistent connection or hub.

Clients Supported by SignalR

To understand which clients are supported by SignalR, it is best to define what *supported* means. In this chapter, we define supported clients as client binaries that are compiled to run with the .NET framework or in a modern-day web browser. With these supported binaries, the following clients are available:

- JavaScript
- Basic .NET 4.0+ applications (such as Win Forms, WPF, and Console applications)
- Silverlight 5
- Windows Store
- Windows Phone 8

There are also nonsupported native clients such as the iPhone and Android that require native SDKs or third-party tools (covered in Chapter 7).

Client Configuration

To get the most from the client, options are available to customize the connection and transport for persistent connections and hubs. The configuration changes are all done to the connection. The options available to configure on the connection are query string parameters, HTTP headers, cookies, certificates, and transports. All the configuration options must be configured before the connection is started. These configuration changes are applied to every request.

Setting Query String Values for a Request

All SignalR clients allow extra query string parameters to be added, and the extra query string parameters will be appended to every communication request sent to the server. A JavaScript example of adding a query string value to a connection is shown in Listing 6-1, in which the ABTest key with a value of V1 is added.

Listing 6-1. JavaScript Client Configuration to Set Query String Parameters

```
var connection = $.hubConnection();
connection.qs = {'ABTest' : 'V1'};
```

Another example of a .NET client that adds a query string parameter is shown in Listing 6-2.

Listing 6-2. Another SignalR Client Configuration to Set Query String Parameters

```
Dictionary<string, string> queryString = new Dictionary<string, string>();
queryString["ABTest"] = "V1";
var connection = new Microsoft.AspNet.SignalR.Client.HubConnection("http://localhost", queryString);
```

For the JavaScript client, query string parameters are set in the qs property of the connection. In other SignalR clients, the query string parameters are set in the connection constructor.

Adding HTTP Headers

Besides the JavaScript client, all clients support adding HTTP headers that are added to the connection object. In Listing 6-3, a header named X-SpecialHeader is added to the request header collection with the value of MyValue. Like query string parameters, the headers are passed on every request sent to the server.

Listing 6-3. Adding HTTP Headers to a Connection

```
var connection = new Microsoft.AspNet.SignalR.Client.HubConnection("http://localhost");
```

connection.Headers.Add("X-SpecialHeader", "MyValue");Adding Cookies to the Request

Cookies are supported by all the clients. For the JavaScript client, cookies are added using the standard JavaScript functions. For other clients, the cookies are added to a CookieContainer to the CookieContainer property of the connection.

The example shown in Listing 6-4 adds a new CookieContainer to the connection. Next, a new cookie is added to the CookieContainer with the name, value, path, and domain specified in the constructor. As with headers and query string parameters, cookies are sent on every request.

Listing 6-4. Example of Setting Cookies on .NET Clients

```
var connection = new Microsoft.AspNet.SignalR.Client.HubConnection("http://localhost");
connection.CookieContainer = new System.Net.CookieContainer();
```

connection.CookieContainer.Add(new System.Net.Cookie("TestCookie", "CookieValue","/","localhost"));Setting Client Certificates

SignalR enables you to configure client certificates to connect to secure servers. The certificate configuration for JavaScript and Silverlight 5 clients is done by the web browser that is hosting the sites. For other clients, it is configured on the connection by calling the AddClientCertificate method.

Listing 6-5 shows a new certificate of type X509Certificate2 being created from a file called Certificate.cer and added to the connection using the AddClientCertificate method.

Listing 6-5. Adding Client Certificate to SignalR Connection

```
var connection = new Microsoft.AspNet.SignalR.Client.HubConnection("http://localhost");
connection.AddClientCertificate(new System.Security.Cryptography.X509Certificates.
X509Certificate2("Certificate.cer"));
```

⬛ **Note**   The X509Certificate2 class was added to the .NET 2.0+ Framework to provide extended functionality to the X509Certificate class.

Customizing the Transport

SignalR provides the functionality to select the priority and types of transports to use for your connection. JavaScript client configuration is different from all the other clients. This configuration option can be used if you have determined the transport(s) that work best for your application. It can also be used to restrict your application to use only certain transports that the application can adequately support. If a transport cannot be successfully negotiated, an error is raised and the connection fails.

The JavaScript client allows four types of transports: webSockets, foreverFrame, serverSendEvents, and longPolling. By default, the connection tries to find the first transport that both the client and server support. This list of transports can be overridden by passing the supported transports to the Start method of the connection. The override supports a single transport, as shown in Listing 6-6.

Listing 6-6. JavaScript Client Configuration for Single Transport

```
var connection = $.hubConnection();
//excluded connection logic
connection.start({ transport: 'webSockets' });
```

The override also supports an array of transports, as shown in Listing 6-7.

Listing 6-7. JavaScript Client Configuration with Multiple Transports for Fail-over

```
var connection = $.hubConnection();
//excluded connection logic
connection.start({ transport: ['webSockets','foreverFrame'] });
```

Other SignalR clients do not have support for the foreverFrame transport, but have the AutoTransport transport. If no transport is configured, the AutoTransport transport is the default. AutoTransport tries to negotiate the best transport out of the available transports. The configuration allows only one transport to be specified in the Start method of the connection. If the client does not support .NET 4.5, the webSockets transport is not available even if the server can support web sockets. Listing 6-8 is an example of how to start a connection using WebSocketTransport to use only web sockets for that connection.

Listing 6-8. .NET 4.5 Configuration of a Web Socket–Only Transport Connection

```
var connection = new Microsoft.AspNet.SignalR.Client.HubConnection("http://localhost");
//excluded connection logic
await connection.Start(new Microsoft.AspNet.SignalR.Client.Transports.WebSocketTransport());
```

Although transports do not usually need to be configured, they have limitations. To configure the clients with different transports or connection logic, a custom class is required. These types of customizations are covered in Chapter 7.

Client and Server Communication

Once a persistent connection or hub has been connected, the communication between client and server is made through connection-specific methods or proxy-generated methods. The persistent connection communication is through a Send method and a Receive event. The hub communication is through proxy methods that call methods on the server or the client.

Persistent Connection Communication

The persistent connection provides a relatively simple format for communication. To send information to the server, the client calls the Send method on the connection. To receive data from the server, the client subscribes to the Receive event. (Examples of sending and subscribing for various clients is available later in the chapter in the respective client section.)

Server Methods Called by the Hub Client

Clients can invoke server methods that are defined in the class that derives from the Hub class. Once a method has been defined on the server, the client calls the method by calling the invoke method on the HubProxy. The invoke method requires the method name and can send zero or more parameters to that method. Each client has an example in the respective client section.

Hub Client Methods Called by the Server

The server can call methods on the client by calling dynamic methods exposed by the HubContext and the client subscribing to the event in the HubProxy. The method can be called with zero or more parameters. Each client has a slightly different way of handling these events, so examples are provided in the respective client section.

Client-side Logging

During SignalR application development, things do not always work as expected. All the clients support some form of logging on the client to provide diagnostic information that should be used only in a non-production environment. For the JavaScript client, this logging is to the web browser console. The other clients log through the TraceWriter.

JavaScript client logging is enabled by setting the logging property on the connection to true, as shown in Listing 6-9. The trace output is then visible in the web browser console.

Listing 6-9. Example of Setting Logging in the JavaScript Client

```
var connection = $.hubConnection();
connection.logging = true;
```

.NET clients have more options when it comes to trace logging. There are multiple levels of tracing: All, Events, Messages, None, and StateChanges. Even the output location of the trace is configurable.

In Listing 6-10, we set the trace level of the client to All, which is all the traceable events. Next, the output of the logging is set to the console window output.

Listing 6-10. Example of Setting Logging in .NET Clients

```
var connection = new Microsoft.AspNet.SignalR.Client.HubConnection("http://localhost");
connection.TraceLevel = Microsoft.AspNet.SignalR.Client.TraceLevels.All;
```

connection.TraceWriter = Console.Out;Connection Lifetime Events

Connection lifetime events are raised during events that affect the state of a connection. Eight possible events can be raised by the clients; two are specific to the JavaScript client, one is specific to the other clients, and the rest of the events are raised by all clients.

The Starting and Disconnected events are specifically raised in the JavaScript client. The Starting event is raised once a successful connection has been negotiated, and the Disconnected event is raised when the connection has been disconnected.

The event specific to the other clients is the Closed event. This event is synonymous with the Disconnected event and is raised when the connection has been disconnected.

The rest of the events are raised by all clients: Received, ConnectionSlow, Reconnecting, Reconnected, and StateChanged. The Received event is raised when data is received from the server. The ConnectionSlow event is raised if the keep-alive signal has not arrived from the server within two-thirds of the connection timeout since the last keep-alive signal was received. The Reconnecting event is raised when the connection attempts to reconnect to the server. The next event is Reconnected, which occurs after a connection has successfully reconnected. The last event is StateChanged, which occurs when the connection has changed state.

Server Example for Clients

The persistent connection and hub server examples are provided for the client examples later in the chapter. These sample server examples should work with all clients of the respective types.

Persistent Connection Server Example

We now reuse the persistent connection server example from Chapter 2. It is a brief overview, so please revisit Chapter 2 if more detail is needed.

1. Create a new ASP.NET web application, as shown in Figure 6-1.

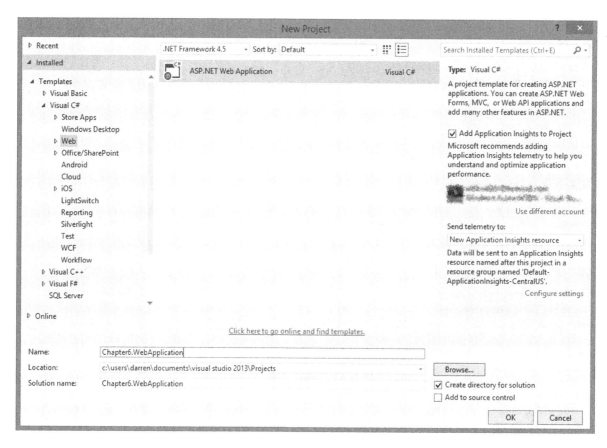

Figure 6-1. *Web application selection window*

2. Choose the MVC template, as shown in Figure 6-2.

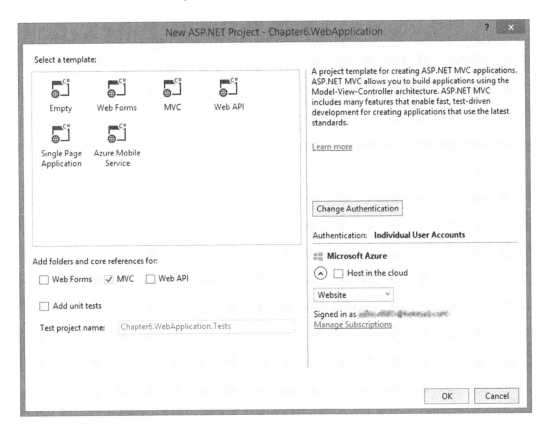

Figure 6-2. *New ASP.NET Project dialog box*

3. Run the following command in the package explorer window to install the necessary SignalR files: Install-Package Microsoft.AspNet.SignalR.

4. Open the Startup.cs file that was added by the NuGet command.

5. Add the code in Listing 6-11 to the Startup class in the Configuration method to register the PersistentConnection.

Listing 6-11. .NET C# PersistentConnection Registration in Configuration Code

```
app.MapSignalR<SamplePersistentConnection>("/SamplePC");
```

6. Create a PersistentConnections folder.

7. Add a new class to the PersistentConnections folder called SamplePersistentConnection.

8. Update the class to look like Listing 6-12.

Listing 6-12. .NET C# PersistentConnection Sample Code

```
public class SamplePersistentConnection : PersistentConnection
    {
        protected override System.Threading.Tasks.Task OnReceived(IRequest request,
         string connectionId, string data)
        {
            return Connection.Broadcast(data);
        }
    }
}
```

9. Add `Microsoft.AspNet.SignalR;` to the class so that the `Broadcast` extension method is available.

We now have a functioning persistent connection example server that works with all the persistent connection client examples in the chapter.

Hub Server Example

In this section, we create a server with hub endpoints to be accessible by all the hub clients. After we complete the following steps, we'll have a working server with hub endpoints.

1. Create a new ASP.NET web application (refer to Figure 6-1).

2. Choose the MVC template (refer to Figure 6-2).

3. Run the following command in the package explorer window to install the necessary SignalR files: `Install-Package Microsoft.AspNet.SignalR`.

4. Open the `Startup.cs` file that was added by the `NuGet` command.

5. Add `app.MapSignalR();` to the class, as shown in Listing 6-13.

Listing 6-13. Startup Class that Configures the SignalR Server

```
[assembly: OwinStartupAttribute(typeof(Chapter6.HubServer.Startup))]
namespace Chapter6.HubServer
{
    public partial class Startup
    {
        public void Configuration(IAppBuilder app)
        {
            ConfigureAuth(app);
            app.MapSignalR();
        }
    }
}
```

6. Create a new folder for the hubs.

7. Create the three classes listed in Listing 6-14.

Listing 6-14. Three Classes Needed to Create the Hub Server Example

```
public class AuctionHub : Microsoft.AspNet.SignalR.Hub
    {
        public AuctionHub()
        {
            BidManager.Start();
        }
        public override System.Threading.Tasks.Task OnConnected()
        {
            Clients.Caller.CloseBid();
            Clients.All.UpdateBid(BidManager.CurrentBid);
            return base.OnConnected();
        }
        public void MakeCurrentBid()
        {
            BidManager.CurrentBid.BidPrice += 1;
            BidManager.CurrentBid.ConnectionId = this.Context.ConnectionId;
            Clients.All.UpdateBid(BidManager.CurrentBid);
        }
        public void MakeBid(double bid)
        {
            if (bid < BidManager.CurrentBid.BidPrice)
            {
                return;
            }
            BidManager.CurrentBid.BidPrice = bid;
            BidManager.CurrentBid.ConnectionId = this.Context.ConnectionId;
            Clients.All.UpdateBid(BidManager.CurrentBid);
        }
    }

    public static class BidManager
    {
        static System.Threading.Timer _timer = new System.Threading.Timer(BidInterval, null, 0, 2000);
        public static Bid CurrentBid { get; set; }
        public static void Start()
        {
            //Empty class to make sure Static class is started
        }
        static void BidInterval(object o)
        {
            var clients = Microsoft.AspNet.SignalR.GlobalHost.ConnectionManager.
            GetHubContext<AuctionHub>().Clients;
            if (BidManager.CurrentBid == null || BidManager.CurrentBid.TimeLeft <= 0)
            {
                BidManager.SetBid();
            }
```

```
        BidManager.CurrentBid.TimeLeft -= 2;
        if (BidManager.CurrentBid.TimeLeft <= 0)
        {
            clients.AllExcept(CurrentBid.ConnectionId).CloseBid();
            if (!string.IsNullOrWhiteSpace(CurrentBid.ConnectionId))
                clients.Client(CurrentBid.ConnectionId).CloseBidWin(CurrentBid);
        }
        clients.All.UpdateBid(BidManager.CurrentBid);
    }
    static List<Bid> _items = new List<Bid>(){
        new Bid(){Name="Bike", Description="10 Speed", TimeLeft = 30, BidPrice = 120.0},
        new Bid(){Name="Car", Description="Sports Car", TimeLeft = 30, BidPrice = 1500.0},
        new Bid(){Name="TV", Description="Big screen TV", TimeLeft = 30, BidPrice = 330.0},
        new Bid(){Name="Boat", Description="Party Boat", TimeLeft = 30, BidPrice = 1200.0}
    };
    public static void SetBid()
    {
        Random rnd = new Random();
        CurrentBid = (Bid)_items[rnd.Next(0, _items.Count - 1)].Clone();
    }
}
}

public class Bid
{
    public Bid Clone()
    {
        return (Bid)MemberwiseClone();
    }
    public string Name { get; set; }
    public string Description { get; set; }
    public double BidPrice { get; set; }
    public int TimeLeft { get; set; }
    public string ConnectionId { get; set; }
}
```

With those steps completed, we now have a fully functional server with a hub endpoint that exposes the basic hub functionality. This example server has the MakeCurrentBid and MakeBid server methods that take zero and one parameter, respectively. The server is also wired up to call the CloseBid, CloseBidWin, and UpdateBid client methods on the client that take zero, one simple type parameter, and one complex type parameter, respectively.

■ **Note**   For the Silverlight example to work, a crossdomain.xml file is needed on the server that contains the content of Listing 6-15.

Listing 6-15. Contents of crossdomain.xml File

```
<?xml version="1.0" ?>
<cross-domain-policy>
  <allow-access-from domain="*" />
</cross-domain-policy>
```

Now that we have created servers to handle persistent connection and hub requests, we can create the clients that consume them.

HTML and JavaScript Clients

SignalR provides support for JavaScript clients using JQuery to provide persistent connection and hub clients to web browsers. These clients function a little differently from the rest of the client types provided by SignalR. This section discusses setting up the JavaScript client examples.

Persistent Connection Client

The persistent connection example in this section shows a simple chat application. It connects to the persistent connection server example created earlier in the chapter.

JavaScript Persistent Connection Example

To create this example, it is easiest to demonstrate using the persistent connection server example as the base. So we complete the following steps on that example:

1. Add a new HTML page to the root of the project.

2. Update the head section to reflect Listing 6-16.

Listing 6-16. Javascript Example Client Script Code

```
<script src="/scripts/jquery-1.8.2.js" type="text/javascript"></script>
<script src="/scripts/jquery.signalR-2.0.0-rc1.js" type="text/javascript"></script>

<script>
    $(function () {
        var connection = $.connection('http://localhost:####/samplepc');

        connection.received(function (data) {
            $('#messages').append('<li>' + data + '</li>');
        });

        connection.start().done(function()
        {
            $("#btnSend").click(function () {
                connection.send($('#name').val() + ': ' + $('#message').val());
            });
        })
    });
</script>
```

3. Update the version numbers of the JQuery and JQuery.SignalR scripts to the appropriate version that is in the Scripts folder.

4. Update #### in the connection to the port in which the example server is running.

5. Update the HTML section to reflect Listing 6-17.

Listing 6-17. Javascript Example Client HTML

```
<ul id="messages" style="border: 1px solid black; height: 250px; width: 450px; overflow:scroll;
list-style:none;"></ul>
<label>Name: </label>
<input id="name" value="User A" />
<label>Message: </label>
<input id="message" />
<button id="btnSend">Send</button>
```

Once we start the server and navigate to the HTML page that we created in multiple tabs or browsers, we can test the communication using a persistent connection (see Figure 6-3).

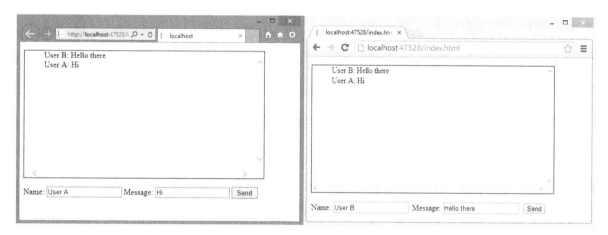

Figure 6-3. *Communication between two JavaScript clients over a persistent connection*

The next step is to create the JavaScript hub client example.

Hub Client

In this section, we go over an example of setting up a JavaScript–based hub client. This example demonstrates an auction by using the hub server example from earlier in the chapter.

Server Methods Called by the Client

The server methods called from the JavaScript client can contain zero or more parameters. Listings 6-18 and 6-19 show the syntax of calling the invoke method with zero or more parameters.

Listing 6-18. JavaScript Example of Calling a Server Method with No Parameters

```
var hubProxy = connection.createHubProxy('SampleHub');
hubProxy.invoke('SampleMethod');
```

Listing 6-19. JavaScript Example of Calling a Server Method with Multiple Parameters and a Complex Type

```
var hubProxy = connection.createHubProxy('SampleHub');
var complexType = {Name: 'Sam', Age: 23};
hubProxy.invoke('SampleMethod', complexType, 5);
```

Client Methods Called by the Server

The server can also "call" methods on a client by the JavaScript client subscribing to events on the HubProxy. Listings 6-20 and 6-21 show calling the on method with zero or more parameters.

Listing 6-20. JavaScript Example of Calling Client Methods from the Server with No Parameters

```
var hubProxy = connection.createHubProxy('SampleHub');
hubProxy.on('ClientMethod',
                 function () {
                 //perform some action on the client
                 });
```

Listing 6-21. JavaScript Example of Calling Client Methods from the Server with Multiple Parameters

```
var hubProxy = connection.createHubProxy('SampleHub');
hubProxy.on('ClientMethod',
                 function (param, anotherParam) {
                 //perform some action on the client
                 //param and anotherParam would be the two parameters passed in from the server
                 });
```

Now that you know the syntax to call methods on the server and client, you can see them in use in the next example.

JavaScript Hub Example

This example creates an auction client using the hub server example to demonstrate the calls from the server to the client and vice versa. This example can be easily added to the server example to show the functionality with the following steps:

1. Add a new HTML page to the root of the project.

2. Update the head section to reflect Listing 6-22.

Listing 6-22. Javascript Example Client Script Code

```
<script src="/scripts/jquery-1.8.2.min.js"></script>
<script src="/scripts/jquery.signalr-2.0.0-rc1.min.js"></script>
<script src="/signalr/hubs"></script>
<script>
    $(document).ready(function () {
        var connection = $.hubConnection();
        var hubProxy = connection.createHubProxy('AuctionHub');

        hubProxy.on('CloseBid', function () {
            UpdateButtons(false);
        })

        hubProxy.on('CloseBidWin', function (data) {
            UpdateButtons(false);
            UpdateBid(data, 1);
        })

        hubProxy.on('UpdateBid', function (data) {
            UpdateBid(data, 0);
            UpdateButtons(true);
        })
        function UpdateBid(bid, updateObject)
        {
            if(bid)
            {
                $('#lblName').text(bid.Name);
                $('#lblDescr').text(bid.Description);
                $('#lblBid').text(bid.BidPrice);
                $('#lblTime').text(bid.TimeLeft);
                if(updateObject > 0)
                {
                    $('#lstWins').append('<li>' + bid.Name + ' at ' + bid.BidPrice + '</li>')
                }
            }
        }
        function UpdateButtons(state) {
            $('#btnCurrentBid').enabled = state;
            $('#btnMakeBid').enabled = state;
        }
        connection.start().done(function () {
            $('#btnCurrentBid').click(function () { hubProxy.invoke('MakeCurrentBid'); });
            $('#btnMakeBid').click(function () { hubProxy.invoke('MakeBid',
            $('#txtBid').val()); });
        });
    });
</script>
```

3. Update the version numbers of the JQuery and JQuery.SignalR scripts to the appropriate version in the Scripts folder.

4. Update the HTML section to reflect Listing 6-23.

Listing 6-23. Javascript Example Client HTML

```
<label id="lblName"></label>
<label id="lblBid"></label><br />
<label id="lblDescr"></label>  
<label>Time Left:</label>
<label id="lblTime"></label><br />
<button id="btnCurrentBid">Current Bid</button>
<button id="btnMakeBid">Make Bid</button>
<input type="text" id="txtBid" />
<ul id="lstWins" style="list-style: none;"></ul>
```

Now when we use the browser and go to the index page, we have an auction client (see Figure 6-4).

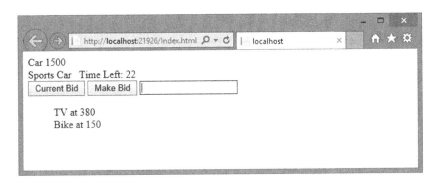

Figure 6-4. *Hub client example after two successful bid wins*

Other clients are very similar, but have small differences that we will show through examples—starting with basic .NET client.

.NET Clients

.NET clients are the core .NET 4.0+ clients such as WPF, Win Forms, and Console applications. Because the Silverlight, Windows Store, and Windows Phone 8 clients use different API wrappers around the .NET functionality, they are described later in their own sections.

Persistent Connection Client

The persistent connection client is fairly straightforward, so we re-create the persistent connection example of a simple chat room as a Win Forms application.

.NET Persistent Connection Example

For .NET SignalR Win Forms clients, you can use either the .NET 4.0 or 4.5 framework. To create the client sample, the following steps should be taken:

1. Create a new Windows Forms project (see Figure 6-5).

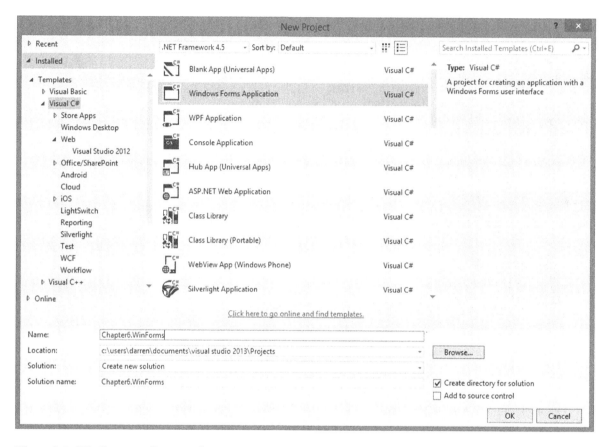

Figure 6-5. *Win Forms application selection menu*

2. Run the following command in the package explorer window: `Install-Package Microsoft.AspNet.SignalR.Client`.

3. Add a couple of text boxes, a button, and a list box to the form to look like Figure 6-6.

Figure 6-6. *Example of Win Forms persistent connection chat application*

4.   Update the form code to look like Listing 6-24.

Listing 6-24. .NET C# Win Forms SignalR Client Code

```
public partial class Form1 : Form
{
    Microsoft.AspNet.SignalR.Client.Connection myConnection = new Microsoft.AspNet.SignalR.Client.
    Connection("http://localhost:####/SamplePC/");

    public Form1()
    {
        InitializeComponent();
        button1.Click += button1_Click;
        myConnection.Received += myConnection_Received;
        myConnection.Start();
    }

    private void button1_Click(object sender, EventArgs e)
    {
        myConnection.Send(textBox1.Text + ":" + textBox2.Text);
    }

    void myConnection_Received(string obj)
    {
        listBox1.Invoke(new Action(() => listBox1.Items.Add(obj)) );
    }
}
```

5.   Update the #### in the connection to the correct port of your server application.

Because we have completed the persistent connection example, the next example is the Win Forms hub example.

Hub Client

In this section, we create a hub client using Win Forms. To show client differences, we use the same examples from the previous client sections—but in the context of the current client.

Server Methods Called by the Client

The server methods called from the Win Forms client can contain zero or more parameters. Listings 6-25 and 6-26 show examples.

Listing 6-25. Win Forms Example of Calling a Server Method with No Parameters

```
Var auctionProxy = hubConnection.CreateHubProxy("AuctionHub");
auctionProxy.Invoke("SampleMethod");
```

Listing 6-26. Win Forms Example of Calling a Server Method with Multiple Parameters and a Complex Type with a Return Value of bool

```
Var auctionProxy = hubConnection.CreateHubProxy("AuctionHub");
int age = 25;
var profile = new Profile("Handle", "Password");
auctionProxy.Invoke<bool>("SampleMethod", profile, age);
```

The Invoke method is what initiates the call. The first parameter listed is the name of the function to invoke on the server. The next parameter is a params, which can take 0 or many objects that are passed as input parameters. These input parameters are provided to the function specified in the first parameter of the invoke call. If the server method returns the type of value defined by the Invoke function's generic definition.

Client Methods Called by the Server

The server can "call" client methods by the Win Forms client subscribing to events on the HubProxy. The HubProxy can be called with zero parameters, as shown in Listing 6-27; and with one or more parameters, as shown in Listing 6-28.

Listing 6-27. Win Forms Example of Calling Client Methods from the Server with No Parameters

```
void Setup(){
    var auctionProxy = _hubConnection.CreateHubProxy("AuctionHub");
    auctionProxy.Subscribe("SampleMethodName").Received += SampleMethod;
}
void SampleMethod (IList<Newtonsoft.Json.Linq.JToken> obj) {
    //Invoke delegate on UI thread with no parameters from the server
    this.Invoke(sampleDelegate);
}
```

Listing 6-28. Win Forms Example of Calling Client Methods from the Server with Multiple Parameters

```
void Setup(){
    var auctionProxy = _hubConnection.CreateHubProxy("AuctionHub");
    auctionProxy.Subscribe("SampleMethodName").Received += SampleMethod;
}
void SampleMethod (IList<Newtonsoft.Json.Linq.JToken> obj) {
    //Invoke delegate on UI thread with the first parameter from the server
    this.Invoke(sampleDelegate, obj[0]);
}
```

The clients subscribe to the Received event with the specified event name. When these events are raised, they are from a thread other than the UI thread, so a delegate must be used to update other threads. In these examples, the delegate is used to update the UI thread. If the server has parameters to pass in, they are contained in the IList<JToken> object and can be accessed by their index position. In the next section, you see these methods in action.

.NET Hub Example

This is an example of the Win Forms client as an auction client connecting to the hub server example.

1. Create a new Windows Form project (refer to Figure 6-5).

2. Run the following command in the package explorer window: Install-Package Microsoft.AspNet.SignalR.Client.

3. Add a couple of buttons named btnCurrentBid and btnMakeBid showing Current Bid and Make Bid, respectively.

4. Add a text box named txtBid.

5. Add a list box named lstWins.

6. Add four labels named lblName, lblDescr, lblBid, and lblTime showing Name, Description, Bid, and Time, respectively.

7. The arrangement of these items can be made to look like Figure 6-7.

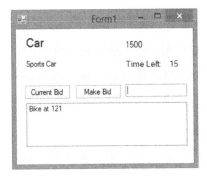

Figure 6-7. *Final output of example hub application*

8. Update the form code to look like Listing 6-29.

Listing 6-29. Win Forms Code of Hub Example

```
public partial class frmAuctionClient : Form
{
    public Microsoft.AspNet.SignalR.Client.HubConnection _hubConnection;
    public Microsoft.AspNet.SignalR.Client.IHubProxy _auctionProxy;
    delegate void UpdateBid(dynamic bid, int formObject);
    delegate void UpdateButtons(bool enabled);
    UpdateBid _updateDelegate;
    UpdateButtons _updateButtonsDelegate;
    public frmAuctionClient()
    {
        InitializeComponent();
        SetupHub();
    }
    private async void SetupHub()
    {
        _updateDelegate = new UpdateBid(UpdateBidMethod);
        _updateButtonsDelegate = new UpdateButtons(UpdateButtonsMethod);
        _hubConnection = new Microsoft.AspNet.SignalR.Client.HubConnection
        ("http://localhost:####");
        _auctionProxy = _hubConnection.CreateHubProxy("AuctionHub");
        _auctionProxy.Subscribe("UpdateBid").Received += UpdateBid_auctionProxy;
        _auctionProxy.Subscribe("CloseBid").Received += CloseBid_auctionProxy;
        _auctionProxy.Subscribe("CloseBidWin").Received += CloseBidWin_auctionProxy;

        await _hubConnection.Start();
    }
    void UpdateBidMethod(dynamic bid, int formObject)
    {
        if (bid != null)
        {
            lblName.Text = bid.Name;
            lblDescr.Text = bid.Description;
            lblBid.Text = bid.BidPrice;
            lblTime.Text = bid.TimeLeft;
            if(formObject > 0)
            {
                lstWins.Items.Add(bid.Name + " at " + bid.BidPrice);
            }
        }
    }
    void UpdateButtonsMethod(bool enabled)
    {
        btnCurrentBid.Enabled = enabled;
        btnMakeBid.Enabled = enabled;
    }
```

```
    void UpdateBid_auctionProxy(IList<Newtonsoft.Json.Linq.JToken> obj)
    {
        this.Invoke(_updateDelegate, obj[0],0);
        this.Invoke(_updateButtonsDelegate, true);
    }
    void CloseBid_auctionProxy(IList<Newtonsoft.Json.Linq.JToken> obj)
    {
        this.Invoke(_updateButtonsDelegate, false);
    }
    void CloseBidWin_auctionProxy(IList<Newtonsoft.Json.Linq.JToken> obj)
    {
        this.Invoke(_updateButtonsDelegate, false);
        this.Invoke(_updateDelegate, obj[0], 1);
    }
    private void btnCurrentBid_Click(object sender, EventArgs e)
    {
        _auctionProxy.Invoke("MakeCurrentBid");
    }

    private void btnMakeBid_Click(object sender, EventArgs e)
    {
        _auctionProxy.Invoke<string>("MakeBid", txtBid.Text);
    }
}
```

9. Update the #### in the connection to the correct port of your server application

Although the examples are simple and straightforward, they require detail depending on the client that is being implemented. The next section shows Silverlight 5 client examples so you can see the difference between them and Win Forms clients.

Silverlight Clients

SignalR supports Silverlight 5 applications that are .NET 4.0 and greater. The Silverlight 5 clients have most of the functionality of the .NET Win Forms clients, but the network features such as the proxy and capability to set the user agent strings are not available.

Persistent Connection Client

The Silverlight 5 persistent connection example shown here is the same chat application running on the default template web page provided by the project.

Silverlight 5 Persistent Connection Example

The Silverlight 5 client sample is very similar to the Win Forms sample due to a lot of shared client code. Follow these steps to create the client sample:

1. Create a new Silverlight 5 project (see Figure 6-8).

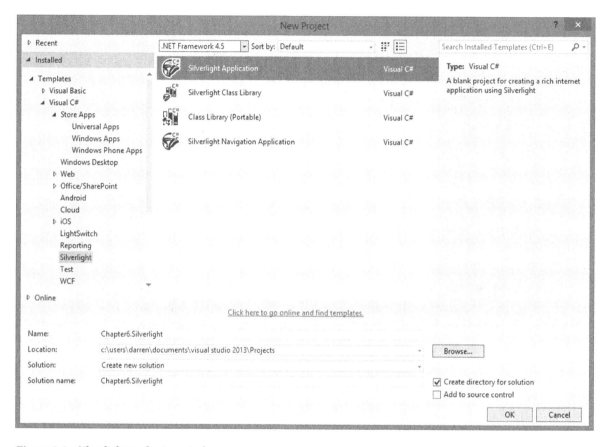

Figure 6-8. *Silverlight 5 selection window*

2. Select to host the application in a new web site, as shown in Figure 6-9.

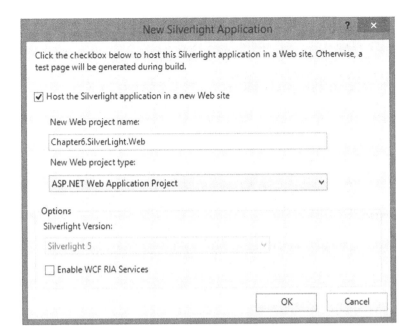

Figure 6-9. Silverlight 5 host selection window

3. After the project is created, select the application as the startup project so that the NuGet install will install the package to this project.

4. Run the following command in the package explorer window: `Install-Package Microsoft.AspNet.SignalR.Client`.

5. After the package is installed, set the web site as the startup project.

6. Update `MainPage.xaml` to look like Listing 6-30.

Listing 6-30. Silverlight 5 Client XAML

```
<UserControl x:Class="SilverlightApplication.MainPage"
    xmlns="http://schemas.microsoft.com/winfx/2006/xaml/presentation"
    xmlns:x="http://schemas.microsoft.com/winfx/2006/xaml"
    xmlns:d="http://schemas.microsoft.com/expression/blend/2008"
    xmlns:mc="http://schemas.openxmlformats.org/markup-compatibility/2006"
    mc:Ignorable="d"
    d:DesignHeight="300" d:DesignWidth="400">
```

```xml
<Grid x:Name="LayoutRoot" Background="White">
    <ListBox Name="lstConvo" HorizontalAlignment="Left" Height="204" Margin="10,63,0,0"
VerticalAlignment="Top" Width="367"/>
        <TextBox Name="txtName" HorizontalAlignment="Left" Height="23" Margin="10,22,0,0"
TextWrapping="Wrap" Text="User A" VerticalAlignment="Top" Width="120"/>
        <TextBox Name="txtMessage" HorizontalAlignment="Left" Height="23" Margin="146,22,0,0"
TextWrapping="Wrap" Text="" VerticalAlignment="Top" Width="120"/>
        <Button Name="btnSend" Content="Send" HorizontalAlignment="Left" Margin="287,22,0,0"
VerticalAlignment="Top" Width="75"/>
    </Grid>
</UserControl>
```

7. Update the `MainPage.cs` class to look like Listing 6-31.

Listing 6-31. Silverlight 5 Client Code

```csharp
public partial class MainPage : UserControl
{
    Microsoft.AspNet.SignalR.Client.Connection myConnection =
    new Microsoft.AspNet.SignalR.Client.Connection("http://localhost:####/SamplePC/");
    public MainPage()
    {
        InitializeComponent();
        btnSend.Click += btnSend_Click;
        myConnection.Received += myConnection_Received;
        myConnection.Start();
    }

    private void btnSend_Click(object sender, RoutedEventArgs e)
    {
        myConnection.Send(txtName.Text + ": " + txtMessage.Text);
    }

    void myConnection_Received(string obj)
    {
        Dispatcher.BeginInvoke(() => { lstConvo.Items.Add(obj); });
    }
}
```

8. Update the #### in the connection to the correct port of your server application.

After the application is complete, you can run it in a browser and it will look like Figure 6-10.

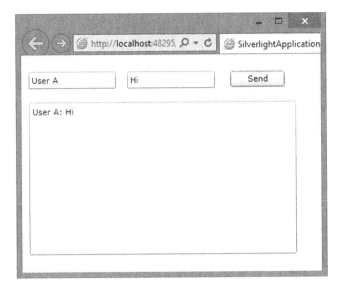

Figure 6-10. *Final result of running Silverlight 5 client application and sending some messages*

■ **Tip** If you run the application in Internet Explorer and you notice that the address bar is accessing the file system instead of a web address such as localhost, you might receive security errors. To correct this problem, access the application using the localhost or web address to run in an Internet Explorer security zone that allows Silverlight applications and enables Internet access from those applications.

This example resembles the .NET client example, but has a different control layout (XAML), has a different mechanism for cross-thread communication, and runs in the web browser. You will continue to see differences in the remaining client examples.

Hub Client

In this section, a hub client is created using Silverlight 5. The hub client example in this section is an auction client using the example hub server.

Server Methods Called by the Client

The server methods called from the Silverlight 5 client can contain zero or more parameters. Examples of calling Invoke with zero parameters and more than one parameter can be seen in Listings 6-32 and 6-33.

Listing 6-32. Silverlight 5 Example of Calling a Server Method with No Parameters

```
Var auctionProxy = hubConnection.CreateHubProxy("AuctionHub");
auctionProxy.Invoke("SampleMethod");
```

Listing 6-33. Silverlight 5 Example of Calling a Server Method with Multiple Parameters and a Complex Type with a Return Value of bool

```
Var auctionProxy = hubConnection.CreateHubProxy("AuctionHub");
int age = 25;
var profile = new Profile("Handle", "Password");
auctionProxy.Invoke<bool>("SampleMethod", profile, age);
```

Client Methods Called by the Server

The server can "call" client methods by the Silverlight 5 client subscribing to events on the HubProxy with zero (see Listing 6-34) or more (see Listing 6-35) parameters.

Listing 6-34. Silverlight 5 Example of Calling Client Methods from the Server with No Parameters

```
void Setup(){
    var auctionProxy = _hubConnection.CreateHubProxy("AuctionHub");
    auctionProxy.Subscribe("SampleMethodName").Received += SampleMethod;
}
void SampleMethod (IList<Newtonsoft.Json.Linq.JToken> obj) {
    //Perform action on UI thread with delegate
    Dispatcher.BeginInvoke(someDelegate);
}
```

Listing 6-35. Silverlight 5 Example of Calling Client Methods from the Server with Multiple Parameters

```
void Setup(){
    var auctionProxy = _hubConnection.CreateHubProxy("AuctionHub");
    auctionProxy.Subscribe("SampleMethodName").Received += SampleMethod;
}
void SampleMethod (IList<Newtonsoft.Json.Linq.JToken> obj) {
     //Perform action on UI thread with delegate
    Dispatcher.BeginInvoke(someDelegate, obj[0]);
}
```

Silverlight 5 Hub Example

As we have done in the previous sections we will use the following steps to create out Silverlight 5 hub example.

1. Create a new Silverlight 5 project (refer to Figure 6-8).

2. Select to host the application in a new web site (refer to Figure 6-9).

3. After the project is created, select the application as the startup project so that the NuGet install will install the package to this project.

4. Run the following command in the package explorer window: `Install-Package Microsoft.AspNet.SignalR.Client`.

5. Run the following command in the package explorer window: `Install-package Microsoft.Bcl.Async`.

6. After the package is installed, set the web site as the startup project.

7. Update `MainPage.xaml` to look like Listing 6-36.

Listing 6-36. Silverlight 5 Client XAML

```
<UserControl x:Class="Chapter6.Silverlight.MainPage"
    xmlns="http://schemas.microsoft.com/winfx/2006/xaml/presentation"
    xmlns:x="http://schemas.microsoft.com/winfx/2006/xaml"
    xmlns:d="http://schemas.microsoft.com/expression/blend/2008"
    xmlns:mc="http://schemas.openxmlformats.org/markup-compatibility/2006"
    mc:Ignorable="d"
    d:DesignHeight="600" d:DesignWidth="500">
    <Grid x:Name="LayoutRoot" Background="Transparent">
        <Grid.RowDefinitions>
            <RowDefinition Height="Auto"/>
            <RowDefinition Height="*"/>
        </Grid.RowDefinitions>
        <StackPanel>
            <Grid>
                <TextBlock HorizontalAlignment="Left" Name="lblName"></TextBlock>
                <TextBlock Margin="0,0,50,0" HorizontalAlignment="Right" Name="lblBid"></TextBlock>
            </Grid>
            <Grid Margin="0,50,0,0">
                <TextBlock HorizontalAlignment="Left" Name="lblDescr"></TextBlock>
                <TextBlock HorizontalAlignment="Center">Time Left:</TextBlock>
                <TextBlock Margin="0,0,50,0" HorizontalAlignment="Right" Name="lblTime"></TextBlock>
            </Grid>
            <Grid  Margin="0,50,0,0">
                <Button Name="btnCurrentBid" HorizontalAlignment="Left" Width="175">Current
                Bid</Button>
                <Button Name="btnMakeBid" HorizontalAlignment="Center" Width="150">Make Bid</Button>
                <TextBox Name="txtBid" HorizontalAlignment="Right" Width="175"/>
            </Grid>
            <ListBox Name="lstWins"></ListBox>
        </StackPanel>
    </Grid>
</UserControl>
```

8. Update the `MainPage.cs` class to look like Listing 6-37.

Listing 6-37. Silverlight 5 Client Code

```
public partial class MainPage : UserControl
    {
        public Microsoft.AspNet.SignalR.Client.HubConnection _hubConnection;
        public Microsoft.AspNet.SignalR.Client.IHubProxy _auctionProxy;
        delegate void UpdateBid(dynamic bid, int formObject);
        delegate void UpdateButtons(bool enabled);
        UpdateBid _updateDelegate;
        UpdateButtons _updateButtonsDelegate;

        public MainPage()
        {
            InitializeComponent();
            btnCurrentBid.Click += btnCurrentBid_Click;
            btnMakeBid.Click += btnMakeBid_Click;
            SetupHub();
        }

        private async void SetupHub()
        {
            _updateDelegate = new UpdateBid(UpdateBidMethod);
            _updateButtonsDelegate = new UpdateButtons(UpdateButtonsMethod);
            _hubConnection = new Microsoft.AspNet.SignalR.Client.HubConnection
            ("http://192.168.1.108:####/");
            _auctionProxy = _hubConnection.CreateHubProxy("AuctionHub");
            _auctionProxy.Subscribe("UpdateBid").Received += UpdateBid_auctionProxy;
            _auctionProxy.Subscribe("CloseBid").Received += CloseBid_auctionProxy;
            _auctionProxy.Subscribe("CloseBidWin").Received += CloseBidWin_auctionProxy;
            await _hubConnection.Start();
        }
        void UpdateBidMethod(dynamic bid, int formObject)
        {
            if (bid != null)
            {
                lblName.Text = (string)bid["Name"];
                lblDescr.Text = (string)bid["Description"];
                lblBid.Text = (string)bid["BidPrice"];
                lblTime.Text = (string)bid["TimeLeft"];
                if (formObject > 0)
                {
                    lstWins.Items.Add((string)bid["Name"] + " at " + (string)bid["BidPrice"]);
                }
            }
        }
        void UpdateButtonsMethod(bool enabled)
        {
            btnCurrentBid.IsEnabled = enabled;
            btnMakeBid.IsEnabled = enabled;
        }
```

```
void UpdateBid_auctionProxy(IList<Newtonsoft.Json.Linq.JToken> obj)
{
    Dispatcher.BeginInvoke(_updateDelegate, obj[0], 0);
    Dispatcher.BeginInvoke(_updateButtonsDelegate, true);
}
void CloseBid_auctionProxy(IList<Newtonsoft.Json.Linq.JToken> obj)
{
    Dispatcher.BeginInvoke(_updateButtonsDelegate, false);
}
void CloseBidWin_auctionProxy(IList<Newtonsoft.Json.Linq.JToken> obj)
{
    Dispatcher.BeginInvoke(_updateButtonsDelegate, false);
    Dispatcher.BeginInvoke(_updateDelegate, obj[0], 1);
}
private void btnCurrentBid_Click(object sender, EventArgs e)
{
    _auctionProxy.Invoke("MakeCurrentBid");
}

private void btnMakeBid_Click(object sender, EventArgs e)
{
    _auctionProxy.Invoke<string>("MakeBid", this.txtBid.Text);
}
}
```

9. Update the #### in the connection to the correct port of your server application

The final product of this example can be seen in Figure 6-11.

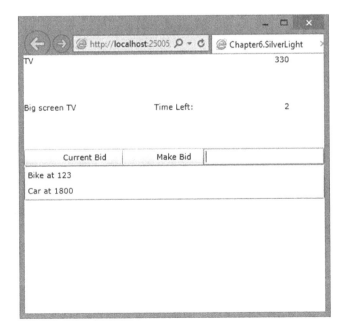

Figure 6-11. *Example of Silverlight 5 hub client*

This is another successful example client that further demonstrates the differences between the various clients. The next clients to be discussed are Windows Store clients.

Windows Store Clients

Both persistent connections and hubs are supported for Windows Store clients. To develop these client applications, Windows 8.1 must be installed to support the newest additions to store apps.

Persistent Connection Client

The Windows Store client applications support persistent connection clients. The following example creates a simple chat application using a Windows Store template.

Windows Store Client Persistent Connection Example

To create the client sample, follow these steps:

1. Create a new Windows Store project with the Blank App template, as shown in Figure 6-12.

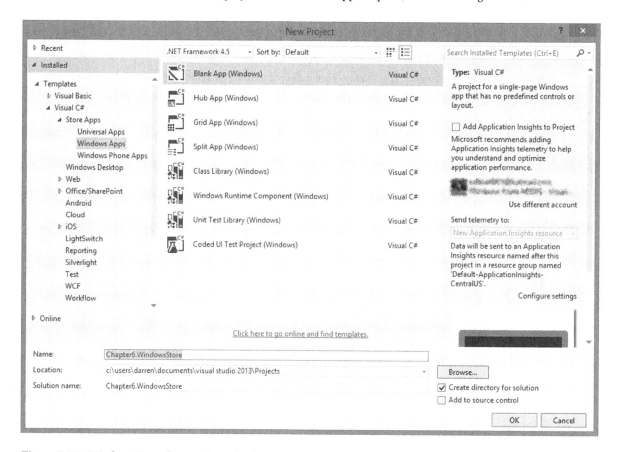

Figure 6-12. *Windows Store client project selection*

2. Run the following command in the package explorer window: `Install-Package Microsoft.AspNet.SignalR.Client`.

3. Update the `MainPage.xaml.cs` class to look like Listing 6-38.

Listing 6-38. .NET C# Windows Store SignalR Client Code

```
public sealed partial class MainPage : Page
    {
        Microsoft.AspNet.SignalR.Client.Connection myConnection = new Microsoft.AspNet.SignalR.
        Client.Connection("http://localhost:####/SamplePC/");
        public MainPage()
        {
            this.InitializeComponent();
            myConnection.Received += myConnection_Received;
            myConnection.Start().Wait();
        }
        private void SendButton_Click(object sender, RoutedEventArgs e)
        {
            myConnection.Send(txtName.Text + ": " + txtInput.Text);
        }
        private void myConnection_Received(string data)
        {
            UpdateList(data);
        }
        private async void UpdateList(string data)
        {
            await itemListBox.Dispatcher.RunAsync(Windows.UI.Core.CoreDispatcherPriority.Normal,
                () =>
                {
                    var item = new ListBoxItem() { Content = data };
                    itemListBox.Items.Add(item);
                });
        }
    }
```

4. Update `MainPage.xaml` to look like Listing 6-39.

Listing 6-39. .NET C# Windows Store Client XAML

```
<Page
    x:Class="Chapter6_WindowsStoreClient.MainPage"
    xmlns="http://schemas.microsoft.com/winfx/2006/xaml/presentation"
    xmlns:x="http://schemas.microsoft.com/winfx/2006/xaml"
    xmlns:local="using:Chapter6_WindowsStoreClient"
    xmlns:d="http://schemas.microsoft.com/expression/blend/2008"
    xmlns:mc="http://schemas.openxmlformats.org/markup-compatibility/2006"
    mc:Ignorable="d">
```

```xml
<Grid Background="{StaticResource ApplicationPageBackgroundThemeBrush}">
    <TextBlock Margin="10,10,0,0">Name:</TextBlock>
    <TextBlock Margin="120,10,0,0">Data:</TextBlock>
    <TextBox x:Name="txtName"
             Text="User A"
             Width="100"
             Height="50"
             HorizontalAlignment="Left"
             VerticalAlignment="Top"
             IsEnabled="True"
             IsReadOnly="False"
             Margin="10,30,0,0"
             TabIndex="1"/>
    <TextBox x:Name="txtInput"
             Width="250"
             Height="50"
             HorizontalAlignment="Left"
             VerticalAlignment="Top"
             IsEnabled="True"
             IsReadOnly="False"
             Margin="120,30,0,0"
             TabIndex="1"/>
    <Button x:Name="btnSend"
            Click="SendButton_Click"
            Width="100"
            Height="50"
            Margin="380,30,0,0"
            VerticalAlignment="Top">Send
    </Button>
    <ListBox
        x:Name="itemListBox"
        AutomationProperties.AutomationId="ItemsListView"
        AutomationProperties.Name="Items"
        Grid.Row="1"
        Margin="0,100,0,0"
        Width="450"
        HorizontalAlignment="Left">
    </ListBox>
</Grid>
</Page>
```

5.   Update the #### in the connection to the correct port of your server application.

If you run the code in the emulator, you should see an example that looks like Figure 6-13.

Figure 6-13. *Example of Windows Store client*

The Windows Store client has a control layout similar to the Silverlight application. But the real difference between the clients is that the Windows Store app runs locally, and Silverlight runs in the browser. Another major difference is the way the threads are dispatched. The Windows Store hub client is discussed next.

Hub Client

In this section, we show how to create a hub client using the Windows Store client application. It is the same auction client that we used in the previous examples so that the clients can be compared.

Server Methods Called by the Client

The server methods called from the Windows Store client can contain zero or more parameters. Examples of calling the Invoke method with zero or one or more parameters can be seen in Listings 6-40 and 6-41, respectively.

Listing 6-40. Windows Store Client Example of Calling a Server Method with No Parameters

```
Var auctionProxy = hubConnection.CreateHubProxy("AuctionHub");
auctionProxy.Invoke("SampleMethod");
```

Listing 6-41. Windows Store Client Example of Calling a Server Method with Multiple Parameters and a Complex Type with a Return Value of bool

```
Var auctionProxy = hubConnection.CreateHubProxy("AuctionHub");
int age = 25;
var profile = new Profile("Handle", "Password");
auctionProxy.Invoke<bool>("SampleMethod", profile, age);
```

Client Methods Called by the Server

The server can "call" client methods by the Windows Store client subscribing to events on the HubProxy (see Listings 6-42 and 6-43).

Listing 6-42. Windows Store Client Example of Calling Client Methods from the Server with No Parameters

```
void Setup(){
    var auctionProxy = _hubConnection.CreateHubProxy("AuctionHub");
    auctionProxy.Subscribe("SampleMethodName").Received += SampleMethod;
}
async void SampleMethod (IList<Newtonsoft.Json.Linq.JToken> obj) {
    await Dispatcher.RunAsync(Windows.UI.Core.CoreDispatcherPriority.Normal, () =>{
    //Perform action on UI thread
    }
}
```

Listing 6-43. Windows Store Client Example of Calling Client Methods from the Server with Multiple Parameters

```
void Setup(){
    var auctionProxy = _hubConnection.CreateHubProxy("AuctionHub");
    auctionProxy.Subscribe("SampleMethodName").Received += SampleMethod;
}
async void SampleMethod (IList<Newtonsoft.Json.Linq.JToken> obj) {
    await Dispatcher.RunAsync(Windows.UI.Core.CoreDispatcherPriority.Normal, () =>{
    //Perform action on UI thread
    this.Age = obj[0];
    }
}
```

Windows Store Client Hub Example

To create the client sample, follow these steps:

1. Create a new Windows Store project with the Blank App template.

2. Run the following command in the package explorer window: `Install-Package Microsoft.AspNet.SignalR.Client`.

3. Update the `MainPage.xaml.cs` class to look like Listing 6-44.

Listing 6-44. Windows Store Client Code

```
public sealed partial class MainPage : Page
{
    public Microsoft.AspNet.SignalR.Client.HubConnection _hubConnection;
    public Microsoft.AspNet.SignalR.Client.IHubProxy _auctionProxy;

    public MainPage()
    {
        InitializeComponent();
        btnCurrentBid.Click += btnCurrentBid_Click;
        btnMakeBid.Click += btnMakeBid_Click;
        SetupHub();
    }

    private async void SetupHub()
    {
        _hubConnection = new Microsoft.AspNet.SignalR.Client.HubConnection
        ("http://192.168.1.108:####/");
        _auctionProxy = _hubConnection.CreateHubProxy("AuctionHub");
        _auctionProxy.Subscribe("UpdateBid").Received += UpdateBid_auctionProxy;
        _auctionProxy.Subscribe("CloseBid").Received += CloseBid_auctionProxy;
        _auctionProxy.Subscribe("CloseBidWin").Received += CloseBidWin_auctionProxy;

        await _hubConnection.Start();
    }
    void UpdateBid(dynamic bid, int formObject)
    {
        if (bid != null)
        {
            lblName.Text = bid.Name;
            lblDescr.Text = bid.Description;
            lblBid.Text = bid.BidPrice;
            lblTime.Text = bid.TimeLeft;
            if(formObject > 0)
            {
                lstWins.Items.Add(bid.Name + " at " + bid.BidPrice);
            }
        }
    }
```

```
void UpdateButtons(bool enabled)
{
    btnCurrentBid.IsEnabled = enabled;
    btnMakeBid.IsEnabled = enabled;
}
async void UpdateBid_auctionProxy(IList<Newtonsoft.Json.Linq.JToken> obj)
{
    await Dispatcher.RunAsync(Windows.UI.Core.CoreDispatcherPriority.Normal,
    () =>{
        UpdateBid(obj[0],0);
        UpdateButtons(true);
    });
}
async void CloseBid_auctionProxy(IList<Newtonsoft.Json.Linq.JToken> obj)
{
    await Dispatcher.RunAsync(Windows.UI.Core.CoreDispatcherPriority.Normal,
    () =>{
        UpdateButtons(false);
    });
}

async void CloseBidWin_auctionProxy(IList<Newtonsoft.Json.Linq.JToken> obj)
{
    await Dispatcher.RunAsync(Windows.UI.Core.CoreDispatcherPriority.Normal,
    () =>
    {
        UpdateButtons(false);
        UpdateBid(obj[0], 1);
    });
}

private void btnCurrentBid_Click(object sender, RoutedEventArgs e)
{
    _auctionProxy.Invoke("MakeCurrentBid");
}

private void btnMakeBid_Click(object sender, RoutedEventArgs e)
{
    _auctionProxy.Invoke<string>("MakeBid", this.txtBid.Text);
}
}
```

4.   Update `MainPage.xaml` to look like Listing 6-45.

Listing 6-45. Windows Store Client XAML

```
<Page
    x:Class="WindowsStore.MainPage"
    xmlns="http://schemas.microsoft.com/winfx/2006/xaml/presentation"
    xmlns:x="http://schemas.microsoft.com/winfx/2006/xaml"
    xmlns:local="using:WindowsStore"
    xmlns:d="http://schemas.microsoft.com/expression/blend/2008"
    xmlns:mc="http://schemas.openxmlformats.org/markup-compatibility/2006"
    mc:Ignorable="d">

    <Grid x:Name="LayoutRoot" Background="Transparent">
        <Grid.RowDefinitions>
            <RowDefinition Height="Auto"/>
            <RowDefinition Height="*"/>
        </Grid.RowDefinitions>
        <StackPanel>
            <Grid Margin="0,50,0,0">
                <TextBlock Name="lblName" Width="150" HorizontalAlignment="Left"></TextBlock>
                <TextBlock Margin="185,0,0,0" >Last Bid:</TextBlock>
                <TextBlock Margin="240,0,0,0" Name="lblBid"></TextBlock>
            </Grid>
            <Grid>
                <TextBlock Name="lblDescr"></TextBlock>
                <TextBlock Margin="185,0,0,0" >Time Left:</TextBlock>
                <TextBlock Margin="240, 0,0,0" Name="lblTime"></TextBlock>
            </Grid>
            <Grid Margin="0,10,0,0">
                <Button Name="btnCurrentBid" Width="175">Current Bid</Button>
                <Button Name="btnMakeBid" Margin="185,0,0,0" Width="150">Make Bid</Button>
                <TextBox Name="txtBid" Margin="360, 0,0,0" Width="175" HorizontalAlignment="Left"/>
            </Grid>
            <ListBox Name="lstWins"></ListBox>
        </StackPanel>
    </Grid>
</Page>
```

5. Update the #### in the connection to the correct port of your server application.

When you view this example in the browser, you see something similar to Figure 6-14.

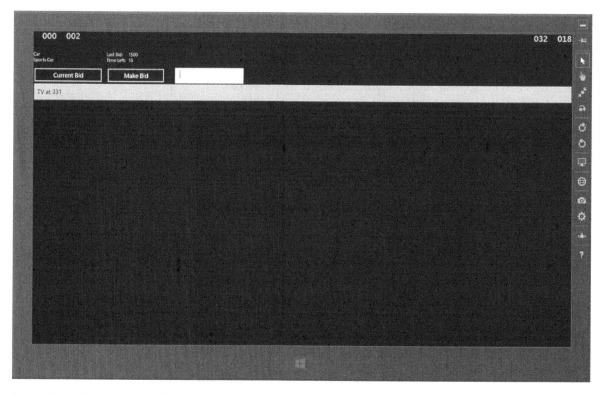

Figure 6-14. *Example of Windows Store hub client*

Now that the Windows Store client examples are complete, we have only one more client variation to show: on the Windows Phone 8 clients.

Windows Phone 8 Clients

SignalR, which is supported on Windows Phone 8 clients, has support for persistent connection and hub applications. For Windows Phone 8 client development, the 64-bit version of Windows 8 is required as well as the Windows Phone 8 SDK.

Persistent Connection Client

The persistent connection client shown in the following example is the same chat application used in previous examples.

Windows Phone 8 Persistent Connection Example

To create the client sample, follow these steps:

1. Create a new Windows Store project with the Windows Phone App template (see Figure 6-15).

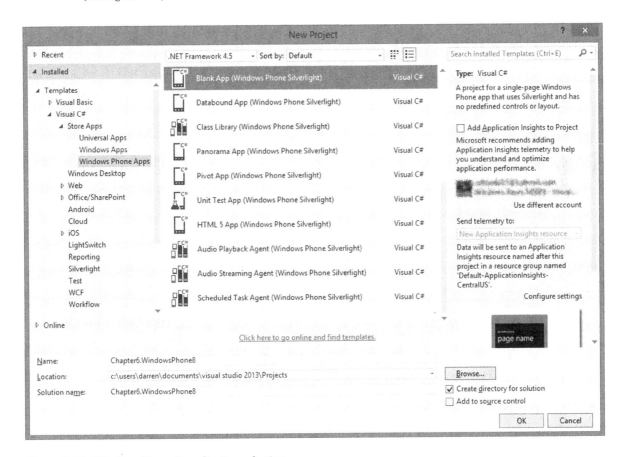

Figure 6-15. *Windows Phone 8 application selection*

2. Select the version of the Windows Phone you want to target. This example targets Windows Phone 8.0 (see Figure 6-16).

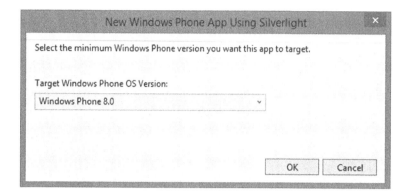

Figure 6-16. *Windows Phone 8 OS version selection*

3. Run the following command in the package explorer window: `Install-Package Microsoft.AspNet.SignalR.Client`.

4. Update the `MainPage.xaml.cs` class to look like Listing 6-46.

Listing 6-46. Windows Phone 8 Client Code

```
public partial class MainPage : PhoneApplicationPage
    {
        Microsoft.AspNet.SignalR.Client.Connection myConnection = new Microsoft.AspNet.SignalR.
        Client.Connection("http://localhost:####/SamplePC/");
        public MainPage()
        {
            this.InitializeComponent();
            myConnection.Received += myConnection_Received;
            myConnection.Start();
        }
        private void SendButton_Click(object sender, RoutedEventArgs e)
        {
            myConnection.Send(txtName.Text + ": " + txtInput.Text);
        }
        private void myConnection_Received(string data)
        {
            UpdateList(data);
        }
        private void UpdateList(string data)
        {
            itemListBox.Dispatcher.BeginInvoke(new Action(() =>
                {
                    var item = new ListBoxItem() { Content = data };
                    itemListBox.Items.Add(item);
                }));
        }
    }
```

5. Update `MainPage.xaml` to look like Listing 6-47.

Listing 6-47. Windows Phone 8 Client XAML

```xml
<phone:PhoneApplicationPage
    x:Class="Chapter6_WindowsPhone.MainPage"
    xmlns="http://schemas.microsoft.com/winfx/2006/xaml/presentation"
    xmlns:x="http://schemas.microsoft.com/winfx/2006/xaml"
    xmlns:phone="clr-namespace:Microsoft.Phone.Controls;assembly=Microsoft.Phone"
    xmlns:shell="clr-namespace:Microsoft.Phone.Shell;assembly=Microsoft.Phone"
    xmlns:d="http://schemas.microsoft.com/expression/blend/2008"
    xmlns:mc="http://schemas.openxmlformats.org/markup-compatibility/2006"
    mc:Ignorable="d"
    FontFamily="{StaticResource PhoneFontFamilyNormal}"
    FontSize="{StaticResource PhoneFontSizeNormal}"
    Foreground="{StaticResource PhoneForegroundBrush}"
    SupportedOrientations="Portrait" Orientation="Portrait"
    shell:SystemTray.IsVisible="True">

    <Grid x:Name="LayoutRoot" Background="Transparent">
        <Grid.RowDefinitions>
            <RowDefinition Height="Auto"/>
            <RowDefinition Height="*"/>
        </Grid.RowDefinitions>
        <TextBlock Margin="10,10,0,0">Name:</TextBlock>
        <TextBlock Margin="120,10,0,0">Data:</TextBlock>
        <TextBox x:Name="txtName"
                Text="User A"
                Width="125"
                Height="75"
                HorizontalAlignment="Left"
                VerticalAlignment="Top"
                IsEnabled="True"
                IsReadOnly="False"
                Margin="10,30,0,0"
                TabIndex="1"/>
        <TextBox x:Name="txtInput"
                Width="250"
                Height="75"
                HorizontalAlignment="Left"
                VerticalAlignment="Top"
                IsEnabled="True"
                IsReadOnly="False"
                Margin="120,30,0,0"
                TabIndex="1"/>
        <Button x:Name="btnSend"
                Click="SendButton_Click"
                Width="100"
                Height="75"
                Margin="380,30,0,0"
                VerticalAlignment="Top">Send
        </Button>
```

```
<ListBox
    x:Name="itemListBox"
    AutomationProperties.AutomationId="ItemsListView"
    AutomationProperties.Name="Items"
    Grid.Row="1"
    Margin="0,100,0,0"
    Width="450"
    HorizontalAlignment="Left">
</ListBox>

    </Grid>
</phone:PhoneApplicationPage>
```

6. Update the #### in the connection to the correct port of your server application

Figure 6-17 shows what the chat application looks like in the Windows Phone emulator.

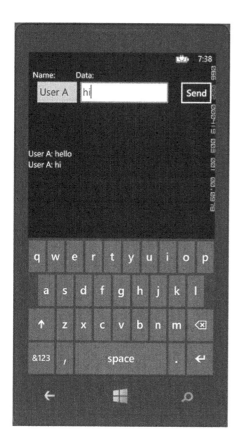

Figure 6-17. *Example of Windows Phone 8 persistent connection client*

■ **Note** If you test the Windows Phone sample application using the emulator, you may need to configure IIS Express and the firewall to get a successful connection. Microsoft has published an article dealing with this issue: `http://msdn.microsoft.com/en-us/library/windowsphone/develop/jj684580.aspx`.

Now that we have created the persistent connection client, the next step is to create the hub client.

Hub Client

This section shows how to create a hub client using a Windows Phone 8 client application. The hub client example in this section is an auction client.

Server Methods Called by the Client

The server methods called from the Windows Phone 8 client can contain zero or more parameters, as shown in Listings 6-48 and 6-49, respectively.

Listing 6-48. Windows Phone 8 Example of Calling a Server Method with No Parameters

```
Var auctionProxy = hubConnection.CreateHubProxy("AuctionHub");
auctionProxy.Invoke("SampleMethod");
```

Listing 6-49. Windows Phone 8 Example of Calling a Server Method with Multiple Parameters and a Complex Type with a Return Value of bool

```
Var auctionProxy = hubConnection.CreateHubProxy("AuctionHub");
int age = 25;
var profile = new Profile("Handle", "Password");
auctionProxy.Invoke<bool>("SampleMethod", profile, age);
```

Client Methods Called by the Server

The server can "call" client methods by the Windows Phone 8 client subscribing to events on the HubProxy. These methods can have zero or one or more parameters, as shown in Listings 6-50 and 6-51, respectively.

Listing 6-50. Windows Phone 8 Example of Calling Client Methods from the Server with No Parameters

```
void Setup(){
    var auctionProxy = _hubConnection.CreateHubProxy("AuctionHub");
    auctionProxy.Subscribe("SampleMethodName").Received += SampleMethod;
}
void SampleMethod (IList<Newtonsoft.Json.Linq.JToken> obj) {
    //Perform action on UI thread with delegate
    Dispatcher.BeginInvoke(someDelegate);
}
```

Listing 6-51. Windows Phone 8 Example of Calling Client Methods from the Server with Multiple Parameters

```
void Setup(){
    var auctionProxy = _hubConnection.CreateHubProxy("AuctionHub");
    auctionProxy.Subscribe("SampleMethodName").Received += SampleMethod;
}
void SampleMethod (IList<Newtonsoft.Json.Linq.JToken> obj) {
    //Perform action on UI thread with delegate
    Dispatcher.BeginInvoke(someDelegate, obj[0]);
}
```

Windows Phone 8 Hub Example

To create the client sample, follow these steps:

1. Create a new Windows Store project with the Windows Phone App template (refer to Figure 6-15).

2. Select the Windows Phone version you want to target; this example targets Windows Phone 8.0 (refer to Figure 6-16).

3. Run the following command in the package explorer window: `Install-Package Microsoft.AspNet.SignalR.Client`.

4. Update the `MainPage.xaml.cs` class to look like Listing 6-52.

Listing 6-52. Windows Phone 8 Client Code

```
public partial class MainPage : PhoneApplicationPage
{
    public Microsoft.AspNet.SignalR.Client.HubConnection _hubConnection;
    public Microsoft.AspNet.SignalR.Client.IHubProxy _auctionProxy;
    delegate void UpdateBid(dynamic bid, int formObject);
    delegate void UpdateButtons(bool enabled);
    UpdateBid _updateDelegate;
    UpdateButtons _updateButtonsDelegate;

    public MainPage()
    {
        InitializeComponent();
        btnCurrentBid.Click += btnCurrentBid_Click;
        btnMakeBid.Click += btnMakeBid_Click;
        SetupHub();
    }

    private async void SetupHub()
    {
        _updateDelegate = new UpdateBid(UpdateBidMethod);
        _updateButtonsDelegate = new UpdateButtons(UpdateButtonsMethod);
        _hubConnection = new Microsoft.AspNet.SignalR.Client.HubConnection
        ("http://192.168.1.108:####/");
        _auctionProxy = _hubConnection.CreateHubProxy("AuctionHub");
        _auctionProxy.Subscribe("UpdateBid").Received += UpdateBid_auctionProxy;
```

```csharp
        _auctionProxy.Subscribe("CloseBid").Received += CloseBid_auctionProxy;
        _auctionProxy.Subscribe("CloseBidWin").Received += CloseBidWin_auctionProxy;

        await _hubConnection.Start();
    }
    void UpdateBidMethod(dynamic bid, int formObject)
    {
        if (bid != null)
        {
            lblName.Text = bid.Name;
            lblDescr.Text = bid.Description;
            lblBid.Text = bid.BidPrice;
            lblTime.Text = bid.TimeLeft;
            if(formObject > 0)
            {
                lstWins.Items.Add(bid.Name + " at " + bid.BidPrice);
            }
        }
    }
    void UpdateButtonsMethod(bool enabled)
    {
        btnCurrentBid.IsEnabled = enabled;
        btnMakeBid.IsEnabled = enabled;
    }
    void UpdateBid_auctionProxy(IList<Newtonsoft.Json.Linq.JToken> obj)
    {
        Dispatcher.BeginInvoke(_updateDelegate, obj[0],0);
        Dispatcher.BeginInvoke(_updateButtonsDelegate, true);
    }
    void CloseBid_auctionProxy(IList<Newtonsoft.Json.Linq.JToken> obj)
    {
        Dispatcher.BeginInvoke(_updateButtonsDelegate, false);
    }
    void CloseBidWin_auctionProxy(IList<Newtonsoft.Json.Linq.JToken> obj)
    {
        Dispatcher.BeginInvoke(_updateButtonsDelegate, false);
        Dispatcher.BeginInvoke(_updateDelegate, obj[0], 1);
    }
    private void btnCurrentBid_Click(object sender, EventArgs e)
    {
        _auctionProxy.Invoke("MakeCurrentBid");
    }

    private void btnMakeBid_Click(object sender, EventArgs e)
    {
        _auctionProxy.Invoke<string>("MakeBid", this.txtBid.Text);
    }
}
```

5. Update `MainPage.xaml` to look like Listing 6-53.

Listing 6-53. Windows Phone 8 Client XAML

```xml
<phone:PhoneApplicationPage
    x:Class="Chapter6.WindowsPhone8.MainPage"
    xmlns="http://schemas.microsoft.com/winfx/2006/xaml/presentation"
    xmlns:x="http://schemas.microsoft.com/winfx/2006/xaml"
    xmlns:phone="clr-namespace:Microsoft.Phone.Controls;assembly=Microsoft.Phone"
    xmlns:shell="clr-namespace:Microsoft.Phone.Shell;assembly=Microsoft.Phone"
    xmlns:d="http://schemas.microsoft.com/expression/blend/2008"
    xmlns:mc="http://schemas.openxmlformats.org/markup-compatibility/2006"
    mc:Ignorable="d"
    FontFamily="{StaticResource PhoneFontFamilyNormal}"
    FontSize="{StaticResource PhoneFontSizeNormal}"
    Foreground="{StaticResource PhoneForegroundBrush}"
    SupportedOrientations="Portrait" Orientation="Portrait"
    shell:SystemTray.IsVisible="True">

    <Grid x:Name="LayoutRoot" Background="Transparent">
        <Grid.RowDefinitions>
            <RowDefinition Height="Auto"/>
            <RowDefinition Height="*"/>
        </Grid.RowDefinitions>
        <StackPanel>
            <Grid>
                <TextBlock HorizontalAlignment="Left" Name="lblName"></TextBlock>
                <TextBlock Margin="0,0,50,0" HorizontalAlignment="Right" Name="lblBid"></TextBlock>
            </Grid>
            <Grid>
                <TextBlock HorizontalAlignment="Left" Name="lblDescr"></TextBlock>
                <TextBlock HorizontalAlignment="Center">Time Left:</TextBlock>
                <TextBlock Margin="0,0,50,0" HorizontalAlignment="Right" Name="lblTime">
</TextBlock>
            </Grid>
            <Grid>
                <Button Name="btnCurrentBid" HorizontalAlignment="Left"
                Width="175">Current Bid</Button>
                <Button Name="btnMakeBid" HorizontalAlignment="Center" Width="150">Make Bid</Button>
                <TextBox Name="txtBid" HorizontalAlignment="Right" Width="175"/>
            </Grid>
            <ListBox Name="lstWins"></ListBox>
        </StackPanel>
    </Grid>
</phone:PhoneApplicationPage>
```

6. Update the #### in the connection to the correct port of your server application.

We have now completed the final example. If we run it with the emulator, it looks similar to Figure 6-18.

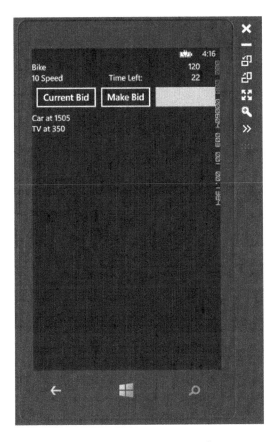

Figure 6-18. *Windows Phone 8 example*

■ **Note**   If you test the Windows Phone sample application using the emulator, you may need to configure IIS Express and the firewall to get a successful connection. Microsoft published an article dealing with this issue: http://msdn.microsoft.com/en-us/library/windowsphone/develop/jj684580.aspx.

We have now gone through the standard list of clients that are supported. iPhone and Android clients are available as well, but they require customization, which is discussed in detail in Chapter 7.

Summary

This chapter showed you what clients are available and how to configure them. The most configurable piece of the client is the connection, which allows us to customize the query string, headers, cookies, certificates, and transport.

We also discussed the communication that occurs between the server and client. In general, the mechanics of the communication is the same for all the clients, but there are subtle differences in consuming the data and moving it off of the connection's thread. We went through the iterations of the examples for each client.

The next chapter will cover using SignalR on non-Windows operating systems that include iPhone and Android clients.

CHAPTER 7

How to Extend and Customize SignalR Functionality

So far, you have seen the basics of SignalR; now it is time to learn the details that will help you customize SignalR to your specific needs. We start the chapter by going over some of the common extensible points. After that, we move on to extending and customizing existing components. If the component cannot be extended to accomplish the task, we discuss replacing the individual components as needed.

Keeping with the theme of expanding SignalR to your needs, we discuss hosting SignalR applications outside of IIS. We also go over how hosting is not limited to just the Windows platform. You'll learn about the Mono framework and how it can be used to run SignalR applications on Linux and OS X. The last section shows you how to use Xamarin for the Visual Studio add-in, which uses a custom version of the Mono framework that runs SignalR clients on Android and iOS devices.

Extensibility of the SignalR Core

As mentioned in earlier chapters, the developers of SignalR have done a great job of engineering the code to be very flexible and customizable. By using a dependency resolver, you can have complete control over what aspects of SignalR you use in your applications. The dependency resolver also allows you to independently replace major core components of SignalR, depending on your needs. As you'll see in the following sections, there are various ways to use a dependency resolver, such as replacing UserIdProvider with an implementation that uses cookies to determine the user.

Implementing a Custom Dependency Resolver

Much of the code in SignalR is abstracted to interfaces, which gives you a lot of control over your implementations. To convert these abstracted interfaces into concrete implementations, additional logic is needed. This is where a dependency resolver comes in.

By default, SignalR is configured to use the DefaultDependencyResolver class for all dependency resolutions. DefaultDependencyResolver implements the IDependencyResolver interface and resolves objects out of a simple container. DefaultDependencyResolver also has a default set of services and hub extensions registered in the constructor that is used in most applications. Even as simple as DefaultDependencyResolver is, it works well for most basic applications.

When the application becomes more complex or integrated with an existing application that already has an IoC container, it may be necessary to replace the DefaultDependencyResolver. If you are adding a new IoC container, there are many choices that can be used, including Ninject, Unity, or StructureMap. Regardless of whether you're using a new or existing IoC container, it must implement the IDependencyResolver interface shown in Listing 7-1 and be configured in the GlobalHost.

Listing 7-1. Interface for IDependencyResolver

```
public interface IDependencyResolver : IDisposable
{
    object GetService(Type serviceType);
    IEnumerable<object> GetServices(Type serviceType);
    void Register(Type serviceType, Func<object> activator);
    void Register(Type serviceType, IEnumerable<Func<object>> activators);
}
```

As an example, we created an implementation of the IDependencyResolver for Unity (see Listing 7-2). Creating your own dependency resolver takes only a little code and can be a great benefit to your application.

Listing 7-2. Dependency Resolver for Unity

```
public class UnityDependencyResolver : DefaultDependencyResolver
{
    IUnityContainer _container = new UnityContainer();

    public override object GetService(Type serviceType)
    {
        try
        {
            return _container.Resolve(serviceType);
        }
        catch
        {
            return base.GetService(serviceType);
        }
    }

    public override IEnumerable<object> GetServices(Type serviceType)
    {
        try
        {
            List<object> services = _container.ResolveAll(serviceType).ToList();
            object defaultService = GetService(serviceType);
            if (defaultService != null) services.Add(defaultService);
            return services;
        }
        catch
        {
            return base.GetServices(serviceType);
        }
    }

    public override void Register(Type serviceType, IEnumerable<Func<object>> activators)
    {
        _container.RegisterType(serviceType, new InjectionFactory((c) => {
            object returnObject = null;
            foreach (Func<Object> activator in activators)
            {
```

```
            object tempObject = activator.Invoke();
            if (tempObject != null)
            {
                returnObject = tempObject;
                break;
            }
        }
        return returnObject;
    }));
    base.Register(serviceType, activators);
}

public override void Register(Type serviceType, Func<object> activator)
{
    _container.RegisterType(serviceType, new InjectionFactory((c) => activator.Invoke()));
    base.Register(serviceType, activator);
}
}
```

This implementation for Unity derives from the DefaultDependencyResolver class, so all registrations that occur in that class are also registered in the Unity container. Now that we have created our own resolver, we register it using the code in Listing 7-3.

Listing 7-3. Code to Register Dependency Resolver

```
Microsoft.AspNet.SignalR.GlobalHost.DependencyResolver = new UnityDependencyResolver();
```

The next step is to use the dependency resolver to help customize SignalR applications. The first approach is to extend existing components, but if more customization is needed, components can be completely replaced.

Extending Existing Components

The most common way to extend SignalR features is to extend existing components. You may have already done this by creating a hub or persistent connection because when you create the hub or persistent connection, you extend the Hub or PersistentConnection class. When these hubs or persistent connections are created for you, they are constructed behind the scenes by the dependency resolver.

These extended classes can be made more functional by injecting the dependent classes or a dependency resolver in the constructor. With the dependency resolver, you can resolve any objects that you have registered in the dependency resolver. For example, you might have an extended class that is for a chat client hub. In the chat client, you can resolve a logger to log all the chat that goes through the hub.

But for complete customization, just extending classes may not be enough. So to take this one step farther, we next show you how to replace SignalR components.

Replacing Individual SignalR Components

In the previous section, you saw how to add on to existing components, but with limited customization. To get the customization you want, it is sometimes necessary to replace classes instead of extending them. When using the DefaultDependencyResolver class, there are 13 general classes registered and 10 hub-specific registrations. So for the out-of-the-box server experience with hubs, there are at least 23 components that can be replaced.

The general classes registered provide functions such as message bus communication management, message serialization/minification, transport and communication management, general configuration, performance and tracing, and client/server identification tracking. The hub-specific registrations provide functions that provide available hubs and their methods, request manipulation into hubs, hub management, and hub pipeline stage management. Some of these interfaces have simple implementations; others have very complex implementations with hundreds of lines and complex thread-safe logic.

You might want to replace a class instead of extending it because the current implementation may not provide access to what you need to change. An example of this is to limit the transports in your application to support only Web Sockets transport for paying customers and long polling transport for non-paying customers. By default, the TransportManager class provides Forever Frame, Server Sent Events, long polling, and Web Sockets transports to all customers. Inheriting from the TransportManager class does not provide the functionality for replacing the default transports. So for this replacement implementation, implement the ITransportManager interface and provide the logic for selecting the correct transport based on the customer type.

For a concrete example, we implement the IUserIdProvider interface with a custom class. The default implementation is the PrincipalUserIdProvider class, which provides a user ID from the name property of the user's identity provided in the request. The CookieUserIdProvider custom class that is implemented in Listing 7-4 retrieves a value from the request's cookies. This value is looked up in an in-memory collection of known mappings. If a key is found, the value for that key is returned as the user ID; otherwise, a null value is returned.

Listing 7-4. Example of a Custom Component Implementing the IUserIdProvider

```
public class CookieUserIdProvider : IUserIdProvider
{
    IUserIdStore _memoryUserIdStore;
    public CookieUserIdProvider(IDependencyResolver resolver)
    {
    _memoryUserIdStore = resolver.Resolve<IUserIdStore>();
    }
    public string GetUserId(IRequest request)
    {
    string returnValue = null;
        Cookie userIdCookie = null;
        if (request.Cookies.TryGetValue("userid", out userIdCookie))
        {
            string strUserId = userIdCookie.Value;
            Guid userGuid;
            if (Guid.TryParse(strUserId, out userGuid))
            {
                returnValue = _memoryUserIdStore.GetUserId(userGuid);
            }
        }
        return returnValue;
    }
}
public interface IUserIdStore
{
    string GetUserId(Guid cookieId);
    void AddUserId(Guid cookieId, string userId);
}
public class MemoryUserIdStore : IUserIdStore
{
    Dictionary<Guid, string> _knownUsers = new Dictionary<Guid, string>();
```

```
public string GetUserId(Guid cookieId)
{
    string returnValue = null;
    if (_knownUsers.ContainsKey(cookieId))
    {
        returnValue = _knownUsers[cookieId];
    }
    return returnValue;
}
public void AddUserId(Guid cookieId, string userId)
{
    _knownUsers[cookieId] = userId;
}
}
```

Once we create the class, we need to register it to replace the default implementation: `PrincipalUserIdProvider`. As shown in Listing 7-5, we register the in-memory collection implementation `MemoryUserIdStore` to the `IUserIdStore` interface and the `CookieUserIdProvider` to the `IUserIdProvider` interface. It is critical that we register `MemoryUserIdStore` so that the dependency can be resolved in the `CookieUserIdProvider` constructor.

Listing 7-5. Example of Code to Register New Component with the DependencyResolver

```
GlobalHost.DependencyResolver.Register(typeof(IUserIdStore),new Func<object>(() => new
MemoryUserIdStore()));
GlobalHost.DependencyResolver.Register(typeof(IUserIdProvider), new Func<object>(() => new
CookieUserIdProvider(GlobalHost.DependencyResolver)));
```

Now that you have seen how to extend the SignalR application by using the dependency resolver, you have a good base for extending and customizing your applications. But there are many other ways to extend your application that are beyond the scope of modifying the code, including hosting outside of IIS and running on other frameworks. We focus on hosting outside of IIS in the next section.

Self-Hosting SignalR Outside of IIS

Internet Information Services (IIS) has been a great host for C# developers for years, but the footprint to deploy it is large and restrictive. So in recent years, developers have worked on a project called the Katana project, adopted by Microsoft to promote the decoupling of web components. This adoption allows the choice of host, server, and middleware components of an OWIN-based application. (As discussed in Chapter 2, WIN is a standard interface between web servers and applications that is not coupled to a specific software implementation.) SignalR implements the OWIN interface and is a middleware component in the Katana project.

In most cases with the Katana components, the host and server can be interchanged with other hosts and servers without having to recompile the application. The middleware pipeline is configured during application startup. This configuration is minimal to allow you to add only the pieces of the pipeline that you want. In this section, we cover how all these pieces work together to enable you to self-host SignalR outside of IIS. We start with a quick example on how easy it is to set up outside of IIS.

Self-Host Example

1. Create a new console application.

2. Run the Package Manager Console.

3. Type **Install-Package Microsoft.AspNet.SignalR.SelfHost**.

4. Type **Install-Package Microsoft.AspNet.SignalR.JS**.

5. Add a new item, Startup.cs, as shown in Figure 7-1.

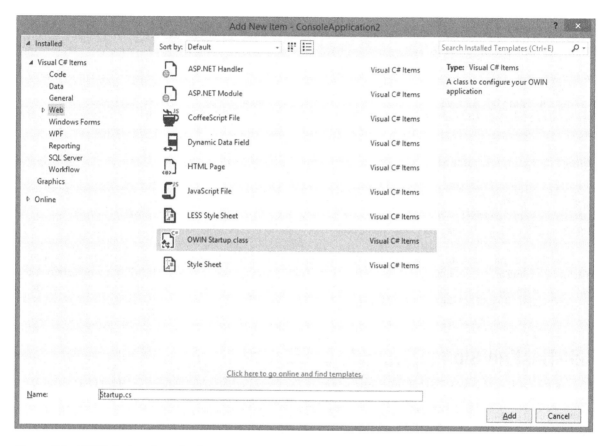

Figure 7-1. *OWIN startup class selection*

6. Update Startup.cs with the code in Listing 7-6.

    Listing 7-6. Self-host Startup Class C# Code

```csharp
public class Startup
{
    public void Configuration(IAppBuilder app)
    {
        app.MapSignalR<ConsoleApplication2.Program.SamplePersistentConnection>
        ("/SamplePC");
        app.Run((context) =>
        {
            if (context.Request.Path.Value.Equals("/", StringComparison.
            CurrentCultureIgnoreCase))
            {
                context.Response.ContentType = "text/html";
                string result = System.IO.File.ReadAllText(System.Environment.
                CurrentDirectory + "\\index.html");
                return context.Response.WriteAsync(result);
            }
            if (context.Request.Path.Value.StartsWith("/scripts/", StringComparison.
            CurrentCultureIgnoreCase))
            {
                context.Response.ContentType = "text/javascript";
                //The requested should be verified but adding for simplicity of
                example.
                string result = System.IO.File.ReadAllText(System.Environment.
                CurrentDirectory + context.Request.Path.Value);
                return context.Response.WriteAsync(result);
            }
            return Task.FromResult<object>(null);
        });
    }
}
```

7.   Add a new HTML page, Index.html, to the root of the project (see Figure 7-2).

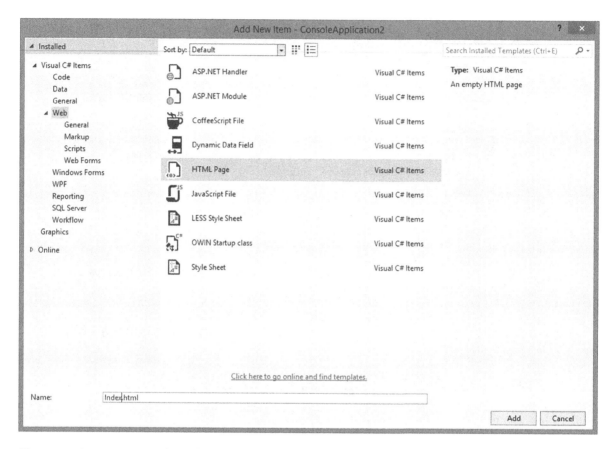

Figure 7-2. *HTML page template selection*

8.   Update the head section in Index.html to reflect Listing 7-7.

Listing 7-7. JavaScript for Index.html

```
<script src="/scripts/jquery-1.6.4.min.js" type="text/javascript"></script>
<script src="/scripts/jquery.signalR-2.0.1.min.js" type="text/javascript"></script>
<script>
    $(function () {
        var connection = $.connection('http://localhost:5045/samplepc');

        connection.received(function (data) {
            $('#messages').append('<li>' + data + '</li>');
        });
```

```
        connection.start().done(function () {
            $("#btnSend").click(function () {
                connection.send($('#name').val() + ': ' + $('#message').val());
            });
        }).fail(function (ex) { alert(ex);})
    });
</script>
```

9. Update the version numbers of the JQuery and JQuery.SignalR scripts to the appropriate version in the Scripts folder.

10. Update the HTML in the Index.html section to reflect Listing 7-8.

Listing 7-8. HTML for Index.html

```
<ul id="messages" style="border: 1px solid black; height: 250px; width: 450px;
overflow:scroll; list-style:none;"></ul>
<label>Name: </label>
<input id="name" value="User A" />
<label>Message: </label>
<input id="message" />
<button id="btnSend">Send</button>
```

11. For each script and index.html in the properties, set Copy to Output to **Copy Always**.

12. Create a new SamplePersistentConnection class and add the code in Listing 7-9.

Listing 7-9. Code for SamplePersistentConnection

```
public class SamplePersistentConnection : PersistentConnection
{
    protected override System.Threading.Tasks.Task OnReceived(IRequest request, string
    connectionId, string data)
    {
        return Connection.Broadcast(data);
    }
}
```

13. Run the following from the command prompt with correct credentials:

```
netsh http add urlacl url=http://+:5045/ user=machine\username
```

163

After implementing the example, you should see results similar to Figure 7-3. Now that you have seen how easy it is to implement, you'll learn about the components that make it up and how they work.

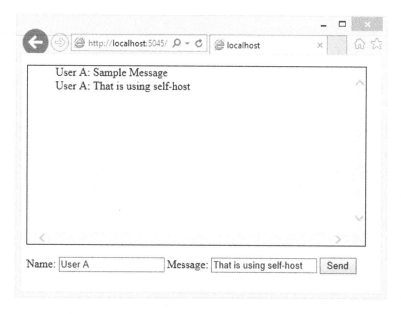

Figure 7-3. Self-host client exampleKatana Project

The Katana project is an open-source project consisting of components that are to be combined to form an OWIN-based application. The project has the components broken down into layers: host, server, middleware, and application. The components need to have the following properties: portable, modular, and scalable.

The layers are divided by functionality and should be exchangeable with other components at the same layer. The following sections discuss the individual layers and the functions they provide with some examples of how they are used. For all layers, there is only one component, but there can be multiple components for the middleware layer.

The properties are provided as guidelines to ensure a consistent experience with components so that any component written should demonstrate these properties.

Host Layer

The host layer is the layer that hosts the application in a process on the operating system. The host is also responsible for setting up a server layer and constructing the OWIN pipeline.

There are currently three supported host scenarios (IIS/ASP.NET, OwinHost.exe, and custom host). With the IIS/ASP.NET host, this configuration runs on the host and server layers because the host also provides the server and cannot be exchanged with other servers. The OwinHost.exe host is a prebuilt host that can be run in a project's directory, and the host attempts to find the startup class. This host can also be configured to run different servers or have the startup class specified by using command-line parameters when starting the host. The custom host can include a variety of processes such as a Windows service, console application, and so on. The custom host needs to have the functionality to start the OWIN-based server and to set up the OWIN pipeline.

Server Layer

The server layer is the layer that opens a network socket, listens as requests come in, and sends the request through the OWIN pipeline. There are two implementations: SystemWeb and HttpListener. The IIS/ASP.NET host is required to use the SystemWeb server, but the other two hosts use the HttpListener by default. The SystemWeb server works by registering an HttpModule and HttpHandler, and it intercepts the requests as they go through the pipeline. HttpListener is a simple class that opens a socket at the specified address and redirects the requests into the OWIN pipeline.

Middleware Layer

The middleware layer is the layer that has one or more middleware components, which are invoked sequentially in the order that they were added to the OWIN pipeline. The only requirement for a middleware component is that it implements the signature in Listing 7-10.

Listing 7-10. Signature Required for a Middleware Component

```
Func<IDictionary<string,object>, Task>
```

There are various middleware components that are very easy for completing frameworks. SignalR is one of those middleware components that is a complete framework. Even though SignalR is a complete framework, there are other popular middleware components that work well in providing additional functionality: WebAPI, Microsoft.Owin. Security.*, and Microsoft.Owin.StaticFiles. These additional components provide the functionality of WebAPI, various forms of security, and hosting of static files, respectively. Regardless of which components are chosen, they are all added and configured in the application layer.

Application Layer

The application layer, which is the actual application that is supported by all the underlying layers, has the logic to configure the middleware. This logic to configure the middleware goes into the startup class. The startup class can be registered multiple ways, but it is generally registered using an assembly tag, as shown in Listing 7-11.

Listing 7-11. Example of Registering a Startup Class with an Assembly Tag

```
[assembly: OwinStartup(typeof(MyApplication.Startup))]
```

Adding middleware components is done by calling Use or the respective extension method provided by the middleware, such as UseSignalR on the IAppBuilder object. The order in which the components are registered in the IAppBuilder is the order in which they will be run for every request that comes in. Once all the layers are selected and configured, the application should be ready to run. There are a few common functionalities that are used in Katana applications that can helpful in your application (discussed next).

Adding Windows Authentication and IIS Pipeline Stages to Applications

Even though the goal of the Katana project is to remove all the extra functionality that is not needed, some commonly used functionality is still needed, so it has to be added back into the application pipeline. The two common functionalities covered here are the Windows authentication middleware and the IIS pipeline event integration.

Windows Authentication

Windows authentication is a critical component that a lot of enterprise applications must support. Currently, there are two Katana servers that support it: SystemWeb and HttpListener. The SystemWeb server is configured in the web.config file for IIS and in the project for IIS Express, and the HttpListener is configured in the application startup class.

The SystemWeb server is the server that is part of the IIS pipeline and is supported only in integrated pipeline mode. Depending on whether you host this on IIS or IIS Express, there are two separate unrelated configurations to change. If your host is IIS, you have to update the web.config file and update the authentication element to have a mode of "Windows" (see Listing 7-12). If this application is hosted in IIS Express, the web site project properties have to be updated. In the properties, Anonymous Authentication needs to be set to Disabled and Windows Authentication needs to be set to Enabled.

Listing 7-12. SystemWeb Server IIS Configuration for Windows Authentication

```
<authentication mode="Windows" />
```

The HttpListener server is different from the SystemWeb server to set up Windows authentication. For the HttpListener configuration, you set it in the startup class, as shown in Listing 7-13.

Listing 7-13. HttpListener Server Configuration for Windows Authentication

```
HttpListener listener = (HttpListener)app.Properties["System.Net.HttpListener"];
listener.AuthenticationSchemes = AuthenticationSchemes.IntegratedWindowsAuthentication;
```

Those settings are all you need to get your application to support Windows authentication. The operating system you run this on also needs the Windows authentication feature turned on as well.

Interaction with IIS Integrated Pipeline

If your SignalR application needs to interact at certain stages in the IIS pipeline, you can use the UseStageMarker function. To use this extension method, add a using statement to the namespace in Listing 7-14.

Listing 7-14. Using Statement Needed for the UseStageMarker Extension Method

```
using Microsoft.Owin.Extensions;
```

You add the UseStageMarker function with the appropriate stage in Listing 7-15 to run the previously registered middleware at that stage in the IIS pipeline. If you are using multiple UseStageMarker method calls, there are several restrictions that must be observed. The first restriction is that a stage can be registered only once. The following is an example of what you should not do. First, register middleware A and B and then call UseStageMarker for the Authorize stage. Next, register middleware C and call UseStageMarker again for the Authorize stage. In this example, the code would be called only for components A and B, therefore making component C useless. The second restriction is that the stages must be registered for the IIS pipeline stages to occur. If they are called out of order, the later stages are ignored and run at the earliest stage that is registered.

Listing 7-15. Integrated Pipeline Stages

```
Authenticate
PostAuthenticate
Authorize
PostAuthorize
ResolveCache
PostResolveCache
MapHandler
PostMapHandler
AcquireState
PostAcquireState
PreHandlerExecute
```

There are many other ways to extend the Katana functionality in your application that are beyond the scope of this book. The next section focuses on what is needed to get a SignalR application on Linux or OS X.

Linux and OS X Support Using the Mono Framework

Recently, Microsoft has been pushing open source; it has even created a subsidiary called Microsoft Open Technologies, Inc. The open-source push has helped get more .NET Framework code decoupled from strongly Windows-centric code. Not only has this provided more standardized and generic implementations of the code but it has also influenced a change in licensing. One of the more recent changes Microsoft Open Technologies was part of was to remove the Windows–only licensing restriction from portable class libraries. So as these libraries open up, they can be used on other platforms such as Linux and OS X with the help of other frameworks.

This section goes over the Mono framework, which allows us to run our code on Linux and OS X. We discuss setting up the development environment to compile our code. Next, we introduce MonoDevelop, which is an IDE for the Mono framework, and show you how to set up a web hosting environment using the Mono framework and demonstrating hosting Mono applications. The section concludes by going over related changes from Linux to OS X.

What Is the Mono Framework?

The Mono framework is an open-source project led by Xamarin to allow cross-platform development. It is based on EMCA standards for C# and Common Language Runtime (CLR) support. The framework is a collection of components that include a compiler, runtime, base class libraries, and Mono class libraries.

The Mono version 3.X compiler accepts C# 1.0 - C# 5.0 code, with some limitations. The compiler currently has limited support for the Windows Presentation Foundation (WPF), Windows Workflow Foundation (WF), and Windows Communication Foundation (WCF). The compiler can generate just-in-time (JIT), ahead-of-time (AOT), and full static compilation, depending on the target OS.

The runtime that the Mono framework provides allows the use of JIT and AOT compilation, garbage collection, threading, and other library functions.

The base class libraries are compatible with the .NET Framework classes using EMCA standards. There are a few framework classes that are not supported because of Windows-specific code or other issues. Examples are the Windows-specific code in the `System.Management` namespace or support for WPF. The page at `http://www.mono-project.com/Compatibility` provides a list of compatibilities with the latest version of Mono.

The Mono class libraries provide support for libraries that may be missing or extend functionality. Examples of this are GTK+ or WinForms, which provide Gnome toolkit and Windows Forms functionality, respectively. So now that you have an idea of what Mono is, we'll cover how to set it up and use it.

Setting Up the Development Environment

This section discusses how to use SignalR on openSUSE 13.1. The reason for choosing openSUSE 13.1 is that it supports Mono version 3.X that supports C# 5.0, which is required for the server components of SignalR. This example starts with a clean install of the operating system, so if the components exist, you should be able to skip those specific steps.

1. Open a new terminal window.

2. Type **sudo zypper install mono-complete** and press Return to install Mono. Confirm package download by pressing y and then pressing Return to confirm the install.

3. Type **sudo zypper install git-core** and press Return to install Git. Confirm package download by pressing y and Return to confirm the install.

4. Type **mozroots --import -sync** and press Return to sync with the Mozilla certificates.

5. Create a directory to work in and navigate to that directory. Type **git clone http:// github.com/SignalR/SignalR.git** and press Return to pull down the SignalR package. The address is case-sensitive.

6. Navigate to the newly created SignalR directory.

7. Type **./build.sh** and press Return to build.

Note   In Linux, file names and commands are case-sensitive. So if something does not run or if you get a missing file error, check the casing.

After completing the preceding steps, you should now have SignalR libraries in a compatible format. Follow these steps to create a SignalR client application:

1. Create a new directory to work in.

2. Copy the newly created files from .\SignalR\src\Microsoft.AspNet.SignalR.Client\ bin\debug to the directory created in step 1.

3. Inside the directory from step 1, type **vi MonoClient.cs** and press Return.

4. Once vi has started, you're in Command mode. Press i to enter Insert mode, which is indicated in the bottom left of the screen with the word INSERT.

5. Enter the code in Listing 7-16.

Listing 7-16. MonoClient.cs Code

```
using System;
public class MonoClient: Form
{
        Button btnSend;
        TextBox txtName;
        TextBox txtMessage;
        ListBox lstMessages;
        Microsoft.AspNet.SignalR.Client.Connection myConnection = new Microsoft.AspNet.
SignalR. Client.Connection("http://localhost:####/SignalR/");
```

```
static public void Main ()
{
        Application.Run (new MonoClient());
}

public MonoClient()
{
    btnSend = new Button() { Text = "Send", Width = 75, Top = 5, Left = 175 };
    txtName = new TextBox() { Width = 75, Top = 5, Left =5 };
    txtMessage = new TextBox() { Width = 75, Top = 5, Left = 90 };
    lstMessages = new ListBox() { Width = 245, Top = 30, Left = 5 };
    btnSend.Click += btnSend_Click;
    myConnection.Received += myConnection_Received;
    this.Controls.Add(btnSend);
    this.Controls.Add(txtName);
    this.Controls.Add(txtMessage);
    this.Controls.Add(lstMessages);
    StartConnection();
}

async void StartConnection()
{
    await myConnection.Start();
}

private void btnSend_Click(object sender, EventArgs e)
{
    myConnection.Send(txtName.Text + ":" + txtMessage.Text);
}

void myConnection_Received(string obj)
{
    lstMessages.Invoke(new Action(() => lstMessages.Items.Add(obj)));
}
}
```

6. Press Esc to exit Insert mode to go back into Command mode.

7. Type **:wq** and press Return to save the file and exit vi.

8. Type **mcs MonoClient.cs -pkg:dotnet -reference:Microsoft.AspNet.SignalR. Client.dll** and press Return to build the Mono client.

9. To launch the client, type **mono MonoClient.exe** and press Return.

■ **Note** In step 8, we tell the compiler to include the dotnet package and to reference the DLL that we created when we compiled the SignalR solution.

Now that there is a client (see Figure 7-4), we need to create a server to connect to. The next section creates a web site that will be hosted via Apache. This example is a bit more complicated than the previous one, so you can take advantage of the MonoDevelop IDE, which can help you manage the numerous files and dependencies for a build rather than trying to manage it manually.

Figure 7-4. *Example of Mono SignalR clientUsing MonoDevelop for More Complex Projects*

As projects grow more complex, it is a good idea to manage them in IDE rather than manually (as in the last section):

1. Open a new terminal window.

2. Type **sudo zypper install monodevelop** and press Return to install MonoDevelop. Confirm the package download by pressing y and pressing Return.

3. Type **sudo zypper install libgnomeui** and press Return to install the gnome UI. Confirm the package download by pressing y and pressing Return.

4. Press Alt+F2 for the runner, type **monodev**, and press Return to run the MonoDevelop IDE, as shown in Figure 7-5.

Figure 7-5. *Shortcut to run the MonoDevelop IDE*

Now that the MonoDevelop IDE is installed, it is ready to use. The MonoDevelop IDE is used in the next section to create a SignalR Mono Server.

Setting Up the Hosting Environment

The following steps set up Apache and XSP for running Mono web sites (if the package is already installed, skip that step):

1. Open a new terminal window.

2. Type **sudo zypper install apache2** and press Return to install the Apache web server. Confirm the package download by pressing y and pressing Return.

3. Type **sudo zypper install xsp** and press Return to install the XSP server. Confirm the package download by pressing y and pressing Return.

4. Type **sudo zypper install apache2-mod_mono** and press Return. to install the Mono module for Apache. Confirm the package download by pressing y and pressing Return.

5. Type **su**, press Return, enter your password, and press Return. This process escalates your command-line privileges.

6. Type **a2enmod mod_mono_auto** and press Return to autoconfigure the Mono module.

7. Navigate to /etc/apache2.

8. Type **vi default-server.conf** and press Return to edit the configuration file.

9. Once vi has started, you are in Command mode, so press i to enter Insert mode, which is indicated in the bottom left of the screen with the word INSERT.

10. Update the two lines that say /srv/www/htdocs to the path where your project will be.

11. Press Esc to exit Insert mode back into Command mode.

12. Type **:wq** and press Return to save the file and exit vi.

Creating a Mono SignalR Server

To create a server, we incorporate the libraries that we compiled when setting up the development section. We will host it in a web application to be run under Apache. Follow these steps:

1. Launch MonoDevelop.

2. Create a new MVC project (see Figure 7-6).

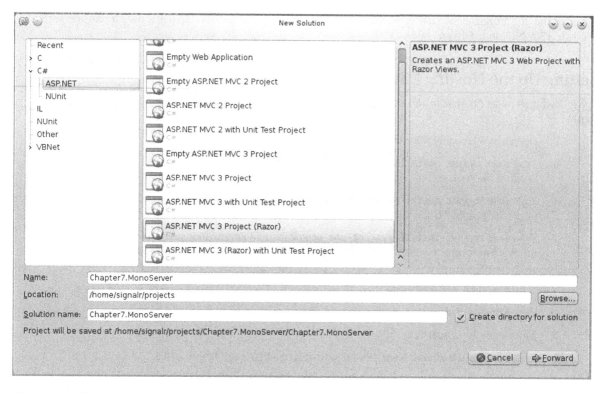

Figure 7-6. *Web project selection in MonoDevelop*

3. Add a new class called Startup with the code in Listing 7-17.

    Listing 7-17. Startup Class for Mono Server Example

    ```
    [assembly: OwinStartupAttribute(typeof(Chapter7.MonoServer.Startup))]
    namespace Chapter7.MonoServer
    {
        public partial class Startup
        {
            public void Configuration(IAppBuilder app)
            {
                app.MapSignalR();
            }
        }
    }
    ```

4. Add a new class called Auction with the code in Listing 7-18.

Listing 7-18. Server Code for Mono Server Example

```
public class AuctionHub : Microsoft.AspNet.SignalR.Hub
    {
        public AuctionHub()
        {
            BidManager.Start();
        }
        public override System.Threading.Tasks.Task OnConnected()
        {
            Clients.Caller.CloseBid();
            Clients.All.UpdateBid(BidManager.CurrentBid);
            return base.OnConnected();
        }
        public void MakeCurrentBid()
        {
            BidManager.CurrentBid.BidPrice += 1;
            BidManager.CurrentBid.ConnectionId = this.Context.ConnectionId;
            Clients.All.UpdateBid(BidManager.CurrentBid);
        }
        public void MakeBid(double bid)
        {
            if (bid < BidManager.CurrentBid.BidPrice)
            {
                return;
            }
            BidManager.CurrentBid.BidPrice = bid;
            BidManager.CurrentBid.ConnectionId = this.Context.ConnectionId;
            Clients.All.UpdateBid(BidManager.CurrentBid);
        }
    }

    public static class BidManager
    {
        static System.Threading.Timer _timer = new System.Threading.Timer(BidInterval,
        null, 0, 2000);
        public static Bid CurrentBid { get; set; }
        public static void Start()
        {
            //Empty class to make sure Static class is started
        }
        static void BidInterval(object o)
        {
            var clients = Microsoft.AspNet.SignalR.GlobalHost.ConnectionManager.
            GetHubContext<AuctionHub>().Clients;
            if (BidManager.CurrentBid == null || BidManager.CurrentBid.TimeLeft <= 0)
            {
                BidManager.SetBid();
            }
            BidManager.CurrentBid.TimeLeft -= 2;
```

```
                if (BidManager.CurrentBid.TimeLeft <= 0)
                {
                    clients.AllExcept(CurrentBid.ConnectionId).CloseBid();
                    if (!string.IsNullOrWhiteSpace(CurrentBid.ConnectionId))
                        clients.Client(CurrentBid.ConnectionId).CloseBidWin(CurrentBid);
                }
                clients.All.UpdateBid(BidManager.CurrentBid);
            }
            static List<Bid> _items = new List<Bid>(){
                new Bid(){Name="Bike", Description="10 Speed", TimeLeft = 30, BidPrice = 120.0},
                new Bid(){Name="Car", Description="Sports Car", TimeLeft = 30, BidPrice = 1500.0},
                new Bid(){Name="TV", Description="Big screen TV", TimeLeft = 30, BidPrice = 330.0},
                new Bid(){Name="Boat", Description="Party Boat", TimeLeft = 30, BidPrice = 1200.0}
            };
            public static void SetBid()
            {
                Random rnd = new Random();
                CurrentBid = (Bid)_items[rnd.Next(0, _items.Count - 1)].Clone();
            }
        }

    public class Bid
    {
        public Bid Clone()
        {
            return (Bid)MemberwiseClone();
        }
        public string Name { get; set; }
        public string Description { get; set; }
        public double BidPrice { get; set; }
        public int TimeLeft { get; set; }
        public string ConnectionId { get; set; }
    }
```

5. Add a reference to the Microsoft.AspNet.SignalR.Core.dll, Microsoft.Owin.dll, Newtonsoft.Json.dll, and Owin.dll.

6. Compile your project.

The application that was created earlier in this chapter can be used to point to http://localhost/SignalR and test the Mono server deployment. To test the server from other machines, make sure that you enable the firewall to allow port 80 to be accessed.

Mono Framework on OS X

Because the OS X operating system supports Linux and Mono version 3.X, you can run the same applications as Linux in this section. The only difference is that the commands to install the libraries on OS X are different from Linux, as you'll see in the next section.

Using the Xamarin Add-in for Visual Studio to Create iOS and Android SignalR Clients

Today, everything is transitioning to mobile, and currently we have shown you only how to support Windows Phone devices. This section changes that by showing how to support SignalR clients with iOS and Android devices. Currently, the easiest way to get SignalR support in these devices is to use a commercial offering from Xamarin. This section is based on the business edition, which is currently priced at $999 per platform, per developer, so that the Xamarin add-in for Visual Studio can be used. The Xamarin product setup for iOS and Android is the same for both platforms, but the iOS platform requires additional steps and an Apple operating system to test devices as well as an Apple Developer account.

Setting Up the Xamarin Add-in for Visual Studio

To get the Xamarin add-in for Visual Studio, you can download it from `http://xamarin.com`. When you install the software, it checks to see whether Java, Xamarin Studio, Android SDKs, and other software packages are installed. If they are not, it downloads and installs necessary software packages. Once the software is installed, you have to update the NuGet package manager so that the SignalR NuGet packages are compatible with portable class libraries. (The NuGet update can be found under Menu Tools ➤ Extensions and Updates and then inside the dialog box under Updates ➤ Visual Studio Gallery.) With these steps done, you should be able to start creating Android applications, but the iOS applications require a little more setup, as described later in the section.

Creating Android Applications

Creating the sample application should be very straightforward. If there are any issues, make sure that all software is up to date, including USB drivers for Android devices, Visual Studio add-ins, SDKs, and so on. The updates may be needed because the speed of development for mobile devices is very fast, and things are always changing. To complete the Android application, complete the following steps:

1. Create a new Android application, as shown in Figure 7-7.

Figure 7-7. *Android application project selection*

2. Type **Install-Package Microsoft.AspNet.SignalR.Client** and press Return in the Package Manager Console.

3. Remove references to System.Threading.Tasks and System.RunTime.

4. Open the properties for the Android application project.

5. Go to the Android Manifest tab and select the Internet permission (see Figure 7-8).

Figure 7-8. Android application manifest properties

6. Replace the code for the `Activity1` class with the code in Listing 7-19. Add any missing using statements.

Listing 7-19. C# Code for Android Example

```csharp
public class Activity1 : Activity
    {
        Button btnCurrentBid;
        Button btnMakeBid;
        txtBid;
        TextView lblName;
        TextView lblDescr;
        TextView lblBid;
        TextView lblTime;
        TextView lblWins;
        Microsoft.AspNet.SignalR.Client.HubConnection _hubConnection;
        Microsoft.AspNet.SignalR.Client.IHubProxy _auctionProxy;
        protected override void OnCreate(Bundle bundle)
```

```csharp
    {
        base.OnCreate(bundle);
        SetContentView(Resource.Layout.Main);
        btnCurrentBid = FindViewById<Button>(Resource.Id.btnCurrentBid);
        btnCurrentBid.Click += delegate { _auctionProxy.Invoke("MakeCurrentBid"); };
        btnMakeBid = FindViewById<Button>(Resource.Id.btnMakeBid);
        btnMakeBid.Click += delegate { _auctionProxy.Invoke<string>("MakeBid",
        txtBid.Text); };
        txtBid = FindViewById<EditText>(Resource.Id.txtBid);
        lblName = FindViewById<TextView>(Resource.Id.lblName);
        lblDescr = FindViewById<TextView>(Resource.Id.lblDescr);
        lblBid = FindViewById<TextView>(Resource.Id.lblBid);
        lblTime = FindViewById<TextView>(Resource.Id.lblTime);
        lblWins = FindViewById<TextView>(Resource.Id.lblWins);
        StartHub();
    }
    async void StartHub()
    {
        _hubConnection = new Microsoft.AspNet.SignalR.Client.HubConnection
         ("http://localhost/signalr");
        _auctionProxy = _hubConnection.CreateHubProxy("AuctionHub");
        _auctionProxy.Subscribe("UpdateBid").Received += UpdateBid_auctionProxy;
        _auctionProxy.Subscribe("CloseBid").Received += CloseBid_auctionProxy;
        _auctionProxy.Subscribe("CloseBidWin").Received += CloseBidWin_auctionProxy;
        await _hubConnection.Start();
    }
    void UpdateBidMethod(Newtonsoft.Json.Linq.JToken bid, int formObject)
    {
        if (bid != null && bid.HasValues)
        {
            lblName.Text = (string)bid["Name"];
            lblDescr.Text = (string)bid["Description"];
            lblBid.Text = (string)bid["BidPrice"];
            lblTime.Text = "Time Left: " + (string)bid["TimeLeft"];
            if (formObject > 0)
            {
                string win = bid["Name"] + " at " + bid["BidPrice"] + "\r\n";
                lblWins.Text += win;
            }
        }
    }
    void UpdateButtonsMethod(bool enabled)
    {
        this.RunOnUiThread(delegate
        {
            btnCurrentBid.Enabled = enabled;
            btnMakeBid.Enabled = enabled;
        });
    }
    void UpdateBid_auctionProxy(IList<Newtonsoft.Json.Linq.JToken> obj)
    {
        this.RunOnUiThread(delegate
```

```
        {
            UpdateBidMethod(obj[0], 0);
            UpdateButtonsMethod(true);
        });
    }
    void CloseBid_auctionProxy(IList<Newtonsoft.Json.Linq.JToken> obj)
    {
        this.RunOnUiThread(delegate
        {
            UpdateButtonsMethod(false);
        });
    }
    void CloseBidWin_auctionProxy(IList<Newtonsoft.Json.Linq.JToken> obj)
    {
        this.RunOnUiThread(delegate
        {
            UpdateButtonsMethod(false);
            UpdateBidMethod(obj[0], 1);
        });
    }
}
```

7. Replace the XML in Resources ➤ Layout ➤ Main.Xaml with the content in Listing 7-20. It may require right-clicking the file and using Open With XML Editor.

Listing 7-20. XAML for Android example

```xml
<?xml version="1.0" encoding="utf-8"?>
<LinearLayout xmlns:android="http://schemas.android.com/apk/res/android"
  android:orientation="vertical"
  android:layout_width="fill_parent"
  android:layout_height="fill_parent">
  <LinearLayout
    android:orientation="horizontal"
    android:layout_width="fill_parent"
    android:layout_height="50px">
    <TextView
      android:id="@+id/lblName"
      android:layout_width="150px"
      android:layout_height="wrap_content"/>
    <TextView
      android:id="@+id/lblBid"
      android:layout_width="150px"
      android:layout_height="wrap_content"/>
  </LinearLayout>
  <LinearLayout
    android:orientation="horizontal"
    android:layout_width="fill_parent"
    android:layout_height="50px">
    <TextView
      android:id="@+id/lblDescr"
      android:layout_width="150px"
```

CHAPTER 7 ■ HOW TO EXTEND AND CUSTOMIZE SIGNALR FUNCTIONALITY

```
                android:layout_height="wrap_content"/>
              <TextView
                android:id="@+id/lblTime"
                android:layout_width="150px"
                android:layout_height="wrap_content"/>
            </LinearLayout>
            <LinearLayout
              android:orientation="horizontal"
              android:layout_width="fill_parent"
              android:layout_height="50px">
              <Button
                android:id="@+id/btnCurrentBid"
                android:layout_width="150px"
                android:layout_height="wrap_content"
                android:text="Current Bid"/>
              <Button
                android:id="@+id/btnMakeBid"
                android:layout_width="150px"
                android:layout_height="wrap_content"
                android:text="Make Bid"/>
              <EditText
                android:id="@+id/txtBid"
                android:layout_width="150px"
                android:layout_height="wrap_content"
                android:textSize ="22px"/>
            </LinearLayout>
            <TextView
              android:id="@+id/lblWins"
              android:layout_width="fill_parent"
              android:layout_height="wrap_content"/>
          </LinearLayout>
```

■ **Note** The emulators for Android devices are very slow. The program includes a warning (see Figure 7-9) that holds true even on high-end systems. So when you are debugging on the emulator, you might have to wait a couple of minutes before your application is deployed and running on the device.

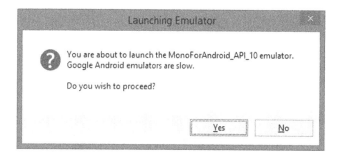

Figure 7-9. *Emulator slowness warning*

180

Now that you have created an Android client application (see Figure 7-10), you can also create a similar application on the iOS devices. You need additional setup steps before you can do that, however.

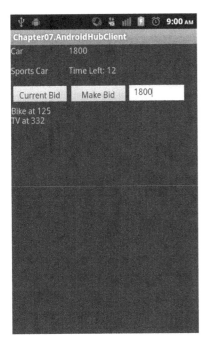

Figure 7-10. *Example of Android hub applicationAdditional Steps for iOS Applications*

For iOS applications, you must have an active Apple operating system on a device such as an iMac, Mac Pro, MacBook, or Mac Mini. This Apple device must be connected and accessible on the same network as your development machine. The first step is to install the Xamarin Studio package on your Apple OS, which is also available from `http://xamarin.com`.

The next step is to join the Apple Developer program, which allows you to deploy software to your provisioned devices. After it is set up, you have to set up the link between Visual Studio and the Apple OS with the Xamarin.iOS Build Host.

Installing Xamarin Studio on Apple OS

The install on your Apple operating system should be very similar to the install for the Windows OS. It checks what components are installed and then installs any missing components. The Apple install has an extra installed program called the Xamarin.iOS Build Host, which is needed to communicate between the Apple OS and the Visual Studio deployment.

Joining the Apple Developer Program

Joining the Apple iOS Developer Program costs $99 at the time of writing. After you register, it might take up to 24 hours to receive the activation e-mail if the registration is successful. Once your account is active, you have to get a developer certificate so that you can provision your devices.

Provisioning Your Devices

There are several ways to provision your devices. (A quick search on the Internet provides many guides that may be even more useful, depending on the number of devices and type of provisioning.) Follow these steps:

1. Connect your device to a machine running OS X and launch Xcode.

2. Inside Xcode, click the Use For Development button in Organizer - Devices.

3. You are asked to associate the device with the Apple Developer account you created. Select the development team you want to provision the device to and click Choose.

4. The software scans for a certificate on the portal (it may not exist if this is the first time).

5. If it does not exist, you can click Request to have one generated for you.

   a. It may take a while to refresh; to speed up the operation, go to `https://developer.apple.com/account/ios/certificate/` and download the Development iOS Team Provisioning Profile to your desktop.

   b. The download link can be made visible by clicking the profile in the list.

   c. Once you have downloaded the provisioning profile, return to Xcode.

   d. Go to Organizer - Devices.

   e. Select Provisioning Profiles and click Add.

   f. Find the file that you downloaded and click Open.

6. Load Xamarin Studio on the OS X machine used in step 1 and go to Preferences on the Xamarin Studio menu.

7. In Preferences, go to the Developer Accounts section.

8. Click the plus sign to add your Apple ID that is associated with the Apple Developer Program.

9. Click OK.

Now that Xamarin is set up, the final step is to set up the Build Host, which is a service that allows Visual Studio to build iOS applications. Next, we show you how to set up the host on the OS X and Windows side.

Setting up the Xamarin.iOS Build Host

1. To set up the link between the Visual Studio and the OS X machine to launch the Xamarin. iOS Build Host, you can locate it by searching for it in Finder (see Figure 7-11).

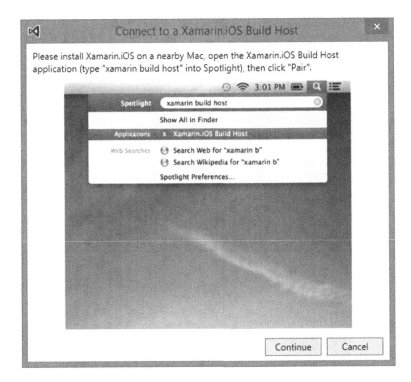

Figure 7-11. *Locating the Xamarin.iOS Build Host on OS X*

2. Once it is running, click the Pair button (see Figure 7-12).

Figure 7-12. *Xamarin.iOS Build Host dialog box*

3. It starts listening for a connection for Visual Studio and displays a PIN (see Figure 7-13) that you need to enter from the Windows machine.

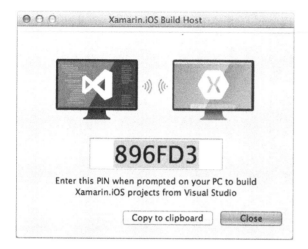

Figure 7-13. *Displaying a PIN in the Xamarin.iOS Build Host dialog box*

4. Return to Windows and launch Visual Studio.

5. Click the Tools menu and click Options.

6. Select the Xamarin tab and then select iOS settings.

7. On this tab, click the Find Mac Build Host button.

8. It displays a message about the Xamarin.iOS Build Host that was launched in an earlier step. Read it; then click Continue.

9. The configuration window attempts to find the host automatically.

10. If the Build Host is not found, you can try to manually enter the information to locate it.

11. If the Build Host is found, click the machine and then click Connect (see Figure 7-14.)

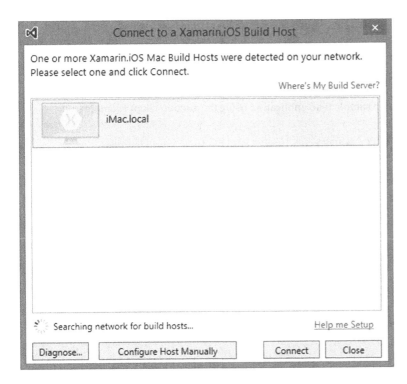

Figure 7-14. *Build Host selection dialog box*

12.   The configuration pops up a dialog box for the PIN (see Figure 7-15) that was displayed earlier on the Apple machine.

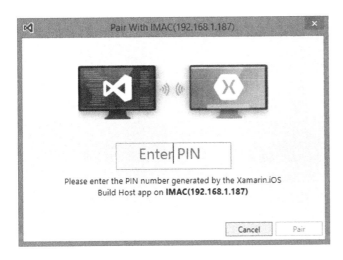

Figure 7-15. *Visual Studio pairing PIN dialog box*

13. Enter the PIN and click Pair. If it paired successfully, click Finish and then OK to exit the Options menu.

Creating a Sample iOS Application

Now that everything is set up, you can create a sample iPad application using the auction client example from Chapter 6:

1. Create a new project of type Visual C# ➤ iOS ➤ iPad and choose the Hello World template, as shown in Figure 7-16.

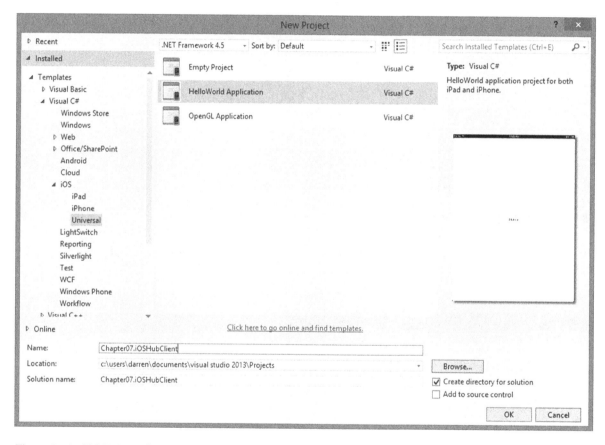

Figure 7-16. *iOS Universal project with HelloWorld template selection*

2. Right-click the project and go to Properties.

3. Click the iOS Application tab.

4. Add an application name, identifier, and version to the respective fields.

5. Choose the appropriate deployment target.

6. Save and close the properties window.

7. Run the Package Manager Console.

8. Type **Install-Package Microsoft.AspNet.SignalR.Client**.

9. Remove System.Runtime, System.Threading.Tasks, and Newtonsoft.Json from the References.

10. Add a reference to Newtonsoft.Json.dll, which can be found under the project root directory\packages\Newtonsoft.Json.X.X.X\lib\portable-net40+sl4+wp7+win8 where the X is the current version of Newtonsoft.Json that exists in your project.

11. Replace the class in MyViewController.cs with the class in Listing 7-21, which will create the UI components of the example.

Listing 7-21. MyViewController C# Code

```
public class MyViewController : UIViewController
{
    UIButton btnCurrentBid;
    UIButton btnMakeBid;
    UITextField txtBid;
    UILabel lblName;
    UILabel lblDescr;
    UILabel lblBid;
    UILabel lblTime;
    UILabel lblWins;
    public override void ViewDidLoad()
    {
        base.ViewDidLoad();

        View.Frame = UIScreen.MainScreen.Bounds;
        View.BackgroundColor = UIColor.LightGray;
        View.AutoresizingMask = UIViewAutoresizing.FlexibleWidth |
        UIViewAutoresizing. FlexibleHeight;

        txtBid = new UITextField(new RectangleF(260, 120, 140, 30)) { BackgroundColor
        = UIColor.White };
        lblName = new UILabel(new RectangleF(20, 20, 200, 30));
        lblBid = new UILabel(new RectangleF(260, 20, 200, 30));
        lblDescr = new UILabel(new RectangleF(20, 60, 200, 30));
        lblTime = new UILabel(new RectangleF(260, 60, 200, 30));
        lblWins = new UILabel(new RectangleF(20, 170, 380, 150)) { BackgroundColor =
        UIColor. White, LineBreakMode = UILineBreakMode.WordWrap, Lines = 0 };
        btnCurrentBid = UIButton.FromType(UIButtonType.System);
        btnCurrentBid.Frame = new RectangleF(20, 120, 100, 30);
        btnCurrentBid.SetTitle("Current Bid", UIControlState.Normal);
        btnCurrentBid.BackgroundColor = UIColor.Gray;
        btnMakeBid = UIButton.FromType(UIButtonType.RoundedRect);
        btnMakeBid.SetTitle("Make Bid", UIControlState.Normal);
        btnMakeBid.Frame = new RectangleF(140, 120, 100, 30);
        btnMakeBid.BackgroundColor = UIColor.Gray;

        View.AddSubview(btnCurrentBid);
        View.AddSubview(btnMakeBid);
```

```
                View.AddSubview(txtBid);
                View.AddSubview(lblName);
                View.AddSubview(lblDescr);
                View.AddSubview(lblBid);
                View.AddSubview(lblTime);
                View.AddSubview(lblWins);
            }
        }
```

12. Add the SignalR Hub client code, which adds what is in Listing 7-22 to the MyViewController class.

Listing 7-22. iOS Code to Wire Up SignalR Hub

```
Microsoft.AspNet.SignalR.Client.HubConnection _hubConnection;
Microsoft.AspNet.SignalR.Client.IHubProxy _auctionProxy;
List<string> winningBids = new List<string>();
async void StartHub()
{
    _hubConnection = new Microsoft.AspNet.SignalR.Client.HubConnection
    ("http://localhost/signalr");
    _auctionProxy = _hubConnection.CreateHubProxy("AuctionHub");
    _auctionProxy.Subscribe("UpdateBid").Received += UpdateBid_auctionProxy;
    _auctionProxy.Subscribe("CloseBid").Received += CloseBid_auctionProxy;
    _auctionProxy.Subscribe("CloseBidWin").Received += CloseBidWin_auctionProxy;
    await _hubConnection.Start();
}

void UpdateBidMethod(Newtonsoft.Json.Linq.JToken bid, int formObject)
{
    if (bid != null && bid.HasValues)
    {
        lblName.Text = (string)bid["Name"];
        lblDescr.Text = (string)bid["Description"];
        lblBid.Text = (string)bid["BidPrice"];
        lblTime.Text = "Time Left: " + (string)bid["TimeLeft"];
        if (formObject > 0)
        {
            string win = bid["Name"] + " at " + bid["BidPrice"] + "\r\n";
            lblWins.Text += win;
        }
    }
}
void UpdateButtonsMethod(bool enabled)
{
    this.InvokeOnMainThread(delegate
    {
btnCurrentBid.Enabled = enabled;
btnMakeBid.Enabled = enabled;
    });
}
void UpdateBid_auctionProxy(IList<Newtonsoft.Json.Linq.JToken> obj)
```

```
{
    this.InvokeOnMainThread(delegate
    {
        UpdateBidMethod(obj[0], 0);
        UpdateButtonsMethod(true);
    });
}
void CloseBid_auctionProxy(IList<Newtonsoft.Json.Linq.JToken> obj)
{
    this.InvokeOnMainThread(delegate
    {
        UpdateButtonsMethod(false);
    });
}
void CloseBidWin_auctionProxy(IList<Newtonsoft.Json.Linq.JToken> obj)
{
    this.InvokeOnMainThread(delegate
    {
        UpdateButtonsMethod(false);
        UpdateBidMethod(obj[0], 1);
    });
}
```

13. After you have the hub proxy in the class, add the code in Listing 7-23 to the bottom of the
    ViewDidLoad method before the View.AddSubview methods. This code associates a UI
    touch event with a corresponding proxy command.

    Listing 7-23. Logic to Associate UI Touch Event to Hub Command

```
btnCurrentBid.TouchUpInside += (object sender, EventArgs e) =>
{
    _auctionProxy.Invoke("MakeCurrentBid");
};

btnMakeBid.TouchUpInside += (object sender, EventArgs e) =>
{
    _auctionProxy.Invoke<string>("MakeBid", txtBid.Text);
};
```

14. The last piece to put in place is the method that connects the hub proxy. The method call
    in Listing 7-24 needs to be added to the top of the ViewDidLoad method.

    Listing 7-24. Logic to Call Hub Start when the UI Loads

```
StartHub();
```

Once this is complete, your application should be ready to run. If your application builds successfully but does not run, and you see No Devices Attached as shown in Figure 7-17, go to the Manager and change the active solution platform to the simulator.

ARCHITECTURE   ANALYZE   WINDOW   HELP

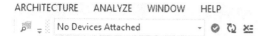

Figure 7-17. *Example of No Devices Attached in device selection*

If the active solution platform is the iPhone (see Figure 7-18), it tries to deploy to the actual device attached if the active solution platform is the iPhone simulator (see Figure 7-19).

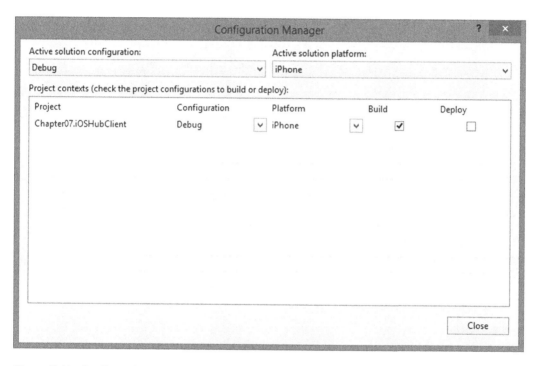

Figure 7-18. *Configuration Manager with actual device selected*

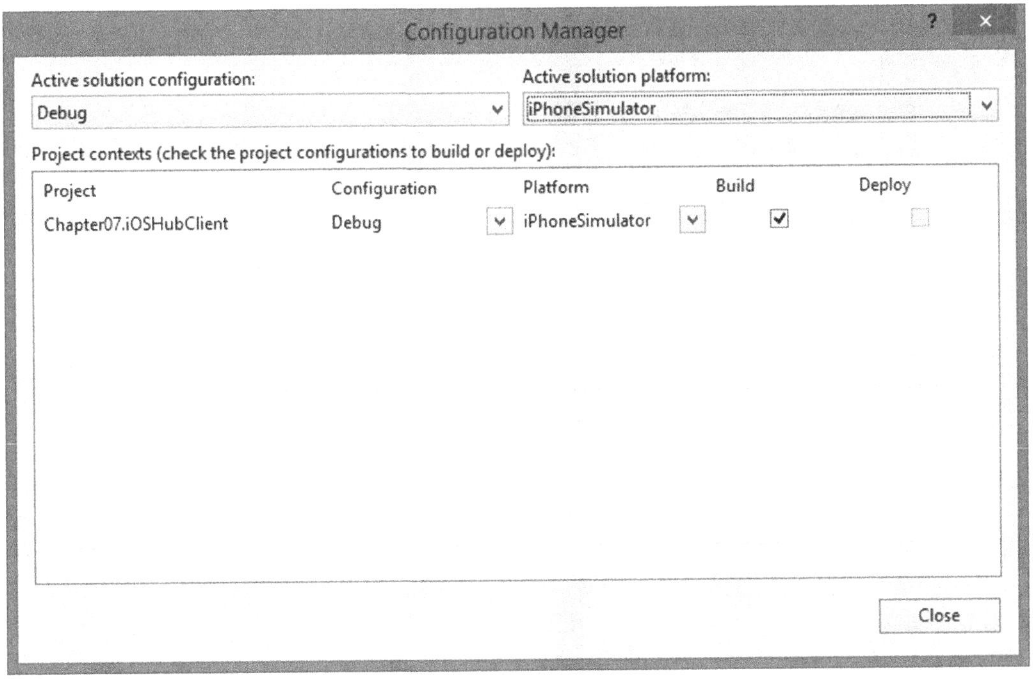

Figure 7-19. *Configuration Manager with simulator selected*

Once the application is deployed, you should see something similar to Figure 7-20. The same code should work for iPhone (just change the deployment target).

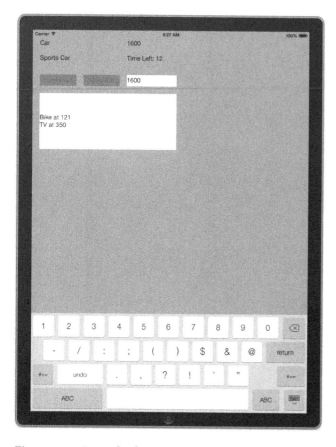

Figure 7-20. *Example of iOS hub applicationSummary*

This chapter showed how to extend and customize SignalR applications so that the applications can fit project requirements. The main component that helps with customizing and extending your application is the dependency resolver.

SignalR, which is considered a middleware component in the Katana project, implements the OWIN interface. The Katana host and server components can easily be changed and can be configured to work with other middleware configured in the pipeline.

You learned that you can use the Mono 3.X Framework to run SignalR libraries on operating systems such as Linux and OS X. Finally, we went over the customized version of the Mono Framework that allows SignalR to run on Android and iOS client devices.

CHAPTER 8

Configuration, Deployment, and Security Aspects of SignalR

In the previous chapters of this book, you learned how to implement an ASP.NET SignalR application using hubs or persistent connections, how to troubleshoot these applications, and how to communicate with ASP.NET SignalR server applications from different client types.

After building and debugging your applications, the final step of developing any software is to configure it to be deployed to production. With this comes the importance of security before you launch an application and expose it to users who can abuse or misuse your software. It also can protect the user from the ill intent of others, depending on the application and its function.

This chapter covers how to secure an ASP.NET SignalR application using authentication and authorization, and how to configure and deploy an ASP.NET SignalR application.

ASP.NET SignalR is designed to be a very customizable and configurable platform to suit different needs. Because an ASP.NET SignalR application consists of several dependent and independent components on the server and client sides, each part comes with different sets of options to be customizable and configurable.

Although the topic of security is not limited to authentication and authorization, ASP.NET SignalR has taken care of many details that developers normally worry about. Authentication and authorization on ASP.NET SignalR applications is integrated into the server-side component in a consistent way like normal authentication and authorization mechanisms in ASP.NET, so being familiar with these topics in ASP.NET web form or ASP.NET MVC is required. As you discover in this chapter, hubs and persistent connections provide mechanisms for authentication and authorization, and there are different techniques to customize them for your needs.

The configuration part of an ASP.NET SignalR application is critical, especially if you are dealing with an enterprise software that has the potential to receive a heavy load from its users. Because ASP.NET SignalR comes with different transport protocols, some of which need a long-held HTTP connection, there are some recommended customizations in the hosting environment (e.g., Internet Information Services [IIS]) to optimize the use of resources. We discuss them in this chapter.

Fortunately, the deployment of ASP.NET SignalR applications is very integrated and similar to other ASP.NET web applications (for web-based applications), and you can easily deploy your applications. We go over this topic briefly as well.

The other topic covered in this chapter is the Open Web Interface for .NET (OWIN) startup in ASP.NET SignalR because it is one of the first Microsoft technologies that supported OWIN. It is important to know how OWIN support works in ASP.NET SignalR.

In a nutshell, the following major topics are covered in this chapter:

- How authentication works in ASP.NET SignalR to prevent anonymous access to hubs and persistent connections

- How to use authorization to limit access to hubs and persistent connections to particular groups or roles of users

- Major configuration aspects of an ASP.NET SignalR application to consider

- Recommended settings for ASP.NET SignalR, IIS, and ASP.NET execution to host ASP.NET SignalR applications

- Deployment considerations for an ASP.NET SignalR application

- How to use performance counters to monitor an ASP.NET SignalR application

- Relationship of OWIN and ASP.NET SignalR

Authentication and Authorization in ASP.NET SignalR

Authentication in ASP.NET SignalR is built on top of authentication in the ASP.NET infrastructure, so all the principles you know about ASP.NET authentication also apply to ASP.NET SignalR. The implementation is slightly different between hubs and persistent connections, as discussed in the following sections.

Authentication and Authorization for Hubs

The `Authorize` attribute located in the `Microsoft.AspNet.SignalR` namespace is a very simple and powerful tool provided in ASP.NET SignalR for authentication and authorization. This attribute can be applied to individual methods on hubs or to the hub itself (in that case, it applies to all the methods defined within that hub). You can pass a comma-separated string list of roles to this attribute to allow access to the hub or individual method for those roles.

Let's see this in an example. We skip some of the general details here about setting up an ASP.NET application with basic cookie authentication, but you can find the full source code in the downloadable samples for this book. Our example applies the ASP.NET project template to generate the default HTML template as well as the basic authentication and authorization code we need. We implement our examples as new views and action methods for the `HomeController`.

Listing 8-1 shows the view that we use for these examples. It is already familiar to you from the previous chapters, with the minor difference that it is now an ASP.NET model-view-controller (MVC) view with some markup in the Razor view engine.

Listing 8-1. ASP.NET MVC View for Hubs Authentication Examples

```
@{
    ViewBag.Title = "Chapter 8 - Authentication and Authorization";
}
<h2>@ViewBag.Title</h2>
<h3>@ViewBag.Message</h3>

<script type="text/javascript" src="@Url.Content("/Scripts/jquery-1.10.2.js")"></script>
<script type="text/javascript" src="@Url.Content("/Scripts/jquery.signalR-2.0.3.min.js")"></script>
<script type="text/javascript" src="@Url.Content("/Signalr/hubs")"></script>

<script type="text/javascript">
    $(function () {
        var chat = $.connection.broadcastHub;

        chat.client.BroadcastMessage = function (message) {
            $('#messages').append('<li>' + message + '</li>');
        };
```

```
    $.connection.hub.start().done(function () {
        $("#broadcast").click(function () {
            chat.server.broadcast($('#msg').val());
        });
    });
});
</script>

<div>
    <input type="text" id="msg" />
    <input type="button" id="broadcast" value="broadcast" />

    <ul id="messages"></ul>
</div>
```

Listing 8-2 shows modifications in the HomeController to handle the new view introduced for the examples.

Listing 8-2. ASP.NET MVC Controller for Hubs Authentication Examples

```
using System.Web.Mvc;

namespace Chapter8.Controllers
{
    public class HomeController : Controller
    {
        public ActionResult Index()
        {
            return View();
        }

        [Authorize]
        public ActionResult AuthenticationHubs()
        {
            ViewBag.Message = "Authentication with Hubs";

            return View();
        }
    }
}
```

We develop a simple broadcasting hub on top of this authentication, but we want to make sure that only authenticated users can broadcast messages to other authenticated users and that anonymous access is prevented.

Listing 8-3 shows how this works. This code is actually the hub implementation for broadcasting.

Listing 8-3. Authentication for Hubs

```
using Microsoft.AspNet.SignalR;

namespace Chapter8.Hubs
{
    public class BroadcastHub : Hub
    {
        [Authorize]
        public void Broadcast(string message)
        {
            Clients.All.broadcastMessage(message);
        }
    }
}
```

This example is the same example we used a few times in the previous chapters of this book, except that it works only when you are logged in; otherwise, the hub throws a 401 (Unauthorized) HTTP status code. (We don't provide the output here because it is similar to what you have already seen in this book.)

You can also apply authorization on top of this example. It is as simple as passing a comma-separated list of roles to the Roles property of the Authorize attribute (see Listing 8-4).

Listing 8-4. Role-based Authorization for Hubs

```
using Microsoft.AspNet.SignalR;

namespace Chapter8.Hubs
{
    public class BroadcastHub : Hub
    {
        [Authorize(Roles="Admins, Users")]
        public void Broadcast(string message)
        {
            Clients.All.broadcastMessage(message);
        }
    }
}
```

You can also use authorization based on usernames rather than roles, and you have to pass the usernames to the Users property of the Authorize attribute (see Listing 8-5).

Listing 8-5. User-based Authorization for Hubs

```
using Microsoft.AspNet.SignalR;

namespace Chapter8.Hubs
{
    public class BroadcastHub : Hub
    {
        [Authorize(Users="keyvan, darren")]
        public void Broadcast(string message)
```

```
        {
            Clients.All.broadcastMessage(message);
        }
    }
}
```

Authentication and Authorization for Persistent Connections

Authentication and authorization for persistent connections is slightly different from hubs, but it relies on the same principles. Just like everything else about persistent connections, you have more control over your security logic as well.

Before discussing the implementation, we show Listing 8-6, in which we update the ASP.NET MVC controller to handle a new action method and view needed for these examples.

Listing 8-6. ASP.NET MVC Controller for Persistent Connection Authentication Examples

```
using System.Web.Mvc;

namespace Chapter8.Controllers
{
    public class HomeController : Controller
    {
        public ActionResult Index()
        {
            return View();
        }

        [Authorize]
        public ActionResult AuthenticationHubs()
        {
            ViewBag.Message = "Authentication with Hubs";

            return View();
        }

        [Authorize]
        public ActionResult AuthenticationPersistentConnections()
        {
            ViewBag.Message = "Authentication with Persistent Connections";

            return View();
        }
    }
}
```

We also introduce a new view for the new action method introduced here (see Listing 8-7). Please note that the reference to the hubs proxy in the listing is present in the master view template.

Listing 8-7. ASP.NET MVC View for Hubs Authentication Examples

```
@{
    ViewBag.Title = "Chapter 8 - Authentication and Authorization";
}
<h2>@ViewBag.Title</h2>
<h3>@ViewBag.Message</h3>

<script type="text/javascript" src="@Url.Content("/Scripts/jquery-1.10.2.js")"></script>
<script type="text/javascript" src="@Url.Content("/Scripts/jquery.signalR-2.0.3.min.js")"></script>

<script type="text/javascript">
    $(function () {
        var connection = $.connection('/broadcast');

        connection.received(function (data) {
            $('#messages').append('<li>' + data + '</li>');
        });

        connection.start().done(function () {
            $("#broadcast").click(function () {
                connection.send($('#msg').val());
            });
        });

    });
</script>

<input type="text" id="msg" />
<input type="button" id="broadcast" value="broadcast" />

<ul id="messages"></ul>
```

Authentication and authorization for persistent connections is as simple as overriding and implementing the AuthorizeRequest method of a persistent connection. This method receives an instance of an IRequest object in SignalR and returns a Boolean value that determines whether a request should have access to that persistent connection.

A basic implementation for authentication is shown in Listing 8-8, but (as you can guess) you can easily build your own complex authorization logic here as well.

Listing 8-8. Authentication for Persistent Connections

```
using Microsoft.AspNet.SignalR;
using System.Threading.Tasks;

namespace Chapter8.PersistentConnections
{
    public class BroadcastConnection : PersistentConnection
    {
        protected override bool AuthorizeRequest(IRequest request)
        {
            return request.User.Identity.IsAuthenticated;
        }
```

```
    protected override Task OnReceived(IRequest request, string connectionId, string data)
    {
        return Connection.Broadcast(data);
    }
  }
}
```

These simple concepts are all you need to know to secure your ASP.NET SignalR application from public access using authentication and authorization (role based or user based).

Configuration Aspects of ASP.NET SignalR Applications

ASP.NET SignalR does not come with many custom configurations specific to this technology. As mentioned throughout the previous chapters of this book, ASP.NET SignalR works closely with ASP.NET applications and derives their configurations for several uses, including security.

ASP.NET SignalR has a set of diagnosis configurations that allow you to trace the whole ecosystem of your application. (We do not repeat these configurations here and refer you to Chapter 5 to read more about them.)

Besides these configurations, there is nothing special about ASP.NET SignalR applications to apply; just configure your application the same way you configure an ASP.NET web application.

Recommended IIS Settings for ASP.NET SignalR Applications

As discussed later in this chapter when we talk about OWIN and ASP.NET SignalR, you probably want to host your ASP.NET SignalR applications in IIS. You know that the nature of ASP.NET SignalR applications is slightly different from typical ASP.NET web applications because they employ the concept of long-held HTTP connections between client(s) and server(s), and this difference can introduce some challenges when configuring a host environment for the best performance.

With this fact in mind, the ASP.NET SignalR team has documented some recommended settings for configuring IIS for the best performance for this type of application.

■ **Note** Although these settings are recommended, you might want to adjust them to better fit your needs, depending on your individual case. The built-in performance counters in ASP.NET SignalR discussed later in this chapter can assist you to monitor the behavior of your own application in the context of your hosting environment and your user base to allow you to adjust these settings accordingly.

The customizations on IIS and your web application have to do with a few different settings, discussed briefly in the following sections.

Default Message Buffer Size

ASP.NET SignalR has a default value of 1,000 messages in memory per hub per connection. Although it is designed for typical messaging scenarios in your application, it might introduce memory issues if the messages are large. In this case, you have to decrease the number of messages you keep in memory, which is a relatively easy change in your configurations (see Listing 8-9).

Listing 8-9. Decreasing the Message Buffer Size for ASP.NET SignalR Applications

```
using Microsoft.AspNet.SignalR;
using Microsoft.Owin;
using Owin;

[assembly: OwinStartupAttribute(typeof(Chapter8.Startup))]
namespace Chapter8
{
    public partial class Startup
    {
        public void Configuration(IAppBuilder app)
        {
            GlobalHost.Configuration.DefaultMessageBufferSize = 500;
            app.MapSignalR();
            ConfigureAuth(app);
        }
    }
}
```

We decreased this value to 500.

Maximum Concurrent Requests per Application

The default number of concurrent requests per application in IIS is 5,000. Increasing this value can enable more resources to serve ASP.NET SignalR applications, especially if you're applying an extensive use of long polling. You can make this IIS configuration change by executing the command in Listing 8-10.

Listing 8-10. Increasing the Maximum Number of Concurrent Requests per Application in IIS

```
cd %windir%\System32\inetsrv\
appcmd.exe set config /section:system.webserver/serverRuntime
        /appConcurrentRequestLimit:10000
```

Here we change this value to 10000 rather than the default 5000 value.

Maximum Concurrent Requests per CPU

You can configure ASP.NET on a server to handle more concurrent requests per CPU available on that server, which can have a positive performance impact on your servers. It can be applied in the aspnet.config file on your server, depending on the version of .NET you use. Listing 8-11 shows how to change this setting.

Listing 8-11. Increasing Maximum Number of Concurrent Requests per CPU in ASP.NET

```
<?xml version="1.0" encoding="UTF-8" ?>
<configuration>
    <system.web>
        <applicationPool maxConcurrentRequestsPerCPU="20000" />
    </system.web>
</configuration>
```

Here we increased this value to 20000.

Request Queue Limit

If the number of incoming requests to each CPU exceeds the limit you defined in the previous section, IIS automatically throttles these requests into a queue. Increasing the size of this queue can improve the performance of an ASP.NET SignalR application as well. As Listing 8-12 shows, you can increase this value in `aspnet.config` by adding an element.

Listing 8-12. Increasing Request Queue Limit in ASP.NET

```
<processModel autoConfig="false" requestQueueLimit="250000" />
```

Here we increased the value to 250000.

Note that we discussed four different performance settings to improve the execution of an ASP.NET SignalR application. The first change (default message buffer size) is an ASP.NET SignalR application change at the application level. The second change (maximum concurrent requests per application) is an IIS change. The third and fourth changes (maximum number of concurrent requests per CPU and request queue limit) are changes at the ASP.NET level at the server level.

Deploying ASP.NET SignalR Applications

Deploying an ASP.NET SignalR application is not very different from deploying any other ASP.NET web application. You can deploy it by using the Deployment option in Visual Studio: right-click on your web project in Solution Explorer and select from file, IIS, or FTP deployments. You can also deploy your application into the cloud.

ASP.NET SignalR applications can be deployed to a variety of hosting environments, including Windows (with the .NET Framework installed) and Linux (with Mono Framework installed). However, you gain the best tools, especially for Web Sockets access, in Windows Server 2012.

If you deploy your SignalR application on a different domain or subdomain from your main web application (in which case you make requests to ASP.NET SignalR application), you have to take care of your cross-domain calls before starting the deployment process.

Make sure that your hosting environment does not override the application path in which your ASP.NET SignalR JavaScript hub proxies are located. If that is the case, you can change this path in your ASP.NET SignalR application or change the settings for your hosting environment.

Performance Counters

Although an application may run with visible issues, in today's software world it is very important to make sure that you have an efficient program that doesn't overuse resources and performs in a reasonable and fast manner. This is particularly important for a real-time web application that needs to communicate data in real time. Any delay caused by a performance issue can have a big impact on the quality of software.

The ASP.NET SignalR team has considered this fact and has bundled a set of performance counters inside the framework that enables software developers and administrators to monitor the performance of the application and make sure that it is running in an efficient manner.

Before talking about these performance counters, we want to emphasize an important point about ASP.NET SignalR hosting (discussed in more detail in the next sections). Because ASP.NET SignalR may use long-polling connections for transport, it has a good potential for having a higher number of concurrent connections with lightweight resource use on IIS or other hosting options. This is in contrast with normal web applications, in which there are fewer concurrent connections with higher resource needs.

With this fact about ASP.NET SignalR applications, having these performance counters can help a lot in determining the quality of the running application.

To install ASP.NET SignalR performance counters, you have to download and install a tool called `SignalR.exe`. The best way to do this is to download it with the NuGet Package Manager. Search for `signalr.util` to find a package called Microsoft ASP.NET SignalR Utilities. After installing this package, you should have the `SignalR.exe` file in the `<project folder>/packages/Microsoft.AspNet.SignalR.Utils.<version>/tools` location on your local drive storage.

If you run the command `signalr.exe ipc` or simply `signalr ipc` as an administrator, the performance counters are installed on your machine (see Figure 8-1).

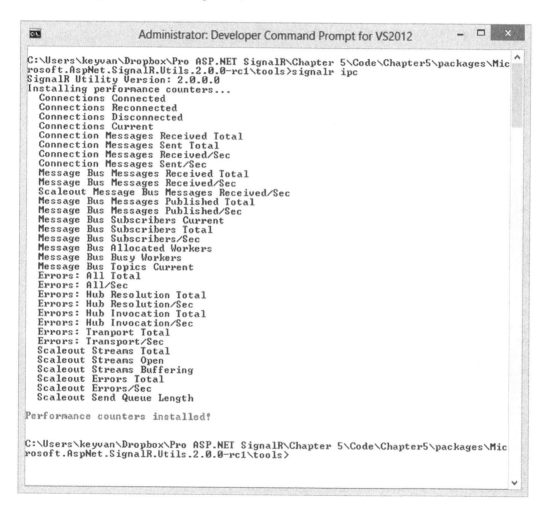

Figure 8-1. *Installing ASP.NET SignalR performance counters*

You can remove these performance counters by running the command `signalr.exe upc` or simply `signalr upc`.

Here is a list of the built-in custom performance counters that come with ASP.NET SignalR:

- Connection counters: Counters for connection lifetime events

    - Connections Connected

    - Connections Reconnected

    - Connections Disconnected

    - Connections Current

- Message counters: Counters for the number of messages generated by ASP.NET SignalR

    - Connection Messages Received Total

    - Connection Messages Sent Total

    - Connection Messages Received/Sec

    - Connection Messages Sent/Sec

- Message bus counters: Counters for messages communicated with the internal ASP.NET SignalR message bus

    - Message Bus Messages Received Total

    - Message Bus Messages Received/Sec

    - Message Bus Messages Published Total

    - Message Bus Messages Published/Sec

    - Message Bus Subscribers Current

    - Message Bus Subscribers Total

    - Message Bus Subscribers/Sec

    - Message Bus Allocated Workers

    - Message Bus Busy Workers

    - Message Bus Topics Current

- Error counters: Counters for errors generated by ASP.NET SignalR applications

    - Errors: All Total

    - Errors: All/Sec

    - Errors: Hub Resolution Total

    - Errors: Hub Resolution/Sec

    - Errors: Hub Invocation Total

    - Errors: Hub Invocation/Sec

    - Errors: Transport Total

    - Errors: Transport/Sec

- Scaleout counters: Counters to measure messages and errors generated by the scaleout provider

  - Scaleout Message Bus Messages Received/Sec

  - Scaleout Streams Total

  - Scaleout Streams Open

  - Scaleout Streams Buffering

  - Scaleout Errors Total

  - Scaleout Errors/Sec

  - Scaleout Send Queue Length

With these counters, you can easily go to the perfmon tool on your Windows machine and add the custom performance counters listed under the SignalR category (see Figure 8-2).

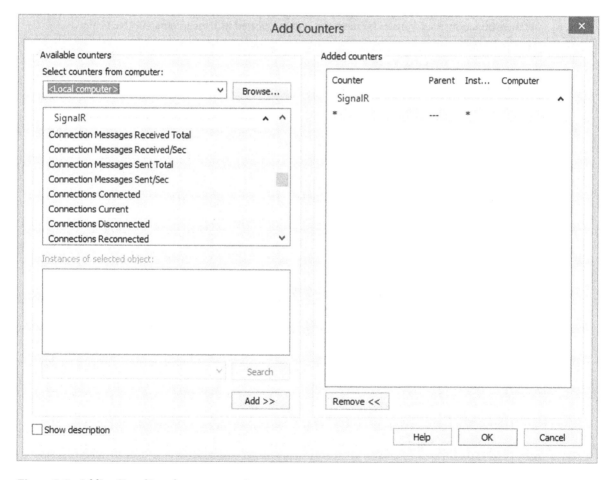

Figure 8-2. Adding SignalR performance counters

Figure 8-3 shows these performance counters working for a simple one-connection application.

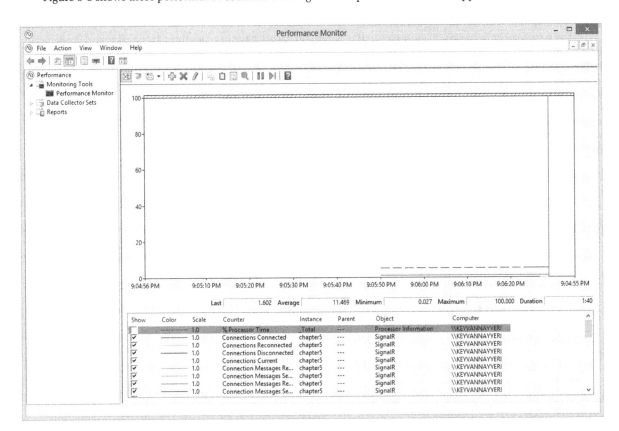

Figure 8-3. *ASP.NET SignalR performance counters monitoring*

OWIN and ASP.NET SignalR

When.NET Framework and ASP.NET were built—and even for almost a decade after that—IIS was an essential part of hosting any ASP.NET application, and there was a close relationship between IIS and ASP.NET. However, in the past few years, the community as well as Microsoft teams have come to the correct conclusion that this level of coupling between ASP.NET, IIS, and the hosting Windows operating system is not beneficial and can introduce limitations.

OWIN can resolve this issue by decoupling the associations between ASP.NET and IIS. OWIN is nothing but a standard defined for communicating between a .NET web application and a web server. This web application can be of any type and can be any server software (IIS or a custom web server on any platform).

Remember that OWIN is nothing but a set of standards; it is not software, components, or anything else. There are implementations of this standard available to developers, though. Microsoft has provided its own implementation for .NET web applications on IIS called Katana (http://katanaproject.codeplex.com). There is also an open-source, community-driven implementation called Nowin (https://github.com/Bobris/Nowin).

Microsoft has been transitioning from the traditional coupled structure in its web platforms with IIS toward OWIN, and ASP.NET SignalR was one of the very first projects that actually adopted this standard and supported OWIN out of the box.

So far in this book, we have been configuring our applications to set up and work and have not discussed how the settings work. Here is a good place to dig further into OWIN in ASP.NET SignalR and learn how to configure your application to work with the hosting environment.

As you remember from several examples in this book, you always have to go to the Startup class and implement a Configuration method similar to that shown in Listing 8-13, which is the implementation for the earlier examples in this chapter.

Listing 8-13. Common OWIN Setup for ASP.NET SignalR Applications

```
using Chapter8.PersistentConnections;
using Microsoft.Owin;
using Owin;

[assembly: OwinStartupAttribute(typeof(Chapter8.Startup))]
namespace Chapter8
{
    public partial class Startup
    {
        public void Configuration(IAppBuilder app)
        {
            app.MapSignalR();
            app.MapSignalR<BroadcastConnection>("/broadcast");
            ConfigureAuth(app);
        }
    }
}
```

The IAppBuilder interface used in the method is in the Microsoft.Owin namespace, in which everything related to OWIN can be found. The IAppBuilder interface comes with a very handy set of methods needed to communicate between the ASP.NET application and the OWIN host (regardless of the implementation for an OWIN standard).

As you can easily guess, it is simple to introduce any hosting environment or platform for an ASP.NET application (hence an ASP.NET SignalR application).

Let's develop a self-hosting environment for ASP.NET SignalR applications to showcase how easy it is to integrate OWIN. We need to implement a self-hosted web server as a Windows console application, so we create a new project for that.

First, we have to execute the NuGet command shown in Listing 8-14 to download the self-hosting components of ASP.NET SignalR in the project.

Listing 8-14. Installing Self-hosting ASP.NET SignalR Components

```
Install-Package Microsoft.AspNet.SignalR.SelfHost
```

Next, we need to install the Microsoft OWIN CORS libraries from NuGet that are responsible for CORS cross-domain communications between clients and a remote server (see Listing 8-15).

Listing 8-15. Installing CORS Components of Microsoft OWIN

```
Install-Package Microsoft.Owin.Cors
```

We are ready to implement the self-hosted server in the console application that we just created. Listing 8-16 shows the very simple implementation of the self-hosted server.

Listing 8-16. Self-hosted OWIN Server

```
using Microsoft.Owin.Hosting;
using System;

namespace SelfHosting
{
    class Program
    {
        static void Main(string[] args)
        {
            string url = "http://localhost:9091";
            using (WebApp.Start(url))
            {
                Console.WriteLine("Self-Hosted server running at {0}", url);
                Console.ReadLine();
            }
        }
    }
}
```

Now we can develop the Startup class for this server (see Listing 8-17).

Listing 8-17. Startup Class for Self-hosted Server

```
using Microsoft.Owin.Cors;
using Owin;

namespace SelfHosting
{
    class Startup
    {
        public void Configuration(IAppBuilder app)
        {
            app.UseCors(CorsOptions.AllowAll);
            app.MapSignalR();
        }
    }
}
```

This is a very familiar code. We use CorsOptions to allow cross-domain communication now that the server is hosted on a different domain.

Finally, we implement a very simple hub inside the console application, which is totally outside ASP.NET and IIS (see Listing 8-18).

Listing 8-18. A Simple Self-hosted Hub

```
using Microsoft.AspNet.SignalR;

namespace SelfHosting
{
    public class BroadcastHub : Hub
    {
        public void Broadcast(string message)
        {
            Clients.All.broadcastMessage(message);
        }
    }
}
```

It is no surprise to see the same hub implementation as before appear in a self-hosted environment because all these implementations are totally independent from the hosting server. We have to worry only about the connections between the application with OWIN and then from OWIN to the server in which we are hosted.

The next step is nothing but a simple change into the client JavaScript code to use this new server in a cross-domain fashion by using the full server URL (see Listing 8-19).

Listing 8-19. Accessing SignalR across different domains

```
@{
    ViewBag.Title = "Chapter 8 - Authentication and Authorization";
}
<h2>@ViewBag.Title</h2>
<h3>@ViewBag.Message</h3>

<script type="text/javascript" src="@Url.Content("/Scripts/jquery-1.10.2.js")"></script>
<script type="text/javascript" src="@Url.Content("/Scripts/jquery.signalR-2.0.3.min.js")"></script>
<script type="text/javascript" src="@Url.Content("http://localhost:9091/signalr/hubs")"></script>

<script type="text/javascript">
    $(function () {
        $.connection.hub.url = "http://localhost:9091/signalr";

        var chat = $.connection.broadcastHub;

        chat.client.BroadcastMessage = function (message) {
            $('#messages').append('<li>' + message + '</li>');
        };

        $.connection.hub.start().done(function () {
            $("#broadcast").click(function () {
                chat.server.broadcast($('#msg').val());
            });
        });
    });
</script>
```

```
<div>
    <input type="text" id="msg" />
    <input type="button" id="broadcast" value="broadcast" />

    <ul id="messages"></ul>
</div>
```

Yes, it is as easy as that. Now we just need to run these two projects simultaneously to get things rolling.

Summary

This chapter discussed securing ASP.NET SignalR applications using authentication and authorization on hubs and persistent connections. We also discussed important topics pertaining to configuring, hosting, and deploying ASP.NET SignalR applications.

This chapter also discussed built-in performance counters for ASP.NET SignalR (for monitoring application performance) and OWIN in ASP.NET SignalR.

CHAPTER 9

Case Study 1: Stock Ticker

Congratulations on making it to this part of the book. So far, you have read chapters dedicated to different aspects of ASP.NET SignalR to have end-to-end knowledge about this powerful technology. Although we tried to focus on all the concepts, principles, and techniques independently with basic examples, you have to apply them all together in practice. Our job is not complete before we provide you with some real-world examples to apply all these principles in action and connect all the dots.

In this chapter and Chapter 11, we discuss two real–world case study examples to demonstrate and apply many of the concepts you learned in the previous chapters. After finishing these two chapters, you will have a very good practical knowledge of ASP.NET SignalR to apply to your day-to-day development tasks.

This chapter provides a case study example of real–time stock updates. The purpose of this case study is to allow users to get real-time updates about recent changes to their stocks. It applies ASP.NET SignalR to push recent stock updates to clients, enabling them to have this information as soon as it becomes available.

This example is built with hubs (although it is certainly doable with persistent connections as well). Here is a brief list of the topics covered in this chapter:

- Overview of the way this application is written
- Main components needed to make this application work
- Server-side implementation of this example, including the hub, hub updater, and domain objects
- Client-side implementation of this example, including the HTML and JavaScript codes

Project Overview

The Microsoft ASP.NET SignalR team has done a great job documenting this technology, and a good part of this documentation is the set of examples provided. One of the best examples of real-world use of ASP.NET SignalR in action is a simple mock stock ticker application (it is commonly called StockTicker) that is released with each update to ASP.NET SignalR and is licensed by Microsoft under an Apache license.

The purpose of this example is to allow developers to get started with ASP.NET SignalR and learn about its concepts in a pragmatic way. We provide a discussion of this sample because we believe it is a great showcase for ASP. NET SignalR.

This sample is available on NuGet, and you can add it to your project from there as we do in this chapter (see Figure 9-1).

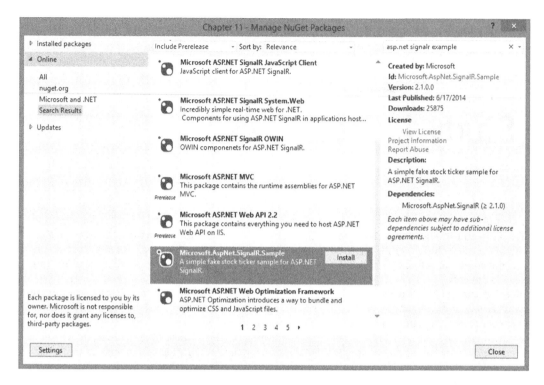

Figure 9-1. *Adding the sample code from NuGet to the project*

After adding this package to your project, you get a new folder called `SignalR.Sample` in your web project along with the other necessary libraries that are required for this sample (e.g., the ASP.NET SignalR library).

You have to take one more step before you can run this example and see the output: add the startup class for StockTicker to your OWIN startup. This is shown in Listing 9-1; you have to add only one line of code to it (shown in bold).

Listing 9-1. Adding StockTicker Startup to Project

```
using Microsoft.Owin;
using Owin;

[assembly: OwinStartupAttribute(typeof(Chapter_11.Startup))]
namespace Chapter_11
{
    public partial class Startup
    {
        public void Configuration(IAppBuilder app)
        {
            Microsoft.AspNet.SignalR.StockTicker.Startup.ConfigureSignalR(app);
            ConfigureAuth(app);
        }
    }
}
```

You can now test this sample before you learn about the different components that make it work. To test this application, navigate to ~/SignalR.Sample/StockTicker.html in two different browsers and click the Open Market button. The output of the browsers (Chrome and Internet Explorer) is shown in Figure 9-2.

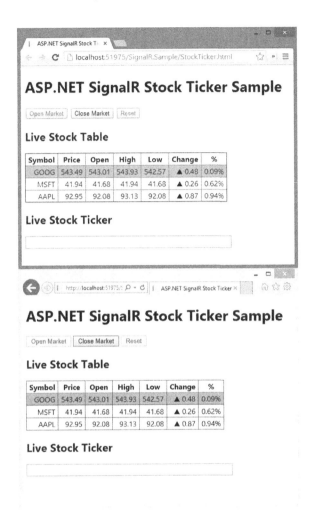

Figure 9-2. *StockTicker output shown in Chrome and Internet Explorer*

Now that the application is running, we discuss different parts of this sample throughout the rest of the chapter. StockTicker is written on top of the hubs ecosystem and a few other helper classes.

StockTicker Server Side

First, we discuss the server-side implementation of StockTicker, which consists of a simple startup class, a hub class, a back-end hub updater class, and a domain class to represent stocks.

Startup

StockTicker comes with its own simple OWIN startup class, which we already called from our web project's OWIN startup to make the sample run. (Refer to Chapter 8.) The code for this startup is shown in Listing 9-2.

Listing 9-2. StockTicker OWIN Startup

```
using Owin;

namespace Microsoft.AspNet.SignalR.StockTicker
{
    public static class Startup
    {
        public static void ConfigureSignalR(IAppBuilder app)
        {
            // For more information on how to configure your application using OWIN startup, visit
            http://go.microsoft.com/fwlink/?LinkID=316888

            app.MapSignalR();
        }
    }
}
```

Stock Domain Class

We need to represent stock in our application, and the best way to do it is to define a new class (see Listing 9-3).

Listing 9-3. Stock Domain Class

```
using System;

namespace Microsoft.AspNet.SignalR.StockTicker
{
    public class Stock
    {
        private decimal _price;

        public string Symbol { get; set; }

        public decimal DayOpen { get; private set; }

        public decimal DayLow { get; private set; }

        public decimal DayHigh { get; private set; }

        public decimal LastChange { get; private set; }
```

```csharp
    public decimal Change
    {
        get
        {
            return Price - DayOpen;
        }
    }

    public double PercentChange
    {
        get
        {
            return (double)Math.Round(Change / Price, 4);
        }
    }

    public decimal Price
    {
        get
        {
            return _price;
        }
        set
        {
            if (_price == value)
            {
                return;
            }

            LastChange = value - _price;
            _price = value;

            if (DayOpen == 0)
            {
                DayOpen = _price;
            }
            if (_price < DayLow || DayLow == 0)
            {
                DayLow = _price;
            }
            if (_price > DayHigh)
            {
                DayHigh = _price;
            }
        }
    }
}
}
```

The properties for a stock are declared here; some properties, such as Change, PercentChange, and Price, are calculated based on other properties in this class.

StockTicker Hub

The next important process of server-side implementation of StockTicker is its hub implementation (see Listing 9-4).

Listing 9-4. StockTicker Hub Implementation

```
using System;
using System.Collections.Generic;
using System.Linq;
using Microsoft.AspNet.SignalR.Hubs;

namespace Microsoft.AspNet.SignalR.StockTicker
{
    [HubName("stockTicker")]
    public class StockTickerHub : Hub
    {
        private readonly StockTicker _stockTicker;

        public StockTickerHub() :
            this(StockTicker.Instance)
        {

        }

        public StockTickerHub(StockTicker stockTicker)
        {
            _stockTicker = stockTicker;
        }

        public IEnumerable<Stock> GetAllStocks()
        {
            return _stockTicker.GetAllStocks();
        }

        public string GetMarketState()
        {
            return _stockTicker.MarketState.ToString();
        }

        public void OpenMarket()
        {
            _stockTicker.OpenMarket();
        }

        public void CloseMarket()
        {
            _stockTicker.CloseMarket();
        }
```

```
        public void Reset()
        {
            _stockTicker.Reset();
        }
    }
}
```

This hub is a very straightforward one that applies a StockTicker class as its back-end business logic and data provider (refer to Chapter 3). It has methods to get all the stocks, get the state of a market (Open or Closed), open a market, close a market, or reset everything. The internal implementation of these methods is done in the StockTicker class that is discussed next. This is a very straightforward and simple hub implementation.

StockTicker Back-end Provider

The main business logic and data provider for StockTicker is a single class called StockTicker (no surprise there). The implementation of this class, which is a little longer, is shown in Listing 9-5. We discuss this implementation piece in the sections that follow.

Listing 9-5. StockTicker Business Logic and Data Provider

```
using System;
using System.Collections.Concurrent;
using System.Collections.Generic;
using System.Threading;
using Microsoft.AspNet.SignalR.Hubs;

namespace Microsoft.AspNet.SignalR.StockTicker
{
    public class StockTicker
    {
        // Singleton instance
        private readonly static Lazy<StockTicker> _instance = new Lazy<StockTicker>(
            () => new StockTicker(GlobalHost.ConnectionManager.GetHubContext<StockTickerHub>().
            Clients));

        private readonly object _marketStateLock = new object();
        private readonly object _updateStockPricesLock = new object();

        private readonly ConcurrentDictionary<string, Stock> _stocks = new
        ConcurrentDictionary<string, Stock>();

        // Stock can go up or down by a percentage of this factor on each change
        private readonly double _rangePercent = 0.002;

        private readonly TimeSpan _updateInterval = TimeSpan.FromMilliseconds(250);
        private readonly Random _updateOrNotRandom = new Random();

        private Timer _timer;
        private volatile bool _updatingStockPrices;
        private volatile MarketState _marketState;
```

```csharp
private StockTicker(IHubConnectionContext<dynamic> clients)
{
    Clients = clients;
    LoadDefaultStocks();
}

public static StockTicker Instance
{
    get
    {
        return _instance.Value;
    }
}

private IHubConnectionContext<dynamic> Clients
{
    get;
    set;
}

public MarketState MarketState
{
    get { return _marketState; }
    private set { _marketState = value; }
}

public IEnumerable<Stock> GetAllStocks()
{
    return _stocks.Values;
}

public void OpenMarket()
{
    lock (_marketStateLock)
    {
        if (MarketState != MarketState.Open)
        {
            _timer = new Timer(UpdateStockPrices, null, _updateInterval, _updateInterval);

            MarketState = MarketState.Open;

            BroadcastMarketStateChange(MarketState.Open);
        }
    }
}
```

```csharp
public void CloseMarket()
{
    lock (_marketStateLock)
    {
        if (MarketState == MarketState.Open)
        {
            if (_timer != null)
            {
                _timer.Dispose();
            }

            MarketState = MarketState.Closed;

            BroadcastMarketStateChange(MarketState.Closed);
        }
    }
}

public void Reset()
{
    lock (_marketStateLock)
    {
        if (MarketState != MarketState.Closed)
        {
            throw new InvalidOperationException("Market must be closed before it can be
            reset.");
        }

        LoadDefaultStocks();
        BroadcastMarketReset();
    }
}

private void LoadDefaultStocks()
{
    _stocks.Clear();

    var stocks = new List<Stock>
    {
        new Stock { Symbol = "MSFT", Price = 41.68m },
        new Stock { Symbol = "AAPL", Price = 92.08m },
        new Stock { Symbol = "GOOG", Price = 543.01m }
    };

    stocks.ForEach(stock => _stocks.TryAdd(stock.Symbol, stock));
}
```

```csharp
private void UpdateStockPrices(object state)
{
    // This function must be re-entrant as it's running as a timer interval handler
    lock (_updateStockPricesLock)
    {
        if (!_updatingStockPrices)
        {
            _updatingStockPrices = true;

            foreach (var stock in _stocks.Values)
            {
                if (TryUpdateStockPrice(stock))
                {
                    BroadcastStockPrice(stock);
                }
            }

            _updatingStockPrices = false;
        }
    }
}

private bool TryUpdateStockPrice(Stock stock)
{
    // Randomly choose whether to udpate this stock or not
    var r = _updateOrNotRandom.NextDouble();
    if (r > 0.1)
    {
        return false;
    }

    // Update the stock price by a random factor of the range percent
    var random = new Random((int)Math.Floor(stock.Price));
    var percentChange = random.NextDouble() * _rangePercent;
    var pos = random.NextDouble() > 0.51;
    var change = Math.Round(stock.Price * (decimal)percentChange, 2);
    change = pos ? change : -change;

    stock.Price += change;
    return true;
}

private void BroadcastMarketStateChange(MarketState marketState)
{
    switch (marketState)
    {
        case MarketState.Open:
            Clients.All.marketOpened();
            break;
```

```
                case MarketState.Closed:
                    Clients.All.marketClosed();
                    break;
                default:
                    break;
            }
        }

        private void BroadcastMarketReset()
        {
            Clients.All.marketReset();
        }

        private void BroadcastStockPrice(Stock stock)
        {
            Clients.All.updateStockPrice(stock);
        }
    }

    public enum MarketState
    {
        Closed,
        Open
    }
}
```

Let's start with a general overview of what this class wants to accomplish. To simplify the implementation, we don't rely on a real data provider for stock data. What we do instead is randomly increase or decrease the stock price by a particular factor. We also want to have mechanisms to open and close markets, and also to reset the whole process and start over. This class does this and also pushes down any data change to all the clients by creating an instance of the StockTickerHub class and calling its methods.

The StockTicker class uses a singleton pattern, so consumers of the class only use one particular instance to get access to methods and properties. It also applies a constructor that loads the list of clients on StockTickerHub into a property to be used throughout the implementation. There are also two lock objects, _marketStateLock and _updateStockPricesLock, which are used to lock access to the market state and stock prices to prevent a race condition in a concurrent call from multiple clients.

The private LoadDefaultStocks() method loads a list of default stocks and initiates this list with Microsoft, Apple, and Google stocks with initial prices. These stocks are added to a concurrent dictionary called _stocks that holds the stocks with the stock names as the key and stock data as the value.

The rest of this class consists of some methods that try to accomplish the goals mentioned before; we outline their purpose here.

The OpenMarket() method uses a lock on the market state object to apply a Timer object to update the stock prices on a regular basis with random data and then broadcasts the change of state for the market to all clients through the BroadcastMarketStateChange() method. On the other hand, the CloseMarket() method follows the same approach to close a market and broadcast this change to all the clients (except that it simply disposes the Timer object).

The Reset() method tries to reset everything if a market is in the Closed state and broadcasts it to all the clients through the BroadcastMarketReset() method.

Finally, the UpdateStockPrices() method applies a lock on the stock prices and uses the TryUpdateStockPrice() method to randomly increase or decrease the price of a given stock by a determined factor. It is broadcast to all clients in BroadcastStockPrice() method.

StockTicker Client Side

This section discusses the client-side implementation of StockTicker, which consists of an HTML file, a CSS file, and some JavaScript code. We do not need to worry about the CSS part because it deals only with the cosmetics of the application; we discuss the HTML and JavaScript aspects only.

HTML

Listing 9-6 shows the HTML code for StockTicker.

Listing 9-6. StockTicker HTML

```
<!DOCTYPE html>
<html xmlns="http://www.w3.org/1999/xhtml">
<head>
    <title>ASP.NET SignalR Stock Ticker</title>
    <link href="StockTicker.css" rel="stylesheet" />
</head>
<body>
    <h1>ASP.NET SignalR Stock Ticker Sample</h1>

    <input type="button" id="open" value="Open Market" />
    <input type="button" id="close" value="Close Market" disabled="disabled" />
    <input type="button" id="reset" value="Reset" />

    <h2>Live Stock Table</h2>
    <div id="stockTable">
        <table border="1">
            <thead>
                <tr><th>Symbol</th><th>Price</th><th>Open</th><th>High</th><th>Low</th><th>Change
                </th><th>%</th></tr>
            </thead>
            <tbody>
                <tr class="loading"><td colspan="7">loading...</td></tr>
            </tbody>
        </table>
    </div>

    <h2>Live Stock Ticker</h2>
    <div id="stockTicker">
        <div class="inner">
            <ul>
                <li class="loading">loading...</li>
            </ul>
        </div>
    </div>

    <script src="jquery-1.10.2.min.js"></script>
    <script src="jquery.color-2.1.2.min.js"></script>
    <script src="../Scripts/jquery.signalR-2.1.0.js"></script>
    <script src="../signalr/hubs"></script>
    <script src="SignalR.StockTicker.js"></script>
</body>
</html>
```

This HTML is a simple one that references the jQuery, ASP.NET SignalR, dynamic hubs proxy, and StockTicker JavaScript files. It also defines three buttons to open, close, and reset the markets; and has definition for a table that holds the stock information. The JavaScript code updates the content of this table in real time.

JavaScript

The last part of this application is the JavaScript code that connects the HTML elements to the dynamic hubs proxy on ASP.NET SignalR and it is shown in Listing 9-7.

Listing 9-7. StockTicker JavaScript

```
/// <reference path="../Scripts/jquery-1.10.2.js" />
/// <reference path="../Scripts/jquery.signalR-2.1.0.js" />

/*!
    ASP.NET SignalR Stock Ticker Sample
*/

// Crockford's supplant method (poor man's templating)
if (!String.prototype.supplant) {
    String.prototype.supplant = function (o) {
        return this.replace(/{([^{}]*)}/g,
            function (a, b) {
                var r = o[b];
                return typeof r === 'string' || typeof r === 'number' ? r : a;
            }
        );
    };
}

// A simple background color flash effect that uses jQuery Color plugin
jQuery.fn.flash = function (color, duration) {
    var current = this.css('backgroundColor');
    this.animate({ backgroundColor: 'rgb(' + color + ')' }, duration / 2)
        .animate({ backgroundColor: current }, duration / 2);
};

$(function () {

    var ticker = $.connection.stockTicker, // the generated client-side hub proxy
        up = '▲',
        down = '▼',
        $stockTable = $('#stockTable'),
        $stockTableBody = $stockTable.find('tbody'),
        rowTemplate = '<tr data-symbol="{Symbol}"><td>{Symbol}</td><td>{Price}</td><td>{DayOpen}
        </td><td>{DayHigh}</td><td>{DayLow}</td><td><span class="dir {DirectionClass}">{Direction}</
        span> {Change}</td><td>{PercentChange}</td></tr>',
        $stockTicker = $('#stockTicker'),
        $stockTickerUl = $stockTicker.find('ul'),
        liTemplate = '<li data-symbol="{Symbol}"><span class="symbol">{Symbol}</
        span> <span class="price">{Price}</span> <span class="change"><span class="dir
        {DirectionClass}">{Direction}
        </span> {Change} ({PercentChange})</span></li>';
```

```
function formatStock(stock) {
    return $.extend(stock, {
        Price: stock.Price.toFixed(2),
        PercentChange: (stock.PercentChange * 100).toFixed(2) + '%',
        Direction: stock.Change === 0 ? '' : stock.Change >=0 ? up : down,
        DirectionClass: stock.Change === 0 ? 'even' : stock.Change >=0 ? 'up' : 'down'
    });
}

function scrollTicker() {
    var w = $stockTickerUl.width();
    $stockTickerUl.css({ marginLeft: w });
    $stockTickerUl.animate({ marginLeft: -w }, 15000, 'linear', scrollTicker);
}

function stopTicker() {
    $stockTickerUl.stop();
}

function init() {
    return ticker.server.getAllStocks().done(function (stocks) {
        $stockTableBody.empty();
        $stockTickerUl.empty();
        $.each(stocks, function () {
            var stock = formatStock(this);
            $stockTableBody.append(rowTemplate.supplant(stock));
            $stockTickerUl.append(liTemplate.supplant(stock));
        });
    });
}

// Add client-side hub methods that the server will call
$.extend(ticker.client, {
    updateStockPrice: function (stock) {
        var displayStock = formatStock(stock),
            $row = $(rowTemplate.supplant(displayStock)),
            $li = $(liTemplate.supplant(displayStock)),
            bg = stock.LastChange < 0
                    ? '255,148,148' // red
                    : '154,240,117'; // green

        $stockTableBody.find('tr[data-symbol=' + stock.Symbol + ']')
            .replaceWith($row);
        $stockTickerUl.find('li[data-symbol=' + stock.Symbol + ']')
            .replaceWith($li);

        $row.flash(bg, 1000);
        $li.flash(bg, 1000);
    },
```

```
    marketOpened: function () {
        $("#open").prop("disabled", true);
        $("#close").prop("disabled", false);
        $("#reset").prop("disabled", true);
        scrollTicker();
    },

    marketClosed: function () {
        $("#open").prop("disabled", false);
        $("#close").prop("disabled", true);
        $("#reset").prop("disabled", false);
        stopTicker();
    },

    marketReset: function () {
        return init();
    }
});

// Start the connection
$.connection.hub.start()
    .then(init)
    .then(function () {
        return ticker.server.getMarketState();
    })
    .done(function (state) {
        if (state === 'Open') {
            ticker.client.marketOpened();
        } else {
            ticker.client.marketClosed();
        }

        // Wire up the buttons
        $("#open").click(function () {
            ticker.server.openMarket();
        });

        $("#close").click(function () {
            ticker.server.closeMarket();
        });

        $("#reset").click(function () {
            ticker.server.reset();
        });
    });
});
```

The first part of this code is simple JavaScript code for some cosmetic effects. The `formatStock()` method simply formats the properties of stock for better presentation. The `scrollTicker()` method creates an animation around the scrolling of stock data, and `stopTicker` stops the data animation on the user interface (UI). The `init()` method performs a common task: connecting the dots between client and ASP.NET SignalR hubs proxy to get the stocks and iterate through them to display each one on the client.

The rest of this JavaScript code is easy to follow: it simply starts the hub, gets the state of a market, and applies the changes necessary whenever a market opens or closes.

Summary

This chapter showed StockTicker, an example provided by Microsoft for ASP.NET SignalR. StockTicker is a real-time stock price system that displays changes in stock prices in real time.

We broke down this application into two parts, server and client, and discussed different components of each part separately to describe how this application works.

CHAPTER 10

Building a Collaborative Drawing Application

This chapter develops a collaborative drawing application with in-depth detail. For this application, there are application requirements that need to be met, as follows:

- Interactively draw in real time
- Chat in real time
- Restrict access to authenticated users
- Scale easily on demand

The project will consist of a server that will be able to support multiple types of clients. Hosting of the project will be done in Microsoft Azure because it has all the necessary PaaS to support all the required features. To ensure that the server can scale the project, we will be able to run as multiple instances with load balancing and use Azure Redis Cache as a backplane.

Project Overview

In this project, we will create a collaborative chat and drawing application. The application lets you create your own canvas/chat room, which we'll refer to later in the code as a canvas room. Inside the canvas room, you'll have a canvas and chat session that is shared with only the people present in the canvas room. You will see people who join and leave the canvas room in the users online section.

An important thing to note about the canvas room is the way to draw. You have your choice of one of four brush actions that must be selected: brush, eraser, fill, and clear all. There is also a choice of eight colors and sizes. None of the drawing actions occurs until you click on the canvas. The color is important only if you're using the brush or fill, and the size is important only if you are using the brush or the eraser.

Note Throughout this chapter, we often describe a large class, section by section, to give you a breakdown of how it works. We then add the complete class to the project as a single step to ensure that the step-by-step instructions are clear and easy to follow.

Now that we have gone over the requirements of the project, let's get started by developing the server.

Developing the Server

The server in this project will be the main hub for all the clients. We will go over the following components and technologies and show how they are used:

- SignalR
- Web API
- OWIN hosting
- OWIN security cookies
- Unity
- Azure Cloud Services (worker role)
- Microsoft SQL database
- Azure Redis Cache

As we go through each component or technology, we will add it into our server solution. To keep the naming simple, we'll use GroupBrush as the solution name and prefix for the projects. There will be six projects in the solution: BL, DL, Entity, Web, Cloud, and Worker. To get the server development started we follow these steps to set up the solution and projects:

1. Create a new solution named GroupBrush using the Blank Solution template.
2. Add a class library project named GroupBrush.Web.
3. Add a class library project named GroupBrush.BL.
4. Add a class library project named GroupBrush.DL.
5. Add a class library project named GroupBrush.Entity.
6. Remove any unneeded Class1.cs files that were added with the class libraries.
7. Add a new Windows Azure Cloud Service project named GroupBrush.Cloud and a worker role that will create a project that should be named GroupBrush.Worker.

Now that we have the projects added to our solution, let's quickly go over what each is used for. The GroupBrush.Web project contains the OWIN components and Unity. GroupBrush.BL contains the business logic encapsulated into services. Many of those services will depend on the next project, GroupBrush.DL, which contains the database logic. The Web, BL, and DL projects all reference their entity objects from the GroupBrush.Entity project. The GroupBrush.Cloud project is the project for cloud configuration, and the GroupBrush.Worker project will host the application in a Worker role on Azure.

Now that we have created the solution and have a general idea of what each project is, we can get started going over the components and the related code. The first component is SignalR, which enables the server to provide real-time interactivity.

Enabling Real-Time Interactivity Using SignalR

Real-time interactivity is the critical requirement that makes the project attractive. We add this interactivity by using a SignalR Hub that will provide the real-time connection between the server and client.

We'll add a hub to our project by creating a class named CanvasHub that derives from the Hub class, using the definition shown in Listing 10-1. We will add this class to the project shortly.

Listing 10-1. CanvasHub Class Definition

```
public class CanvasHub : Hub
```

To add some extra functionality to our class, we'll inject a couple of services into the class constructor that will provide user and canvas services. The rest of the CanvasHub class will consist of a couple of helper functions, connection events, and server-side methods.

Before implementing the SignalR code, the projects folder structure is implemented by following these steps:

1. Run the following command from the Package Manager Console for the Default package of GroupBrush.Web and GroupBrush.Worker:

    ```
    Install-Package Microsoft.AspNet.SignalR.Core
    ```

2. Add a solution folder named Hubs to the GroupBrush.Web project.

3. Add a solution folder named Users to the GroupBrush.BL and GroupBrush.DL projects.

4. Add a solution folder named Canvases to the GroupBrush.BL and GroupBrush.DL projects.

5. Add a solution folder named Storage to the GroupBrush.BL project.

With the structure and dependencies out of the way, we'll look first at the constructor in Listing 10-2. The constructor is very simple; it takes the IUserService and ICanvasRoomService parameters and assigns them to their respective private variables.

Listing 10-2. Constructor and Private Variables of the CanvasHub Class

```
private IUserService _userService;
private ICanvasRoomService _canvasRoomService;
public CanvasHub(IUserService userService, ICanvasRoomService canvasRoomService)
{
    _userService = userService;
    _canvasRoomService = canvasRoomService;
}
```

The constructor's first dependency is the IUserService shown in Listing 10-3, which provides the signatures for user services. These services provide the creation of a user, validation of a user login, and retrieval of a user's name from an ID. The hub uses only the GetUserNameFromId method in this interface.

Listing 10-3. IUserService Interface

```
public interface IUserService
{
    int? CreateAccount(string userName, string password);
    bool ValidateUserLogin(string userName, string password, out int? userId);
    string GetUserNameFromId(int id);
}
```

The second dependency is the ICanvasRoomService interface that provides canvas room services shown in Listing 10-4. The services provided by this interface allow brush actions performed by the user to be added to the canvas room, data retrieval to synchronize to a last known command position, and ability to add/remove users from the canvas room.

Listing 10-4. ICanvasRoomService Interface

```
public interface ICanvasRoomService
{
    CanvasBrushAction AddBrushAction(string canvasId, CanvasBrushAction brushData);
    CanvasSnapshot SyncToRoom(string canvasId, int currentPosition);
    void AddUserToCanvas(string canvasId, string id);
    void RemoveUserFromCanvas(string canvasId, string id);
}
```

The implementation for these services will be added later in the chapter. Next, add the interfaces with these steps:

1. Add an interface named IUserService to the GroupBrush.BL project in the Users folder with the contents of Listing 10-3.

2. Add an interface named ICanvasRoomService to the GroupBrush.BL project in the Canvases folder with the contents of Listing 10-4.

After the CanvasHub class constructor, there are two helper methods, two events, and four server-side methods in this class that we will discuss before adding them into our project. The two helper methods are GetCanvasIdFromQueryString and GetUserNameFromContext. They are added so that common code specific to the CanvasHub class is not repeated in multiple places in the class.

The first helper method, GetCanvasIdFromQueryString shown in Listing 10-5, looks in the query string for the key canvasid; if it is found and is valid, Guid will return that canvasid.

Listing 10-5. GetCanvasIdFromQueryString Helper Method

```
private string GetCanvasIdFromQueryString()
{
    Guid validationGuid = Guid.Empty;
    string groupId = Context.QueryString["canvasid"];
    if (!string.IsNullOrWhiteSpace(groupId) && Guid.TryParse(groupId,out validationGuid))
    {
        return groupId;
    }
    throw new ArgumentException("Invalid Canvas Id");
}
```

The second helper method, GetUserNameFromContext shown in Listing 10-6, gets the username of the current user from the request. This is accomplished by retrieving the ID from Context.Request.User.Identity.Name, which is the current request's identity object Name property that is populated by an OWIN security middleware (discussed later in the chapter). Once this ID is obtained, it is passed into the IUserService to look up a username for that ID. If the name is found, it is returned; otherwise, the method returns an empty string for the username.

Listing 10-6. GetUserNameFromContext Helper Method

```
private string GetUserNameFromContext()
{
    string strUserId = Context.Request.User.Identity.Name;
    int userId = 0;
    if (int.TryParse(strUserId, out userId))
    {
        return _userService.GetUserNameFromId(userId);
    }
    return string.Empty;
}
```

Next are the OnConnected and OnDisconnected events shown in Listing 10-7 and 10-8, respectively. These events override the base class events and have three main actions: to add or remove the user from the canvas, to add or remove the connection ID from the canvas group, and to notify all canvas group members of the user connecting or disconnecting.

Listing 10-7. OnConnected Event

```
public override Task OnConnected()
{
    _canvasRoomService.AddUserToCanvas(GetCanvasIdFromQueryString(), GetUserNameFromContext());
    Groups.Add(Context.ConnectionId.ToString(), GetCanvasIdFromQueryString());
    Clients.Group(GetCanvasIdFromQueryString()).UserConnected(GetUserNameFromContext());
    return base.OnConnected();
}
```

Listing 10-8. OnDisconnected Event

```
public override Task OnDisconnected(bool stopCalled)
{
    _canvasRoomService.RemoveUserFromCanvas(GetCanvasIdFromQueryString(), GetUserNameFromContext());
    Groups.Remove(Context.ConnectionId.ToString(), GetCanvasIdFromQueryString());
    Clients.Group(GetCanvasIdFromQueryString()).UserDisconnected(GetUserNameFromContext());
    return base.OnDisconnected(stopCalled);
}
```

The last parts of the CanvasHub class are the four server-side methods, which are methods that are publicly exposed to the SignalR clients.

MoveCursor, shown in Listing 10-9, takes two parameters: the cursor x and y values of the current user. The method sends a client message of MoveOtherCursor to all the members of the canvas group with the current user's x and y cursor coordinates and username.

Listing 10-9. MoveCursor Method

```
public void MoveCursor(double x, double y)
{
    Clients.Group(GetCanvasIdFromQueryString()).MoveOtherCursor(GetUserNameFromContext(), x, y);
}
```

The second method, SendChatMessage shown in Listing 10-10, takes one parameter: the message to send. The method prepends the username and a colon to the message and sends it to all the members of the canvas group by the UserChatMessage client method.

Listing 10-10. SendChatMessage Method

```
public void SendChatMessage(string message)
{
    Clients.Group(GetCanvasIdFromQueryString()).UserChatMessage(GetUserNameFromContext() + ":
" + message);
}
```

The third method, SendDrawCommand shown in Listing 10-10, takes one parameter, CanvasBrushAction, which is defined in Listing 10-12. It contains the brush information and the affected positions of the brush, as defined in the Position class in Listing 10-13. The first step of this method is to save the information provided by the parameter by calling the AddBrushAction method on the ICanvasRoomService service. Once the information is saved, we can send the parameter information to all the canvas group users by using the DrawCanvasBrushAction client method.

Listing 10-11. SendDrawCommand Method

```
public void SendDrawCommand(CanvasBrushAction brushData)
{
    CanvasBrushAction canvasBrushAction =
    _canvasRoomService.AddBrushAction(GetCanvasIdFromQueryString(), brushData);
    Clients.Group(GetCanvasIdFromQueryString()).DrawCanvasBrushAction(canvasBrushAction);
}
```

Listing 10-12. CanvasBrushAction Entity Class

```
public class CanvasBrushAction
{
    public int Sequence { get; set; }
    public Int64 ClientSequenceId { get; set; }
    public int Type { get; set; }
    public string Color { get; set; }
    public int Size { get; set; }
    public List<Position> BrushPositions { get; set; }
}
```

Listing 10-13. Position Entity Class

```
public class Position
    {
        public double X { get; set; }
        public double Y { get; set; }
    }
```

The last method, SyncToRoom shown in Listing 10-14, takes in one parameter: the client's last known drawing history position. It returns all the canvas brush data as a CanvasSnapshot, defined in Listing 10-15, from the value of the position parameter to the latest entry in storage. The information is retrieved by using the SyncToRoom method on the ICanvasRoomService service and is returned only to the calling user.

Listing 10-14. SyncToRoom Method

```
public CanvasSnapshot SyncToRoom(int currentPosition)
{
    return _canvasRoomService.SyncToRoom(GetCanvasIdFromQueryString(), currentPosition);
}
```

Listing 10-15. CanvasSnapshot Entity Class

```
public class CanvasSnapshot
{
    public string CanvasName { get; set; }
    public string CanvasDescription { get; set; }
    public List<string> Users { get; set; }
    public List<CanvasBrushAction> Actions { get; set; }
}
```

The CanvasHub class, shown in Listing 10-16, is the main SignalR class for our project. It will provide the real-time functionality for the drawing, chatting, and online user state of the canvas room.

Listing 10-16. Complete CanvasHub Class

```
public class CanvasHub : Hub
{
    private IUserService _userService;
    private ICanvasRoomService _canvasRoomService;
    public CanvasHub(IUserService userService, ICanvasRoomService canvasRoomService)
    {
        _userService = userService;
        _canvasRoomService = canvasRoomService;
    }
    private string GetCanvasIdFromQueryString()
    {
        Guid validationGuid = Guid.Empty;
        string groupId = Context.QueryString["canvasid"];
        if (!string.IsNullOrWhiteSpace(groupId) && Guid.TryParse(groupId,out validationGuid))
        {
            return groupId;
        }
        throw new ArgumentException("Invalid Canvas Id");
    }
    private string GetUserNameFromContext()
    {
        string strUserId = Context.Request.User.Identity.Name;
        int userId = 0;
        if (int.TryParse(strUserId, out userId))
        {
            return _userService.GetUserNameFromId(userId);
        }
        return string.Empty;
    }
    public override Task OnConnected()
    {
        _canvasRoomService.AddUserToCanvas(GetCanvasIdFromQueryString(), GetUserNameFromContext());
        Groups.Add(Context.ConnectionId.ToString(), GetCanvasIdFromQueryString());
        Clients.Group(GetCanvasIdFromQueryString()).UserConnected(GetUserNameFromContext());
        return base.OnConnected();
    }
```

```
public override Task OnDisconnected(bool stopCalled)
{
    _canvasRoomService.RemoveUserFromCanvas(GetCanvasIdFromQueryString(),
    GetUserNameFromContext());
    Groups.Remove(Context.ConnectionId.ToString(), GetCanvasIdFromQueryString());
    Clients.Group(GetCanvasIdFromQueryString()).UserDisconnected(GetUserNameFromContext());
    return base.OnDisconnected(stopCalled);
}
public void MoveCursor(double x, double y)
{
    Clients.Group(GetCanvasIdFromQueryString()).MoveOtherCursor(GetUserNameFromContext(), x, y);
}
public void SendChatMessage(string message)
{
    Clients.Group(GetCanvasIdFromQueryString()).UserChatMessage(GetUserNameFromContext()
    + ": " + message);
}
public void SendDrawCommand(CanvasBrushAction brushData)
{
    CanvasBrushAction canvasBrushAction =
    _canvasRoomService.AddBrushAction(GetCanvasIdFromQueryString(), brushData);
    Clients.Group(GetCanvasIdFromQueryString()).DrawCanvasBrushAction(canvasBrushAction);
}
public CanvasSnapshot SyncToRoom(int currentPosition)
{
    return _canvasRoomService.SyncToRoom(GetCanvasIdFromQueryString(), currentPosition);
}
}
```

Now that we have discussed the sections that make up the CanvasHub class, they need to be added to our project by following these steps:

1. Add a class named CanvasBrushAction to the GroupBrush.Entity project with the contents of Listing 10-12.

2. Add a class named Position to the GroupBrush.Entity project with the contents of Listing 10-13.

3. Add a class named CanvasSnapshot to the GroupBrush.Entity project with the contents of Listing 10-15.

4. Add a class named CanvasHub to the GroupBrush.Web project under the Hubs folder with the contents of Listing 10-16.

The services for CanvasHub provide the internal workings that allow the canvas room and user data to be retrieved and persisted. (We'll go over user service implementation in the next section and focus on the canvas data in this section.) ICanvasRoomService is implemented in this project as a class named CanvasRoomService, as shown in Listing 10-17.

Listing 10-17. CanvasRoomService Class Definition

```
public class CanvasRoomService : ICanvasRoomService
```

CanvasRoomService needs additional dependencies that will be injected into the constructor, as seen in Listing 10-18, as it was with CanvasHub. The dependencies are represented by the IMemStorage and IGetCanvasDescriptionData interfaces, which are defined in Listings 10-19 and 10-20, respectively. As with the constructor in CanvasHub, the dependencies will be assigned to local variables in the constructor.

Listing 10-18. Constructor and Private Variables for CanvasRoomService

```
IMemStorage _ memStorage;
   IGetCanvasDescriptionData _getCanvasDescriptionData;
   public CanvasRoomService(IMemStorage memStorage, IGetCanvasDescriptionData
   getCanvasDescriptionData)
   {
       _ memStorage = memStorage;
       _getCanvasDescriptionData = getCanvasDescriptionData;
   }
```

Listing 10-19. IMemStorage Interface

```
public interface IMemStorage
{
    CanvasBrushAction AddBrushAction(string canvasId, CanvasBrushAction brushData);
    List<CanvasBrushAction> GetBrushActions(string canvasId, int currentPosition);
    List<string> GetCanvasUsers(string canvasId);
    void AddUserToCanvas(string canvasId, string id);
    void RemoveUserFromCanvas(string canvasId, string id);
    string GetUserName(int id);
    void StoreUserName(int id, string userName);
}
```

Listing 10-20. IGetCanvasDescriptionData Interface

```
public interface IGetCanvasDescriptionData
{
    CanvasDescription GetCanvasDescription(Guid canvasId);
}
```

Listing 10-21 shows that the logic for most of the methods of the CanvasRoomService is to call the corresponding method on the IMemStorage dependency. The exception to this is the SyncToRoom method, which calls the IGetCanvasDescriptionData dependency to retrieve a CanvasDescription object (defined in Listing 10-22), and the IMemStorage dependency to retrieve the canvas data. The data from these three calls are combined into one class and returned. The storage logic is fairly abstracted from this class because we want to provide two different storage implementations: an in-memory storage that works for only one instance and a Redis-based memory storage that allows scaling to multiple instances.

Listing 10-21. Complete CanvasRoomService Class

```
public class CanvasRoomService : ICanvasRoomService
{
    IMemStorage _memStorage;
    IGetCanvasDescriptionData _getCanvasDescriptionData;
    public CanvasRoomService(IMemStorage memStorage, IGetCanvasDescriptionData
```

```
getCanvasDescriptionData)
{
    _memStorage = memStorage;
    _getCanvasDescriptionData = getCanvasDescriptionData;
}
public CanvasBrushAction AddBrushAction(string canvasId, CanvasBrushAction brushData)
{
    return _memStorage.AddBrushAction(canvasId, brushData);
}
public CanvasSnapshot SyncToRoom(string canvasId, int currentPosition)
{
    CanvasDescription canvasDescription =
    _getCanvasDescriptionData.GetCanvasDescription(Guid.Parse(canvasId));
    List<CanvasBrushAction> actions = new List<CanvasBrushAction>();
    actions = _memStorage.GetBrushActions(canvasId, currentPosition);
    List<string> users = new List<string>();
    users = _memStorage.GetCanvasUsers(canvasId);
    return new CanvasSnapshot() { Users = users, Actions = actions, CanvasName =
    canvasDescription.Name, CanvasDescription = canvasDescription.Description };
}
public void AddUserToCanvas(string canvasId, string id)
{
    _memStorage.AddUserToCanvas(canvasId, id);
}

public void RemoveUserFromCanvas(string canvasId, string id)
{
    _memStorage.RemoveUserFromCanvas(canvasId, id);
}
}
```

Listing 10-22. CanvasDescription Entity Class

```
public class CanvasDescription
{
    public string Name { get; set; }
    public string Description { get; set; }
}
```

Before we go into more detail about that, let's catch up with what we have done so far:

1. Added an interface named IMemStorage to the GroupBrush.BL project under the Storage folder with the contents of Listing 10-19.

2. Added an interface named IGetCanvasDescriptionData to the GroupBrush.DL project under the Canvases folder with the contents of Listing 10-20.

3. Added a class named CanvasRoomService to the GroupBrush.BL project under the Canvases folder with the contents of Listing 10-21.

4. Added a class named CanvasDescription to the GroupBrush.Entity project with the contents of Listing 10-22.

There are two possible implementations for the IMemStorage interface, depending on the number of instances we want to deploy. We discuss the in-memory solution here and the Redis implementation in the "Scaling the Server" section later in the chapter.

The first requirement for this class, which we call MemoryStorage, is to implement the IMemStorage, as shown in Listing 10-23. Unlike most of the other classes we have covered so far, this class does not have any dependencies injected in the constructor. However, it does have four ConcurrentDictionary collections that we will use to persist the canvas room data (see Listing 10-24).

Listing 10-23. MemoryStorage Class Definition

```
public class MemoryStorage : IMemStorage
```

Listing 10-24. MemoryStorage Private Variables

```
private ConcurrentDictionary<string, int> canvasTransactions =
new ConcurrentDictionary
<string, int>();
private ConcurrentDictionary<string, ConcurrentBag<CanvasBrushAction>> canvasActions =
new ConcurrentDictionary<string, ConcurrentBag<CanvasBrushAction>>();
private ConcurrentDictionary<string, ConcurrentDictionary<string,string>> canvasUsers =
new ConcurrentDictionary<string, ConcurrentDictionary<string,string>>();
private ConcurrentDictionary<int, string> userNames = new ConcurrentDictionary<int, string>();
```

The class contains seven public methods that satisfy the IMemStorage interface contract. Two methods, AddBrushAction and GetBrushActions, are used specifically for canvas room data; three methods are for users in a canvas room; and two methods are for username data.

The AddBrushAction method shown in Listing 10-25 stores client brush actions for a specific canvas room into memory. For drawings to look correct, we need to ensure that brush actions are applied in order. To ensure this order, we need to store the sequence as a unique number for each CanvasBrushAction. So in the top of the method, we check to see whether we have a canvasTransactions entry for the canvas ID. If there is no existing entry, we add one, starting at 0.

Listing 10-25. AddBrushAction Method

```
public CanvasBrushAction AddBrushAction(string canvasId, CanvasBrushAction brushData)
{
    if (!canvasTransactions.ContainsKey(canvasId))
    {
        canvasTransactions[canvasId] = 0;
    }
    int transactionNumber = canvasTransactions[canvasId] = canvasTransactions[canvasId]++;
    if (!canvasActions.ContainsKey(canvasId))
    {
        canvasActions[canvasId] = new ConcurrentBag<CanvasBrushAction>();
    }
    brushData.Sequence = transactionNumber;
    canvasActions[canvasId].Add(brushData);
    return brushData;
}
```

We take the entry, increment it by 1, and use it as the transactionNumber variable. Now that we have a transaction, we have to see whether there is a canvasActions entry to store the client brush actions. If there is no entry, we add a new entry of ConcurrentBag<CanvasBrushAction> to the collection.

Next we add transactionNumber to brushData. We now add the updated brushData to the canvasActions entry. Finally we return the updated brushData.

The second method, GetBrushActions shown in Listing 10-26, gets the brush actions that have occurred for a specific canvas since a position in the canvas history. The method starts by creating a List<CanvasBrushAction> named actions to store the returned brush action entries. The next part of the method checks to see whether a canvasActions collection entry exists for the canvasId parameter. If the entry exists, all entries that are greater than or equal to the currentPosition parameter are added to the actions collection, and that collection is then sorted by sequence number. Finally, regardless of whether an entry existed, the actions collection is returned.

Listing 10-26. GetBrushActions Method

```
public List<CanvasBrushAction> GetBrushActions(string canvasId, int currentPosition)
{
    List<CanvasBrushAction> actions = new List<CanvasBrushAction>();
    if (canvasActions.ContainsKey(canvasId))
    {
        ConcurrentBag<CanvasBrushAction> storedActions = canvasActions[canvasId];
        actions.AddRange(storedActions.Where(x => x.Sequence >= currentPosition));
        actions.Sort(new Comparison<CanvasBrushAction>((a, b) => { return
        a.Sequence.CompareTo (b.Sequence); }));
    }
    return actions;
}
```

The third method, GetCanvasUsers shown in Listing 10-27, gets the current list of usernames in a canvas. This method also starts with creating a List<string> named returnValue, which will be returned at the end of the method. All the logic for this method depends on there being an entry in the canvasUsers collection. If there is an entry found, the collection is enumerated, and the username data that is stored as the key is added to a HashSet to ensure uniqueness. The returnValue collection is then overridden with a new list generated from the HashSet. Finally, the returnValue parameter is returned.

Listing 10-27. GetCanvasUsers Method

```
public List<string> GetCanvasUsers(string canvasId)
{
    List<string> returnValue = new List<string>();
    if (canvasUsers.ContainsKey(canvasId))
    {
        HashSet<string> uniqueList = new HashSet<string>();
        ConcurrentDictionary<string, string> users = canvasUsers[canvasId];
        foreach (KeyValuePair<string, string> user in users)
        {
            uniqueList.Add(user.Key);
        }
        returnValue = uniqueList.ToList<string>();
    }
    return returnValue;
}
```

The fourth method, AddUserToCanvas shown in Listing 10-28, adds users to a canvas room. This method starts by checking for the existence of an entry in the canvasUsers collection. If an entry does not exist, it adds a new ConcurrentDictionary<string,string> to the canvasUsers collection for the canvasId parameter. This ensures that the lookup in canvasUsers by canvasId always returns a ConcurrentDictionary<string, string> for the specified canvas. The returned collection is checked for the existence of the id parameter. If it does not exist in the collection, it is added to the collection.

Listing 10-28. AddUserToCanvas Method

```
public void AddUserToCanvas(string canvasId, string id)
{
    if (!canvasUsers.ContainsKey(canvasId))
    {
        canvasUsers[canvasId] = new ConcurrentDictionary<string, string>();
    }
    ConcurrentDictionary<string, string> users = canvasUsers[canvasId];
    if (!users.ContainsKey(id))
    {
        users[id] = id;
    }
}
```

The fifth method, RemoveUserFromCanvas shown in Listing 10-29, removes users from a canvas room. It starts by checking for the existence of an entry in the canvasUsers collection. If an entry does exist and contains a key for the id parameter, the method attempts to remove the id from the entry.

Listing 10-29. RemoveUserFromCanvas Method

```
public void RemoveUserFromCanvas(string canvasId, string id)
{
    if (canvasUsers.ContainsKey(canvasId))
    {
        ConcurrentDictionary<string, string> users = canvasUsers[canvasId];
        if (users.ContainsKey(id))
        {
            string tempValue = null;
            users.TryRemove(id, out tempValue);
        }
    }
}
```

The methods GetUserName and StoreUserName are simple methods shown in Listing 10-30 to store and retrieve usernames based on the user ID. These methods are not dependent on a canvasId. The GetUserName method checks the userNames collection for an ID; if it exists, it returns the username; otherwise, it returns null. The StoreUserName method stores the username in the collection at the key specified.

Listing 10-30. GetUserName and StoreUserName Methods

```
public string GetUserName(int id)
{
    if (userNames.ContainsKey(id))
    {
        return userNames[id];
    }
    return null;
}
public void StoreUserName(int id, string userName)
{
    userNames[id] = userName;
}
```

Now let's add this class to our project with the following step:

1. Add a class named MemoryStorage to the GroupBrush.BL project under the Storage folder with the contents of Listing 10-31.

Listing 10-31. Complete MemoryStorage Class

```
public class MemoryStorage : IMemStorage
{
    private ConcurrentDictionary<string, int> canvasTransactions = new ConcurrentDictionary<string, int>();
    private ConcurrentDictionary<string, ConcurrentBag<CanvasBrushAction>> canvasActions = new
    ConcurrentDictionary<string, ConcurrentBag<CanvasBrushAction>>();
    private ConcurrentDictionary<string, ConcurrentDictionary<string,string>> canvasUsers = new
    ConcurrentDictionary<string, ConcurrentDictionary<string,string>>();
    private ConcurrentDictionary<int, string> userNames = new ConcurrentDictionary<int, string>();

    public CanvasBrushAction AddBrushAction(string canvasId, CanvasBrushAction brushData)
    {
        if (!canvasTransactions.ContainsKey(canvasId))
        {
            canvasTransactions[canvasId] = 0;
        }
        int transactionNumber = canvasTransactions[canvasId] = canvasTransactions[canvasId]++;
        if (!canvasActions.ContainsKey(canvasId))
        {
            canvasActions[canvasId] = new ConcurrentBag<CanvasBrushAction>();
        }
        brushData.Sequence = transactionNumber;
        canvasActions[canvasId].Add(brushData);
        return brushData;
    }
    public List<CanvasBrushAction> GetBrushActions(string canvasId, int currentPosition)
    {
        List<CanvasBrushAction> actions = new List<CanvasBrushAction>();
        if (canvasActions.ContainsKey(canvasId))
        {
            ConcurrentBag<CanvasBrushAction> storedActions = canvasActions[canvasId];
            actions.AddRange(storedActions.Where(x => x.Sequence >= currentPosition));
        }
        actions.Sort(new Comparison<CanvasBrushAction>((a, b) => { return
        a.Sequence.CompareTo(b.Sequence); }));
        return actions;
    }
    public List<string> GetCanvasUsers(string canvasId)
    {
        List<string> returnValue = new List<string>();
        if (canvasUsers.ContainsKey(canvasId))
        {
            HashSet<string> uniqueList = new HashSet<string>();
            ConcurrentDictionary<string, string> users = canvasUsers[canvasId];
            foreach (KeyValuePair<string, string> user in users)
```

```
        {
            uniqueList.Add(user.Key);
        }
        returnValue = uniqueList.ToList<string>();
    }
    return returnValue;
}
public void AddUserToCanvas(string canvasId, string id)
{
    if (!canvasUsers.ContainsKey(canvasId))
    {
        canvasUsers[canvasId] = new ConcurrentDictionary<string, string>();
    }

    ConcurrentDictionary<string, string> users = canvasUsers[canvasId];
    if (!users.ContainsKey(id))
    {
        users[id] = id;
    }
}
public void RemoveUserFromCanvas(string canvasId, string id)
{
    if (canvasUsers.ContainsKey(canvasId))
    {
        ConcurrentDictionary<string, string> users = canvasUsers[canvasId];
        if (users.ContainsKey(id))
        {
            string tempValue = null;
            users.TryRemove(id, out tempValue);
        }
    }
}
public string GetUserName(int id)
{
    if (userNames.ContainsKey(id))
    {
        return userNames[id];
    }
    return null;
}
public void StoreUserName(int id, string userName)
{
    userNames[id] = userName;
}
}
```

The final class for the SignalR implementation is the GetCanvasDescriptionData class shown in Listing 10-32. This class provides the data layer access to retrieve the CanvasDescription data. This class has a dependency of a string in the constructor, which we will use to inject the connection string.

Listing 10-32. GetCanvasDescriptionData Class

```
public class GetCanvasDescriptionData : IGetCanvasDescriptionData
    {
        private string _connectionString;
        public GetCanvasDescriptionData(string connectionString)
        {
            _connectionString = connectionString;
        }
        public CanvasDescription GetCanvasDescription(Guid canvasId)
        {
            CanvasDescription returnValue = null;
            using(SqlConnection connection = new SqlConnection(_connectionString))
            using (SqlCommand command = new SqlCommand())
            {
                command.Connection = connection;
                command.CommandText = "dbo.GetCanvasDescription";
                command.CommandType = System.Data.CommandType.StoredProcedure;
                SqlParameter prmCanvasId = new SqlParameter("@CanvasId", SqlDbType.UniqueIdentifier)
                { Direction = ParameterDirection.Input, Value = canvasId };
                SqlParameter prmCanvasName = new SqlParameter("@CanvasName", SqlDbType.NVarChar,
                100) { Direction = ParameterDirection.Output};
                SqlParameter prmCanvasDescription = new SqlParameter("@CanvasDescription",
                SqlDbType.NVarChar, 100) { Direction = ParameterDirection.Output };
                command.Parameters.Add(prmCanvasId);
                command.Parameters.Add(prmCanvasName);
                command.Parameters.Add(prmCanvasDescription);
                connection.Open();
                command.ExecuteNonQuery();
                returnValue = new CanvasDescription();
                if (prmCanvasName != null && prmCanvasName.Value != DBNull.Value && prmCanvasName.
                Value is string)
                {
                    returnValue.Name = (string)prmCanvasName.Value;
                }
                if (prmCanvasDescription != null && prmCanvasDescription.Value != DBNull.Value &&
                prmCanvasDescription.Value is string)
                {
                    returnValue.Description = (string)prmCanvasDescription.Value;
                }
            }
            return returnValue;
        }
    }
```

The method is a very straightforward data layer class: it creates a new SqlConnection and SqlCommand inside of using statements that will properly dispose of the classes and close the connection. The SqlConnection is created with the connection string that was injected.

The next part of the class sets up the parameters of the command with the connection, the stored procedure name, and the type of command to be executed. We add the canvasId as a SQL input parameter and create an output SQL parameter for the canvas name and canvas description. Once everything is set up, we open the connection and execute the query. A CanvasDescription return value is created, and the Name and Description values are set if the CanvasName and CanvasDescription parameters come back with proper values and types. This return value is then returned.

This class needs to be added to our project with the following steps:

1. Add a class named GetCanvasDescriptionData to the GroupBrush.DL project under the Canvases folder with the contents of Listing 10-32.

2. In GroupBrush.BL, add a project reference to the GroupBrush.Entity project.

3. In GroupBrush.DL, add a project reference to the GroupBrush.Entity project.

4. In GroupBrush.BL, add a project reference to the GroupBrush.DL project.

5. In GroupBrush.Web, add a project reference to the GroupBrush.BL project.

6. In GroupBrush.Web, add a project reference to the GroupBrush.Entity project.

We have now created the classes that support the real-time functionality, but we still need a way to provide other data that is not real-time and is not called very often. To do that, we can use the Web API to provide the needed endpoints to create and join canvases.

Adding API Endpoints

Sometimes we do not have a connection to a hub or want to create one, but we still need to access data from the application. Instead of creating a hub connection every time, we need data to hold a hub connection open for a few requests. We can use Web API endpoints for this data access.

In this section, we will add the endpoints for creating and joining a canvas. To create these endpoints, we have to add a little more to our project. The following steps add more folder structure and install the needed dependencies:

1. Add a solution folder named Public to the GroupBrush.Web project.

2. Add a solution folder named Controllers to the Public folder in the GroupBrush.Web project.

3. Run the following command from the Package Manager Console for the Default package of the GroupBrush.Web and GroupBrush.Worker projects:

    ```
    Install-Package Microsoft.AspNet.WebApi.Owin
    ```

4. Run the following command from the Package Manager Console for the Default package of the GroupBrush.Web and GroupBrush.Worker projects:

    ```
    Install-Package Microsoft.AspNet.WebApi.SelfHost
    ```

The first place to start with the Web API endpoints is the controller class, which derives from the ApiController class that lets us create a Web API endpoint. We will create a class named CanvasController that derives from ApiController (see Listing 10-33).

Listing 10-33. CanvasController Class

```
public class CanvasController : ApiController
    {
        ICanvasService _canvasService;
        public CanvasController(ICanvasService canvasService)
        {
            _canvasService = canvasService;
        }
```

```
[Route("api/canvas")]
[HttpPost]
public Guid? CreateCanvas(CanvasDescription canvasDescription)
{
    Guid? canvasId = null;
    if (canvasDescription != null)
    {
        canvasId = _canvasService.CreateCanvas(canvasDescription);
    }
    return canvasId;
}


[Route("api/canvas")]
[HttpPut]
public Guid? LookUpCanvas(CanvasName canvasName)
{
    Guid? canvasId = null;
    if (canvasName != null)
    {
        canvasId = _canvasService.LookUpCanvas(canvasName.Name);
    }
    return canvasId;
}
}
```

Like many other classes, this class has dependencies injected in the constructor. The dependency that is injected into the constructor of the CanvasController class is the ICanvasService interface in Listing 10-34, which will allow us to create and join canvases from Web API endpoints. This injected dependency is set to a private variable in the CanvasController class.

Listing 10-34. ICanvasService Interface

```
public interface ICanvasService
{
    Guid? CreateCanvas(CanvasDescription canvasDescription);
    Guid? LookUpCanvas(string canvasName);
}
```

The controller is fairly simple and contains only two methods, CreateCanvas and LookUpCanvas, which return data from the injected service.

Because we are using attribute routing for our Web API controller, both of these methods are accessible through the URL *hostname* + /api/canvas. But to give our API more of rest feel, we limit access to these methods using the HttpPost and HttpPut attributes. These attributes allow access only if the HTTP verb in the request is Post or Put. (The Post and Put verbs are for creating and joining, respectively.)

A type mapping will occur behind the scenes to populate the data that is passed into the methods. Sometimes the data is ambiguous, and the controller cannot map value types properly. We are giving it a little help with the LookUpCanvas method. In this method, we tell the controller that we're expecting a type of CanvasName, which is just a single string (see Listing 10-35).

Listing 10-35. CanvasName Entity Class

```
public class CanvasName
{
    public string Name;
}
```

Now that we know the controller just calls the ICanvasService interface, we need to look at the implementation. For the implementation, there is a class named CanvasService (shown in Listing 10-36), which derives from the ICanvasService interface. It also has two dependencies injected into the constructor: ICreateCanvasData and ILookUpCanvasData (shown in Listings 10-37 and 10-38, respectively). These dependencies are the interfaces for accessing the database to create or join a canvas, respectively, which set private variables for use by the class.

Listing 10-36. CanvasService class

```
public class CanvasService : ICanvasService
{
    ICreateCanvasData _createCanvasData;
    ILookUpCanvasData _lookUpCanvasData;
    public CanvasService(ICreateCanvasData createCanvasData,ILookUpCanvasData lookUpCanvasData)
    {
        _createCanvasData = createCanvasData;
        _lookUpCanvasData = lookUpCanvasData;
    }
    public Guid? CreateCanvas(CanvasDescription canvasDescription)
    {
        Guid? canvasId = null;
        if (canvasDescription != null && !string.IsNullOrWhiteSpace(canvasDescription.Name) &&
        !string.IsNullOrWhiteSpace(canvasDescription.Description))
        {
            canvasId = _createCanvasData.CreateCanvas(canvasDescription.Name,
            canvasDescription.Description);
        }
        return canvasId;
    }
    public Guid? LookUpCanvas(string canvasName)
    {
        Guid? canvasId = null;
        if(!string.IsNullOrWhiteSpace(canvasName))
        {
            canvasId = _lookUpCanvasData.LookUpCanvas(canvasName);
        }
        return canvasId;
    }
}
```

Listing 10-37. ICreateCanvasData Interface

```
public interface ICreateCanvasData
{
    Guid? CreateCanvas(string canvasName, string Description);
}
```

Listing 10-38. ILookUpCanvasData Interface

```
public interface ILookUpCanvasData
{
    Guid? LookUpCanvas(string canvasName);
}
```

The logic for the methods in this class checks to make sure the data passed into them is valid by not being null or an empty string. If the data is valid, they call the respective data layer services and return the values from those services.

The CreateCanvasData class in Listing 10-39 implements the ICreateCanvasData interface that our project uses to create a new canvas. This class is very simple: it has the connection string injected in the constructor, which sets the connection string to a local variable. The CreateCanvas method takes two parameters, canvasName and canvasDescription, which it passes directly into the stored procedure. If the return value is 0, which means successful creation of a canvas, and a valid Guid is returned for the canvasId parameter, the canvasId parameter is returned, which signals a successful canvas creation. If the return value is not 0 or the canvasId parameter is null, the canvas was not created, and a null is returned for the Guid value.

Listing 10-39. CreateCanvasData Class

```
public class CreateCanvasData : ICreateCanvasData
    {
        private string _connectionString;
        public CreateCanvasData(string connectionString)
        {
            _connectionString = connectionString;
        }
        public Guid? CreateCanvas(string canvasName, string description)
        {
            Guid? returnValue = null;
            using(SqlConnection connection = new SqlConnection(_connectionString))
            using (SqlCommand command = new SqlCommand())
            {
                command.Connection = connection;
                command.CommandText = "dbo.CreateCanvas";
                command.CommandType = System.Data.CommandType.StoredProcedure;
                SqlParameter prmReturnValue = new SqlParameter("@ReturnValue", SqlDbType.Int) {
                Direction = ParameterDirection.ReturnValue };
                SqlParameter prmCanvasName = new SqlParameter("@CanvasName", SqlDbType.NVarChar,
                100) { Direction = ParameterDirection.Input, Value = canvasName };
                SqlParameter prmCanvasDescription = new SqlParameter("@CanvasDescription",
                SqlDbType.NVarChar, 255) { Direction = ParameterDirection.Input, Value =
                description };
                SqlParameter prmCanvasId = new SqlParameter("@CanvasId", SqlDbType.UniqueIdentifier)
                { Direction = ParameterDirection.Output };
                command.Parameters.Add(prmReturnValue);
                command.Parameters.Add(prmCanvasName);
                command.Parameters.Add(prmCanvasDescription);
                command.Parameters.Add(prmCanvasId);
                connection.Open();
                command.ExecuteNonQuery();
```

```
            if (prmReturnValue != null && prmReturnValue.Value != DBNull.Value &&
            prmReturnValue.Value is int && (int)prmReturnValue.Value == 0)
            {
                if (prmCanvasId != null && prmCanvasId.Value !=
                DBNull.Value && prmCanvasId.Value is Guid)
                {
                    returnValue = (Guid)prmCanvasId.Value;
                }
            }
        }
        return returnValue;
    }
}
```

The LookUpCanvasData class shown in Listing 10-40 implements the ILookUpCanvas data interface that our project uses to join a canvas. This class is very simple: the connection string is injected in the constructor, which sets the connection string to a local variable. When the LookUpCanvas method is called, it will pass the canvasName parameter to the database to see whether a canvas exists with that name. If the return value is 0 (which means a canvas was successfully found and a valid Guid is returned for the canvasId parameter), the value of the canvasId parameter is returned; otherwise, a null value is returned.

Listing 10-40. LookUpCanvasData Class

```
public class LookUpCanvasData : ILookUpCanvasData
    {
        private string _connectionString;
        public LookUpCanvasData(string connectionString)
        {
            _connectionString = connectionString;
        }
        public Guid? LookUpCanvas(string canvasName)
        {
            Guid? returnValue = null;
            using(SqlConnection connection = new SqlConnection(_connectionString))
            using (SqlCommand command = new SqlCommand())
            {
                command.Connection = connection;
                command.CommandText = "dbo. LookUpCanvas";
                command.CommandType = System.Data.CommandType.StoredProcedure;
                SqlParameter prmReturnValue = new SqlParameter("@ReturnValue", SqlDbType.Int) {
                Direction = ParameterDirection.ReturnValue };
                SqlParameter prmCanvasName = new SqlParameter("@CanvasName", SqlDbType.NVarChar,
                100) { Direction = ParameterDirection.Input, Value = canvasName };
                SqlParameter prmCanvasId = new SqlParameter("@CanvasId", SqlDbType.UniqueIdentifier)
                { Direction = ParameterDirection.Output };
                command.Parameters.Add(prmReturnValue);
                command.Parameters.Add(prmCanvasName);
                command.Parameters.Add(prmCanvasId);
                connection.Open();
                command.ExecuteNonQuery();
```

```
                if (prmReturnValue != null && prmReturnValue.Value != DBNull.Value &&
                prmReturnValue.Value is int && (int)prmReturnValue.Value == 0)
                {
                    if (prmCanvasId != null && prmCanvasId.Value != DBNull.Value &&
                    prmCanvasId.Value is Guid)
                    {
                        returnValue = (Guid)prmCanvasId.Value;
                    }
                }
            }
            return returnValue;
        }
}
```

Now is a good time to update our project to include the classes we discussed. We can accomplish this with the following steps:

1. Add the ICanvasService interface with the contents in Listing 10-34 to the GroupBrush.BL project in the Canvases folder.

2. Add the CanvasController class with the contents in Listing 10-33 to the GroupBrush.Web project in the Controllers folder nested under the Public folder.

3. Add the CanvasName class with the contents in Listing 10-35 to the GroupBrush.Entity project.

4. Add the ICreateCanvasData interface with the contents in Listing 10-36 to the GroupBrush.DL project in the Canvases folder.

5. Add the ILookUpCanvasData interface with the contents in Listing 10-37 to the GroupBrush.DL project in the Canvases folder.

6. Add the CanvasService class with the contents in Listing 10-38 to the GroupBrush.BL project in the Canvases folder.

7. Add the CreateCanvasData class with the contents in Listing 10-39 to the GroupBrush.DL project in the Canvases folder.

8. Add the LookUpCanvasData class with the contents in Listing 10-40 to the GroupBrush.DL project in the Canvases folder.

The next step is to add users to authenticate with. We can set up user registration and authentication access via the ASP.NET Web API, which we do in the next section.

Securing the Server

To secure the server, we add two Web API controllers, which allow us to register and authenticate users. Both of these controllers have the IUserService interface shown in Listing 10-41 injected into them. Both controllers also derive from the ApiController class. The dependency injection will provide the needed user services to create an account and validate a user's login, and the ApiController class will allow these classes to implement Web API endpoints.

Listing 10-41. IUserService Interface

```
public interface IUserService
{
    int? CreateAccount(string userName, string password);
    bool ValidateUserLogin(string userName, string password, out int? userId);
    string GetUserNameFromId(int id);
}
```

We have to add some required dependencies with the following step:

1. Run the following command from the Package Manager Console for the Default package
    of GroupBrush.Web and GroupBrush.Worker.

    ```
    Install-Package Microsoft.Owin.Security.Cookies
    ```

The first controller class is the RegisterController class shown in Listing 10-42. This class has a single endpoint represented by the CreateUser method. The purpose of this method is to create a new user and return success message with a logged-in cookie. The endpoint is accessed by the URL of *hostname* + /public/api/user. What is important about this URL is that after we lock down the server, only the entries with a root of public will be accessible without a valid cookie.

Listing 10-42. RegisterController Class

```
public class RegisterController : ApiController
    {
        IUserService _userService;
        public RegisterController(IUserService userService)
        {
            _userService = userService;
        }

        [Route("public/api/user")]
        [HttpPost]
        public HttpResponseMessage CreateUser(User user)
        {
            HttpResponseMessage response = new HttpResponseMessage();
            response.StatusCode = System.Net.HttpStatusCode.Forbidden;
            if (user != null)
            {
                int? userId = null;
                userId = _userService.CreateAccount(user.UserName, user.Password);
                if(userId.HasValue && userId.Value > -1)
                {
                    var identity = new ClaimsIdentity(CookieAuthenticationDefaults.
                    AuthenticationType);
                    identity.AddClaim(new Claim(ClaimTypes.Name, userId.ToString()));
                    OwinHttpRequestMessageExtensions.GetOwinContext(this.Request).Authentication.
                    SignIn(identity);
                    response.StatusCode = System.Net.HttpStatusCode.OK;
```

```
                    response.Content = new StringContent("Success");
                }
            }
            return response;
        }
    }
```

The CreateUser method takes an entity class of User (defined in Listing 10-43) so that the Web API will bind the data from the request to a usable object. Once we have the user object, we use the user service to validate the username and password. If the user service returns a positive user ID, we use that as an indicator of a successful account creation and return a message of "Success" with a logged-in cookie. If the user is null or a negative user ID is returned, we'll return an HTTP status code of Forbidden. (The logic of creating the cookie will be examined when we discuss the login endpoint).

Listing 10-43. User Entity Class

```
public class User
{
    public string UserName { get; set; }
    public int UserId { get; set; }
    public string Password { get; set; }
}
```

Now that we can register users, we need to create some endpoints to log in, log off, and validate the current cookie. To consolidate our login endpoints to one controller, we'll create a LoginController class, which will have the IUserService dependency injected, as shown in Listing 10-44. We'll use this user service to validate login requests.

Listing 10-44. LoginController Class Constructor

```
IUserService _userService;
public LoginController(IUserService userService)
{
    _userService = userService;
}
```

Looking at the login endpoint/method in Listing 10-45, we see that this endpoint will take a Post request from the URL *hostname* + /public/api/login. This method uses the UserLogin entity shown in Listing 10-46 to get the needed login information. If the user service can validate the login from the data in the UserLogin object, it will return a message of "Success" with a logged-in cookie. If the UserLogin object is not valid or the user service could not validate the login, an HTTP status code of Unauthorized is returned.

Listing 10-45. Login Method

```
[Route("public/api/login")]
[HttpPost]
public HttpResponseMessage Login(UserLogin login)
{
    HttpResponseMessage response = new HttpResponseMessage();
    response.StatusCode = System.Net.HttpStatusCode.Unauthorized;
    if (login != null)
    {
        int? userId;
        if (_userService.ValidateUserLogin(login.UserName, login.Password, out userId))
```

```
        {
            var identity = new ClaimsIdentity(CookieAuthenticationDefaults.AuthenticationType);
            identity.AddClaim(new Claim(ClaimTypes.Name, userId.ToString()));
            OwinHttpRequestMessageExtensions.GetOwinContext(this.Request).Authentication.
            SignIn(identity);
            response.StatusCode = System.Net.HttpStatusCode.OK;
            response.Content = new StringContent("Success");
        }
    }
    return response;
}
```

Listing 10-46. UserLogin Entity

```
public class UserLogin
{
    public string UserName { get; set; }
    public string Password { get; set; }
}
```

In the event of a successful login, a new ClaimsIdentity for cookies is created. Next, a claim with the key of "Name" and data of the user ID is added to ClaimsIdentity, which is passed in to the SignIn method of OWIN authentication middleware. For this example, the authentication middleware is Microsoft OWIN security cookies. So the calling SignIn method will create a cookie that is returned in the response.

Sometimes a client might have a cookie, but that does not mean that the cookie is still valid. To allow the client to see whether the login is still valid, we expose the URL hostname + /public/api/loginStatus for Get requests. If the server can validate the cookie in the request, a message of "loggedIn" is returned; otherwise, a message of "loggedOut" is returned (see Listing 10-47).

Listing 10-47. GetLoginStatus Method

```
[Route("public/api/loginStatus")]
[HttpGet]
public string GetLoginStatus()
{
    if (User != null && User.Identity.IsAuthenticated)
    {
        return "loggedIn";
    }
    else
    {
        return "loggedOut";
    }
}
```

When it is time for a user to log out, there is an endpoint that is available for Post requests at *hostname* + /public/api/logout. This endpoint tells the OWIN cookie security to sign out the current request, which gets rid of the cookie by logging the user out. Once this is complete, a message of "Success" is returned (see Listing 10-48).

Listing 10-48. Logout Method

```
[Route("public/api/logout")]
[HttpPost]
public string Logout()
{
OwinHttpRequestMessageExtensions.GetOwinContext(this.Request).Authentication.SignOut
(CookieAuthenticationDefaults.AuthenticationType);
    return "Success";
}
```

With all the components together, you see the output of the complete LoginController class in Listing 10-49. For a more detailed look at what is occurring in the register and login controllers, we use the UserService class.

Listing 10-49. Complete LoginController Class

```
public class LoginController : ApiController
    {
        IUserService _userService;
        public LoginController(IUserService userService)
        {
            _userService = userService;
        }
        [Route("public/api/loginStatus")]
        [HttpGet]
        public string GetLoginStatus()
        {
          . if (User != null && User.Identity.IsAuthenticated)
            {
                return "loggedIn";
            }
            else
            {
                return "loggedOut";
            }
        }

        [Route("public/api/login")]
        [HttpPost]
        public HttpResponseMessage Login(UserLogin login)
        {
            HttpResponseMessage response = new HttpResponseMessage();
            response.StatusCode = System.Net.HttpStatusCode.Unauthorized;
            if (login != null)
            {
                int? userId;
                if (_userService.ValidateUserLogin(login.UserName, login.Password, out userId))
                {
                    var identity = new ClaimsIdentity(CookieAuthenticationDefaults.AuthenticationType);
                    identity.AddClaim(new Claim(ClaimTypes.Name, userId.ToString()));
```

```
                    OwinHttpRequestMessageExtensions.GetOwinContext(this.Request).Authentication.
                    SignIn(identity);
                    response.StatusCode = System.Net.HttpStatusCode.OK;
                    response.Content = new StringContent("Success");
                }
            }
            return response;
        }


        [Route("public/api/logout")]
        [HttpPost]
        public string Logout()
        {
        OwinHttpRequestMessageExtensions.GetOwinContext(this.Request).Authentication.SignOut(CookieA
        uthenticationDefaults.AuthenticationType);
            return "Success";
        }
    }
```

A critical service of the canvas, registration, and login classes is the UserService class, which allows creation, validation, and name look-up for users. All these actions depend on the database for persistent storage of this information.

This class has three data layer project interfaces and the IMemStorage interface injected in the constructor to provide this data. The data layer interfaces are listed in Listings 10-50, 10-51, and 10-52, which provide the CreateUser, ValidateUser, and GetUserName methods, respectively.

Listing 10-50. ICreateUserData Interface

```
public interface ICreateUserData
{
    int? CreateUser(string userName, string password);
}
```

Listing 10-51. IValidateUserData Interface

```
public interface IValidateUserData
{
    bool ValidateUser(string userName, string password, out int? userId);
}
```

Listing 10-52. IGetUserNameFromIdData Interface

```
public interface IGetUserNameFromIdData
{
    string GetUserName(int id);
}
```

The class logic shown in Listing 10-53 is relatively simple: CreateAccount and ValidateUserLogin return the data passed through to the data layer interfaces. The GetUserName method is not much more complex; it checks the IMemStorage implementation for the username. If it does not exist or is an empty string, it will query the data layer for this information. If the username is found in the data layer, it is stored in the IMemStorage implementation and then returned from the method.

Listing 10-53. UserService Class

```
public class UserService : IUserService
    {
        ICreateUserData _createUserData;
        IValidateUserData _validateUserData;
        IGetUserNameFromIdData _getUserNameFromIdData;
        IMemStorage _memStorage;

        public UserService(ICreateUserData createUserData, IValidateUserData validateUserData,
        IGetUserNameFromIdData getUserNameFromIdData, IMemStorage memStorage)
        {
            _createUserData = createUserData;
            _validateUserData = validateUserData;
            _getUserNameFromIdData = getUserNameFromIdData;
            _memStorage = memStorage;
        }
        public int? CreateAccount(string userName, string password)
        {
            return _createUserData.CreateUser(userName, password);
        }
        public bool ValidateUserLogin(string userName, string password, out int? userId)
        {
            return _validateUserData.ValidateUser(userName, password, out userId);
        }
        public string GetUserNameFromId(int id)
        {
            string userName = _memStorage.GetUserName(id);
            if (string.IsNullOrWhiteSpace(userName))
            {
                userName = _getUserNameFromIdData.GetUserName(id);
                if (!string.IsNullOrWhiteSpace(userName))
                {
                    _memStorage.StoreUserName(id, userName);
                }
            }
            return userName;
        }
    }
```

Now we discuss creating concrete class implementations of data layer interfaces. The first implementation is the CreateUserData class shown in Listing 10-54, which implements the ICreateUserData interface.

The class will have the connection string injected in the constructor and will pass the userName and password parameters to the database via the CreateUser stored procedure. The stored procedure returns two output parameters, ReturnValue and UserId, which are used to determine whether a user was created successfully. If the ReturnValue parameter is equal to 0, and the UserId parameter is a positive integer, the value from the UserId parameter is returned. If the ReturnValue parameter is equal to 0, and the UserId parameter is not populated, it will return a value of -1 to indicate an error. If ReturnValue is not valid, the method will return null.

Listing 10-54. CreateUserData Class

```
public class CreateUserData : ICreateUserData
{
    private string _connectionString;
    public CreateUserData(string connectionString)
    {
        _connectionString = connectionString;
    }
    public int? CreateUser(string userName, string password)
    {
        int? returnValue = null;
        using(SqlConnection connection = new SqlConnection(_connectionString))
        using (SqlCommand command = new SqlCommand())
        {
            command.Connection = connection;
            command.CommandText = "dbo.CreateUser";
            command.CommandType = System.Data.CommandType.StoredProcedure;
            SqlParameter prmReturnValue = new SqlParameter("@ReturnValue", SqlDbType.Int) {
            Direction = ParameterDirection.ReturnValue };
            SqlParameter prmName = new SqlParameter("@Name", SqlDbType.NVarChar, 100) { Direction =
            ParameterDirection.Input, Value = userName };
            SqlParameter prmPassword = new SqlParameter("@Password", SqlDbType.NVarChar, 255) {
            Direction = ParameterDirection.Input, Value = password };
            SqlParameter prmUserId = new SqlParameter("@UserId", SqlDbType.Int) { Direction =
            ParameterDirection.Output };
            command.Parameters.Add(prmReturnValue);
            command.Parameters.Add(prmName);
            command.Parameters.Add(prmPassword);
            command.Parameters.Add(prmUserId);
            connection.Open();
            command.ExecuteNonQuery();
            if(prmReturnValue != null && prmReturnValue.Value != DBNull.Value && prmReturnValue.
            Value is int && (int)prmReturnValue.Value == 0)
            {
                if(prmUserId != null && prmUserId.Value != DBNull.Value && prmUserId.Value is int)
                {
                    returnValue = (int)prmUserId.Value;
                }
                else
                {
                    returnValue = -1;
                }
            }
        }
        return returnValue;
    }
}
```

The ValidateUserData class shown in Listing 10-55 has the connection string injected in the constructor. The class will pass the userName and password parameters to the database via the ValidateUser stored procedure while expecting three output parameters: ReturnValue, ValidUser, and UserId. If the ValidUser parameter is equal to 1, and the UserId parameter is populated with a valid value, the out userId parameter is set with the value from the UserId parameter and the method returns true. Otherwise, the out userId parameter is null and false is returned from the method.

Listing 10-55. ValidateUserData Class

```
public class ValidateUserData : IValidateUserData
    {
        private string _connectionString;
        public ValidateUserData(string connectionString)
        {
            _connectionString = connectionString;
        }
        public bool ValidateUser(string userName, string password, out int? userId)
        {
            bool returnValue = false;
            userId = null;
            using(SqlConnection connection = new SqlConnection(_connectionString))
            using (SqlCommand command = new SqlCommand())
            {
                command.Connection = connection;
                command.CommandText = "dbo.ValidateUser";
                command.CommandType = System.Data.CommandType.StoredProcedure;
                SqlParameter prmName = new SqlParameter("@Name", SqlDbType.NVarChar, 100) {
                Direction = ParameterDirection.Input, Value = userName };
                SqlParameter prmPassword = new SqlParameter("@Password", SqlDbType.NVarChar, 255) {
                Direction = ParameterDirection.Input, Value = password };
                SqlParameter prmValidUser = new SqlParameter("@ValidUser", SqlDbType.Int) {
                Direction = ParameterDirection.Output };
                SqlParameter prmUserId = new SqlParameter("@UserId", SqlDbType.Int) { Direction =
                ParameterDirection.Output };
                command.Parameters.Add(prmName);
                command.Parameters.Add(prmPassword);
                command.Parameters.Add(prmValidUser);
                command.Parameters.Add(prmUserId);
                connection.Open();
                command.ExecuteNonQuery();
                if (prmValidUser != null && prmValidUser.Value != DBNull.Value && prmValidUser.Value
                is int && (int)prmValidUser.Value == 1)
                {
                    if (prmUserId != null && prmUserId.Value != DBNull.Value && prmUserId.Value is int)
                    {
                        userId = (int)prmUserId.Value;
                        returnValue = true;
                    }
                }
            }
            return returnValue;
        }
    }
```

The GetUserNameFromIdData class shown in Listing 10-56 has the connection string injected in the constructor. The class will pass the id parameter to the database via the GetUserName stored procedure. The procedure is expecting one output parameter of UserName. If the UserName parameter is a string value, it is returned for the method; otherwise, null is returned.

Listing 10-56. GetUserNameFromIdData Class

```
public class GetUserNameFromIdData : IGetUserNameFromIdData
    {
        private string _connectionString;
        public GetUserNameFromIdData(string connectionString)
        {
            _connectionString = connectionString;
        }
        public string GetUserName(int id)
        {
            string returnValue = null;
            using (SqlConnection connection = new SqlConnection(_connectionString))
            using (SqlCommand command = new SqlCommand())
            {
                command.Connection = connection;
                command.CommandText = "dbo.GetUserName";
                command.CommandType = System.Data.CommandType.StoredProcedure;
                SqlParameter prmUserId = new SqlParameter("@UserId", SqlDbType.Int) { Direction =
                ParameterDirection.Input, Value = id };
                SqlParameter prmUserName = new SqlParameter("@UserName", SqlDbType.NVarChar, 100) {
                Direction = ParameterDirection.Output };
                command.Parameters.Add(prmUserName);
                command.Parameters.Add(prmUserId);
                connection.Open();
                command.ExecuteNonQuery();
                if (prmUserName != null && prmUserName.Value != DBNull.Value && prmUserName.Value
                is string)
                {
                    returnValue = (string)prmUserName.Value;
                }
            }
            return returnValue;
        }
    }
```

Now that we have covered all the logic to secure the server, let's add it to our project with the following steps:

1. Add the RegisterController class with the contents in Listing 10-42 to the GroupBrush.Web project in the Controllers folder nested under the Public folder.

2. Add the User class with the contents in Listing 10-43 to the GroupBrush.Entity project.

3. Add the UserLogin class with the contents in Listing 10-46 to the GroupBrush.Entity project.

4. Add the LoginController class with the contents in Listing 10-49 to the GroupBrush.Web project in the Controllers folder nested under the Public folder.

5. Add the ICreateUserData interface with the contents in Listing 10-50 to the GroupBrush.DL project in the Users folder.

6. Add the IValidateUserData interface with the contents in Listing 10-51 to the GroupBrush.DL project in the Users folder.

7. Add the IGetUserNameFromIdData interface with the contents in Listing 10-52 to the GroupBrush.DL project in the Users folder.

8. Add the UserService class with the contents in Listing 10-53 to the GroupBrush.BL project in the Users folder.

9. Add the CreateUserData class with the contents in Listing 10-54 to the GroupBrush.DL project in the Users folder.

10. Add the ValidateUserData class with the contents in Listing 10-55 to the GroupBrush.DL project in the Users folder.

11. Add the GetUserNameFromIdData class with the contents in Listing 10-56 to the GroupBrush.DL project in the Users folder.

Now that we have all the components, we'll show you how to set up the dependency resolver, which will allow the constructor dependency injection to have the implemented classes we intended.

Setting Up the Dependency Resolver

For this project, we will be using the Unity container. We add it to our project with the following steps:

1. Add a solution folder named Unity to the GroupBrush.Web project.

2. Run the following command from the Package Manager Console for the Default package of GroupBrush.Web and GroupBrush.Worker:

```
Install-Package Unity
```

For Unity to work in our project, we have to create an adapter to work with both the SignalR and Web API dependency resolver interfaces and a helper class to configure our container registrations. Both classes will be added to the GroupBrush.Web project.

Looking at the UnityDependencyResolver class definition shown in Listing 10-57 you can see that we're deriving from the SignalR DefaultDependencyResolver and implementing the Web API IDependencyResolver interface, which enables us to have shared functionality. This works well in most cases, but it is missing the default registrations that the Web API would normally have from the DefaultDependencyResolver Web API.

Listing 10-57. UnityDependencyResolver Class Definition

```
public class UnityDependencyResolver : DefaultDependencyResolver,
System.Web.Http.Dependencies.IDependencyResolver
```

The next parts of the resolver are the constructor and private variables. Listing 10-58 shows two constructors. The first constructor is an empty constructor that uses the internal Unity container. The second constructor takes in a container that it will use for that class, which is necessary to provide functionality for the Web API BeginScope method (see Listing 10-61).

Listing 10-58. UnityDependencyResolver Constructor and Private Variables

```
IUnityContainer _container = new UnityContainer();
public UnityDependencyResolver()
{ }
public UnityDependencyResolver(IUnityContainer container)
{
    _container = container;
}
```

Next are the overrides of the SignalR DefaultDependencyResolver. We use these methods to attempt to resolve or register using the Unity container.

In the resolve methods GetService and GetServices in Listing 10-59, there is not a friendly way to see whether Unity can resolve a type, so a try-catch statement must be used, falling back to the base class if the resolution fails.

Listing 10-59. UnityDependencyResolver SignalR DefaultDependencyResolver Overrides

```
public override object GetService(Type serviceType)
{
    try
    {
        return _container.Resolve(serviceType);
    }
    catch
    {
        return base.GetService(serviceType);
    }
}

public override IEnumerable<object> GetServices(Type serviceType)
{
    try
    {
        List<object> services = _container.ResolveAll(serviceType).ToList();
        object defaultService = GetService(serviceType);
        if (defaultService != null) services.Add(defaultService);
        return services;
    }
    catch
    {
        return base.GetServices(serviceType);
    }
}

public override void Register(Type serviceType, IEnumerable<Func<object>> activators)
{
    _container.RegisterType(serviceType, new InjectionFactory((c) =>
    {
        object returnObject = null;
        foreach (Func<Object> activator in activators)
        {
            object tempObject = activator.Invoke();
            if (tempObject != null)
```

```
            {
                returnObject = tempObject;
                break;
            }
        }
        return returnObject;
    }));
    base.Register(serviceType, activators);
}
```

The registration function adapts the DefaultDependencyResolver Register method to register the services in the Unity container and then in the base class. This is useful because if an object can be resolved out of the Unity container, it avoids the exception penalty of resolving it from the base class.

Every dependency injection container has its own syntax to provide registration, resolution, and container lifetime management. So to use some of the features of Unity, we created methods to expose the Unity methods shown in Listing 10-60. The first method allows us to register an interface to an implementation. The second method does the same as the first, but also allows us to control the LifeTimeManager of our registration. The third method allows us to register types to an activation function that we define.

Listing 10-60. Helpful Unity Registration Methods

```
public void RegisterType<TFrom,TTo>(params InjectionMember [] injectionMembers) where TTo : TFrom
{
    _container.RegisterType<TFrom, TTo>(injectionMembers);
}
public void RegisterType<TFrom, TTo>(LifetimeManager lifetimeManager, params InjectionMember[]
injectionMembers) where TTo : TFrom
{
    _container.RegisterType<TFrom, TTo>(lifetimeManager, injectionMembers);
}
public override void Register(Type serviceType, Func<object> activator)
{
    _container.RegisterType(serviceType, new InjectionFactory((c) => activator.Invoke()));
    base.Register(serviceType, activator);
}
public void RegisterInstance<TInterface>(TInterface instance)
{
    _container.RegisterInstance<TInterface>(instance);
}
```

The last part of DependencyResolver is the BeginScope method shown in Listing 10-61 that is added for Web API compatibility. It allows the creation of a child container per request that comes in. This allows unique registration and resolution per request. If the resolution does not succeed in the child container, it will bubble up to the parent containers to look for the resolution.

Listing 10-61. Web API IDependencyResolver Method

```
public IDependencyScope BeginScope()
{
    return new UnityDependencyResolver(_container.CreateChildContainer());
}
```

Now that all the methods are together, you can see a complete DependencyResolver class like the one in Listing 10-62. To use the new resolver, we will configure the registration in a static class (discussed next).

Listing 10-62. Complete UnityDependencyResolver Class

```
public class UnityDependencyResolver : DefaultDependencyResolver, System.Web.Http.Dependencies.
IDependencyResolver
    {
        IUnityContainer _container = new UnityContainer();
        public UnityDependencyResolver()
        { }
        public UnityDependencyResolver(IUnityContainer container)
        {
            _container = container;
        }
        public override object GetService(Type serviceType)
        {
            try
            {
                return _container.Resolve(serviceType);
            }
            catch
            {
                return base.GetService(serviceType);
            }
        }

        public override IEnumerable<object> GetServices(Type serviceType)
        {
            try
            {
                List<object> services = _container.ResolveAll(serviceType).ToList();
                object defaultService = GetService(serviceType);
                if (defaultService != null) services.Add(defaultService);
                return services;
            }
            catch
            {
                return base.GetServices(serviceType);
            }
        }

        public override void Register(Type serviceType, IEnumerable<Func<object>> activators)
        {
            _container.RegisterType(serviceType, new InjectionFactory((c) =>
            {
                object returnObject = null;
                foreach (Func<Object> activator in activators)
                {
                    object tempObject = activator.Invoke();
```

```
                    if (tempObject != null)
                    {
                        returnObject = tempObject;
                        break;
                    }
                }
                return returnObject;
            }));
            base.Register(serviceType, activators);
        }
        public void RegisterType<TFrom,TTo>(params InjectionMember [] injectionMembers)
        where TTo : TFrom
        {
            _container.RegisterType<TFrom, TTo>(injectionMembers);
        }
        public void RegisterType<TFrom, TTo>(LifetimeManager lifetimeManager, params
        InjectionMember[] injectionMembers) where TTo : TFrom
        {
            _container.RegisterType<TFrom, TTo>(lifetimeManager, injectionMembers);
        }
        public override void Register(Type serviceType, Func<object> activator)
        {
            _container.RegisterType(serviceType, new InjectionFactory((c) => activator.Invoke()));
            base.Register(serviceType, activator);
        }
        public void RegisterInstance<TInterface>(TInterface instance)
        {
            _container.RegisterInstance<TInterface>(instance);
        }
        public IDependencyScope BeginScope()
        {
            return new UnityDependencyResolver(_container.CreateChildContainer());
        }
    }
}
```

The UnityWireupConfiguration class in Listing 10-63 is a very simple registration for most types. But there are a few registrations that are different.

Listing 10-63. UnityWireupConfiguration Class

```
public class UnityWireupConfiguration
    {
        public static void WireUp(UnityDependencyResolver dependencyResolver)
        {
            string groupBrushSQLConnectionString = CloudConfigurationManager.
            GetSetting("GroupBrushDB");
            dependencyResolver.RegisterType<IUserService, UserService>(new
            ContainerControlledLifetimeManager());
            dependencyResolver.RegisterType<ICanvasService,CanvasService>();
            dependencyResolver.RegisterType<ICanvasRoomService, CanvasRoomService>();
```

```
        dependencyResolver.RegisterType<IMemStorage, MemoryStorage>(new
        ContainerControlledLifetimeManager());
        dependencyResolver.Register(typeof(IGetUserNameFromIdData), () => new
        GetUserNameFromIdData(groupBrushSQLConnectionString));
        dependencyResolver.Register(typeof(IGetCanvasDescriptionData), () => new
        GetCanvasDescriptionData(groupBrushSQLConnectionString));
        dependencyResolver.Register(typeof(ICreateUserData), () => new
        CreateUserData(groupBrushSQLConnectionString));
        dependencyResolver.Register(typeof(IValidateUserData), () => new
        ValidateUserData(groupBrushSQLConnectionString));
        dependencyResolver.Register(typeof(ICreateCanvasData), () => new
        CreateCanvasData(groupBrushSQLConnectionString));
        dependencyResolver.Register(typeof(ILookUpCanvasData), () => new
        LookUpCanvasData(groupBrushSQLConnectionString));
    }
}
```

The first line of the WireUp method retrieves configuration settings from a CloudConfigurationManager that provides compatibility with App.Config and cloud configurations. These configuration values can then be passed to the registration as with the SQL connection string.

The second line provides a ContainerControlledLifeTimeManager to that registration. That means the object will live the entire life of the container, whereas the other registration types are re-created with every request.

Finally, the order in which types are registered is important; registrations that are dependent for other registrations should be registered first.

Once again, it is time to add the Unity container classes to our project with the following steps:

1. Add the UnityDependencyResolver class with the contents in Listing 10-62 to the GroupBrush.Web project in the Unity folder.

2. Add the UnityWireupConfiguration class with the contents in Listing 10-63 to the GroupBrush.Web project in the Unity folder.

3. Add a reference from the GroupBrush.Web project to the GroupBrush.DL project.

4. Add a reference to the Microsoft.WindowsAzure.Configuration assembly in the GroupBrush.Web project.

Next, we have to set up the OWIN pipeline so the application can handle the requests with the correct order and logic.

Setting Up the OWIN Pipeline

The StartUp class sets up the OWIN pipeline, which will handle every request that comes in. The StartUp class has a special assembly attribute to indicate that the OWIN pipeline should use this class for configuration. (You can see an example of this attribute in Listing 10-64.) The configuration for our project has four setup areas: dependency resolver, authentication, Web API, and SignalR. Similar to the Unity setup, the order in which things are registered to IAppBuilder is important.

Listing 10-64. OwinStart Attribute

```
[assembly: OwinStartup(typeof(GroupBrush.Web.Startup))]
```

The first thing to set up in the StartUp configuration is the dependency resolver, which is done by using the three lines in Listing 10-65 and one line in Listing 10-67 (shown later). The first line creates the dependency resolver that we will use for SignalR and the Web API. We can configure it using the UnityWireupConfiguration static WireUp method, which is done in the second line. The third line configures SignalR to use the dependency resolver we created in the first line. (There is a fourth line of configuration needed for the Web API, which will be discussed in the Web API section).

Listing 10-65. Dependency Resolver Setup

```
var dependencyResolver = new UnityDependencyResolver();
UnityWireupConfiguration.WireUp(dependencyResolver);
GlobalHost.DependencyResolver = dependencyResolver;
```

The next thing to add to the StartUp class is the authentication shown in Listing 10-66. For authentication, create a configuration class for the cookie authentication. In this configuration, we want the default cookie authentication type and for any login/logout redirect to return to the root path. With our cookie configuration, we set up the first entry in the OWIN pipeline with the UseCookieAuthentication method. The next entry we add to the OWIN pipeline allows requests to the root or public folder to continue to the next middleware in the pipeline. If the request did not continue to the next middleware, and the user is null or unauthenticated, the request is stopped with a 401 response. Finally, if the request has made it this far, it is continued to the next middleware in the pipeline.

Listing 10-66. Authentication Setup

```
var options = new CookieAuthenticationOptions()
{
    AuthenticationType = CookieAuthenticationDefaults.AuthenticationType,
    LoginPath = new PathString("/"),
    LogoutPath = new PathString("/")
};
app.UseCookieAuthentication(options);

app.Use(async (context, next) =>
{
    if (context.Request.Path.Value.Equals("/") ||
    context.Request.Path.Value.StartsWith("/public", StringComparison.CurrentCultureIgnoreCase))
    {
        await next();
    }
    else if (context.Request.User == null || !context.Request.User.Identity.IsAuthenticated)
    {
        context.Response.StatusCode = 401;
    }
    else
    {
        await next();
    }
});
```

After the authentication is set up, the Web API is the next middleware that we want to run. We use the setup in Listing 10-67 to create a configuration for the Web API middleware. In that configuration, we add the dependency resolver that we created in Listing 10-65 so the Web API will use that dependency resolver. Next, we tell the configuration to MapHttpAttributeRoutes, which will enable us to use the Web API attribute routing features. We add the Web API to the OWIN pipeline using the UseWebApi extension method.

Listing 10-67. Web API Setup

```
HttpConfiguration webApiConfiguration = new HttpConfiguration();
webApiConfiguration.DependencyResolver = dependencyResolver;
webApiConfiguration.MapHttpAttributeRoutes();
app.UseWebApi(webApiConfiguration);
```

Finally, we add SignalR middleware with one line, as demonstrated in Listing 10-68.

Listing 10-68. SignalR Setup

```
app.MapSignalR();
```

If you take the four sections in the correct order, you will end up with a complete StartUp class like Listing 10-69. But don't forget the OwinStartUp attribute in Listing 10-64, which is critical for the application to know which configuration to use.

Listing 10-69. Complete StartUp Class

```
public class Startup
{
    public void Configuration(IAppBuilder app)
    {
        var dependencyResolver = new UnityDependencyResolver();
        UnityWireupConfiguration.WireUp(dependencyResolver);
        GlobalHost.DependencyResolver = dependencyResolver;

        var options = new CookieAuthenticationOptions()
        {
            AuthenticationType = CookieAuthenticationDefaults.AuthenticationType,
            LoginPath = new PathString("/"),
            LogoutPath = new PathString("/")
        };
        app.UseCookieAuthentication(options);

        app.Use(async (context, next) =>
        {
            if (context.Request.Path.Value.Equals("/") ||
            context.Request.Path.Value.StartsWith("/public", StringComparison.CurrentCultureIgnoreCase))
            {
                await next();
            }
            else if (context.Request.User == null || !context.Request.User.Identity.IsAuthenticated)
            {
                context.Response.StatusCode = 401;
            }
```

```
        else
        {
            await next();
        }
    });

    HttpConfiguration webApiConfiguration = new HttpConfiguration();
    webApiConfiguration.DependencyResolver = dependencyResolver;
    webApiConfiguration.MapHttpAttributeRoutes();
    app.UseWebApi(webApiConfiguration);

    app.MapSignalR();
    }
}
```

To add the `StartUp` configuration, we follow these steps:

1. Add an OWIN `StartUp` class to the root of the `GroupBrush.Web` project with the contents of Listing 10-69.

2. Ensure that the `OwinStartUp` attribute is included in the `StartUp.cs` file created in step 1 and is similar to Listing 10-64.

We have now created all the code that is necessary to run the server, but need an application to host it in. For this application, we will be hosting in an Azure cloud service worker role (discussed next).

Hosting the Server in Azure

For this project, the Microsoft Azure cloud is a great candidate to support all the platforms we need to have a scalable, reliable, and easily maintainable application. We will use the cloud services platform to host our application in a worker role.

We will cover the following five areas of the worker role that are essential to the project:

- Implementing the `RoleEntryPoint` class
- Creating the cloud service
- Configuring the worker role
- Testing our deployment locally
- Deploying our application to the cloud

After covering these five areas, we will have a fully deployed application running in a worker role.

Implementing the RoleEntryPoint Class

First, we want to implement the `RoleEntryPoint` class. Azure uses this class as an entry point to start, stop, and run the code in the worker role. When we created the `GroupBrush.Worker` project, it created a `WorkerRole` class that derives from the `RoleEntryPoint` class. We will use this class to host our application. When this is running in the cloud, we can start and stop our application using the `OnStart` and `OnStop` methods, respectively.

Because the WorkerRole class is already created, we will use it and add a few changes. The first change is to add a variable that will be responsible for disposing of the WebApp. The next change is starting the WebApp by calling the WebApp generic static Start method with our OWIN StartUp class and configuration. The configuration provided is the endpoint from which the WebApp should be hosted. We determine the endpoint by looking for SignalREndpoint in the endpoints configured for the instance.

Finally, we want to have a way to stop the application; we do that by calling the dispose method on the IDisposable object that was returned from the start method. Once all this is complete, the code will look similar to Listing 10-70.

Listing 10-70. WorkerRole Class

```
public class WorkerRole : RoleEntryPoint
{
    IDisposable _webApp = null;
    public override void Run()
    {
        while (true)
        {
            Thread.Sleep(10000);
            Trace.TraceInformation("Working");
        }
    }

    public override bool OnStart()
    {
        ServicePointManager.DefaultConnectionLimit = 12;
        RoleInstanceEndpoint signalREndpoint = null;
        if (RoleEnvironment.CurrentRoleInstance.InstanceEndpoints.TryGetValue("SignalREndpoint",
        out signalREndpoint))
        {
            _webApp = WebApp.Start<Startup>(string.Format("{0}://{1}", signalREndpoint.Protocol,
            signalREndpoint.IPEndpoint));
        }
        else
        {
            throw new KeyNotFoundException("Could not find SignalREndpoint");
        }
        return base.OnStart();
    }
    public override void OnStop()
    {
        if (_webApp != null)
        {
            _webApp.Dispose();
        }
        base.OnStop();
    }
}
```

Let's add these changes to our project with the following steps:

1. Update the WorkerRole class in the GroupBrush.Worker project with the contents of Listing 10-70.

2. Add a reference from the GroupBrush.Worker project to the GroupBrush.Web project.

3. Run the following command from the Package Manager Console for the Default package of GroupBrush.Worker:

```
Install-Package Microsoft.Owin.Hosting
Install-Package Microsoft.Owin.Host.HttpListener
```

That is all the code it takes to start and stop our application in the cloud. Now that we have our code, we have to create a host in the cloud to run it.

Creating the Cloud Service

Because we already have code for a worker role, we need to create a cloud service on Azure to host it. There are numerous ways to create a cloud service, but we'll use Server Explorer in Visual Studio to do it.

A cloud service can be created only once for a project by using the following steps:

1. Sign in to Visual Studio with the account that is associated to the Azure account.

2. Open the Server Explorer and navigate to Cloud Services, as shown in Figure 10-1.

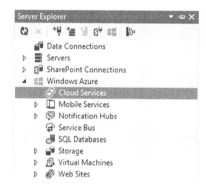

***Figure 10-1.** Azure components in Server Explorer*

3. Right-click on Cloud Services to display the context menu and then click Create Cloud Service, as shown in Figure 10-2.

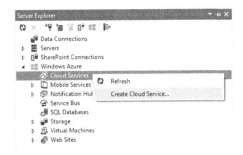

Figure 10-2. *Cloud Services context menu*

4. Complete the following on the Create Cloud Service dialog box, as shown in Figure 10-2:

   a. Choose the subscription that you want this cloud service to be associated with.

   b. Enter a name for the cloud service.

   c. Choose where you want this cloud service deployed.

5. Finally, click Create after all the correct information is entered.

Figure 10-3. *Create Cloud Service dialog box*

There should now be a cloud service ready to use in Azure. Now we need to create a database that will persist our data in the cloud.

Creating the Azure SQL Database

In our application, we need to persist data such as users and canvases, so we will use the Azure SQL database. Creating the database is very simple; we follow these steps:

1. Log in to http://portal.azure.com.

2. Click the New(+) button in the bottom left.

3. Click SQL Database (see Figure 10-4).

4. In the SQL database tab, do the following, as shown in Figure 10-5:

Figure 10-4. *Creating a new SQL Database*

    a.   Enter the database name.

    b.   Click the server button to configure the server.

Figure 10-5. *Creating a new SQL database configuration*

5. In the Server tab, click Create a New Server.

6. In the New Server tab, do the following:

    a. Enter server name.

    b. Enter server admin name.

    c. Enter admin password.

    d. Enter admin password again to confirm.

    e. Click OK.

7. Click Create.

We store two sets of records for our application: users and canvases. So we need to create two tables in our database: one for users and the other for canvases.

The Users table consists of three values per record, as seen in Listing 10-71: the user ID, the name, and password of the user.

Listing 10-71. Users Table Create Script

```
USE [GroupBrush]
GO

CREATE TABLE [dbo].[Users](
        [UserId] [int] IDENTITY(1,1) NOT NULL PRIMARY KEY,
        [Name] [nvarchar](100) NOT NULL,
        [Password] [nvarchar](255) NOT NULL
) ON [PRIMARY]

GO
```

The Canvases table shown in Listing 10-72 is very simple as well. It contains the canvas table ID, canvas ID, canvas name, and canvas description.

Listing 10-72. Canvases Table Create Script

```
USE [GroupBrush]
GO

CREATE TABLE [dbo].[Canvases](
        [CanvasTableId] [bigint] IDENTITY(1,1) NOT NULL PRIMARY KEY,
        [CanvasId] [uniqueidentifier] NOT NULL,
        [CanvasName] [nvarchar](100) NOT NULL,
        [CanvasDescription] [nvarchar](100) NOT NULL
) ON [PRIMARY]

GO
```

To add these tables to our database, follow these steps:

1. Connect to the database using SQL Server Management Studio.

2. Run the complete script in Listing 10-71 to add the Users table.

3. Run the complete script in Listing 10-72 to add the Canvases table.

Note When using MS SQL in Azure, a table must have a primary key before you can use it.

Now that the tables are created, we can create the stored procedures to support the data layer functions. Because the stored procedures are simplified, we will not go into the details of each procedure and give only a short description:

- CreateUser, shown in Listing 10-73, creates a new user returning the user ID.

- ValidateUser, shown in Listing 10-74, validates the user login.

- GetUserName, shown in Listing 10-75, gets the username from the user ID.

- CreateCanvas, shown in Listing 10-76, creates a new canvas returning the canvas ID.

- LookUpCanvas, shown in Listing 10-77, gets the canvas ID of a canvas from the name.

- GetCanvasDescription, shown in Listing 10-78, gets the canvas name and description from the canvas ID.

Listing 10-73. CreateUser Stored Procedure

```
USE [GroupBrush]
GO

CREATE Procedure [dbo].[CreateUser](
@Name nchar(100),
@Password nchar(255),
@UserId int output
)

As
Begin

Declare @ReturnValue int = -1
If Exists(Select 1 From dbo.Users Where Name = @Name)
Begin
        Set @ReturnValue = 1
End
Else
Begin
        Declare @UserIds Table (userId int)
        INSERT INTO [dbo].[Users]
                        ([Name]
                        ,[Password])
                Output Inserted.UserId Into @UserIds(userId)
                  VALUES
                        (@Name
                        ,@Password)
        Select @ReturnValue = 0, @UserId = userId From @UserIds
End
Return @ReturnValue
End

GO
```

Listing 10-74. ValidateUser Stored Procedure

```
USE [GroupBrush]
GO

CREATE Procedure [dbo].[ValidateUser](
@Name nchar(100),
@Password nchar(255),
@UserId int  = NULL output,
@ValidUser bit output
)

As
Begin
        Select @UserId = UserId From dbo.Users Where Name = @Name and Password = @Password
        If (@UserId Is Not Null)
        Begin
                Set @ValidUser = 1
        End
        Else
        Begin
                Set @ValidUser = 0
        End
End

GO
```

Listing 10-75. GetUserName Stored Procedure

```
USE [GroupBrush]
GO

Create Procedure [dbo].[GetUserName](
@UserId Int,
@UserName NVarChar(100) Output
)

As
Begin

Select @UserName = Name From dbo.Users where UserId = @UserId

End
GO
```

Listing 10-76. CreateCanvas Stored Procedure

```
USE [GroupBrush]
GO

CREATE Procedure [dbo].[CreateCanvas](
@CanvasName nchar(100),
@CanvasDescription nchar(255),
@CanvasId UniqueIdentifier output
)
```

```
As
Begin

Declare @ReturnValue int = -1
If Exists(Select 1 From dbo.Canvases Where CanvasName = @CanvasName)
Begin
        Set @ReturnValue = 1
End
Else
Begin
        Declare @CanvasIds Table (CanvasId UniqueIdentifier)
        INSERT INTO [dbo].[Canvases]
          ([CanvasId]
          ,[CanvasName]
                 ,[CanvasDescription])
        Output Inserted.CanvasId Into @CanvasIds(CanvasId)
     VALUES
           (NewID()
           ,@CanvasName
                  ,@CanvasDescription)
        Select  @ReturnValue = 0,
                        @CanvasId = CanvasId
                        From @CanvasIds
End
Return @ReturnValue
End

GO
```

Listing 10-77. LookUpCanvas Stored Procedure

```
USE [GroupBrush]
GO

CREATE Procedure [dbo].[LookUpCanvas](
@CanvasName nvarchar(100),
@CanvasId UniqueIdentifier = NULL output
)

As
Begin
Declare @ReturnValue int = -1
Select @CanvasId = CanvasId From dbo.Canvases Where CanvasName = @CanvasName
If @CanvasId Is Not Null
Begin
        Set @ReturnValue = 0
End

Return @ReturnValue
End

GO
```

Listing 10-78. GetCanvasDescription Stored Procedure

```
USE [GroupBrush]
GO

Create Procedure [dbo].[GetCanvasDescription](
@CanvasId UniqueIdentifier,
@CanvasName NVarChar(100) Output,
@CanvasDescription NVarChar(100) Output
)

As
Begin

Select @CanvasName = CanvasName, @CanvasDescription = CanvasDescription
From dbo.Canvases
Where CanvasId = @CanvasId

End
GO
```

Now we know which stored procedures are needed, so let's add them to our database with the following steps:

1. Connect to the database using SQL Server Management Studio.

2. Run the complete script in Listing 10-73 to add the CreateUser stored procedure.

3. Run the complete script in Listing 10-74 to add the ValidateUser stored procedure.

4. Run the complete script in Listing 10-75 to add the GetUserName stored procedure.

5. Run the complete script in Listing 10-76 to add the CreateCanvas stored procedure.

6. Run the complete script in Listing 10-77 to add the LookUpCanvas stored procedure.

7. Run the complete script in Listing 10-78 to add the GetCanvasDescription stored procedure.

Now with the database work complete, let's move on to configuring the worker role.

Configuring the Worker Role

For the worker role to work correctly, we have to add some settings at runtime. These settings can also change, depending on the environment in which we are running. This section briefly covers the following configuration tabs: Settings, Endpoints, and Configuration. The configuration for a worker role can be found under the properties of that worker role (see Figure 10-6).

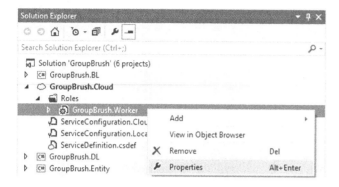

Figure 10-6. *Worker role context menu*

For application configuration, it is very common to have different settings, based on where the code is running. To accommodate for this, we can configure the configuration for All Configurations, Cloud, Local, or add our own service configuration. All Configurations applies the configuration to all configurations regardless of where it is running, but it is possible to overwrite in a specific configuration.

The Cloud configuration is used when the worker role is run on Azure. The Local configuration is used when the application is run locally for testing. Each configuration tab allows a Service Configuration setting for all the configuration values that the tab will let you configure.

The first tab is the Settings tab (see Figure 10-7), in which strings and connection strings can be added. It is a very simple configuration: for each entry, we give it a name, the type of entry it is, and the value. This tab stores simple settings or connection strings to databases that can be retrieved by name.

Figure 10-7. *Azure worker role Settings tab*

This configuration tab is where we set the connection string for the database with the following steps:

1. Go to the Settings tab in the worker role configuration.

2. Click Add Setting.

3. On the newly added setting, change the name to **GroupBrushDB**.

4. Change the type to **String**.

5. Change the value to be the value of the connection string of the database created in the previous section.

The next tab is the Endpoints tab shown in Figure 10-8. The settings are used to determine what endpoints are allowed for a worker role. The endpoints have a name, the type (direction), public port, private port, and SSL certificate name. We need to add an endpoint so that the worker has a port that is exposed to the Internet to take requests.

Figure 10-8. *Azure worker role Endpoints tab*

To add the endpoint, follow these steps:

1. Go to the Endpoints tab in the worker role configuration.

2. Click Add Endpoint.

3. On the newly added Endpoint entry, change the name to **SignalREndpoint**.

4. Change the type to **Input**.

5. Change the protocol to **http**.

6. Make the public and private ports **80**.

7. Leave the SSL certificate name blank.

8. Press Ctrl+S to save your settings.

With the endpoint added, there is one last tab: the Configuration tab (see Figure 10-9). This is the tab used to choose the size and number of instances of the worker role that we want running by default.

Figure 10-9. *Azure worker role Configuration tab*

Although we did not cover all the possible configuration tabs available to the worker role, we discussed the most common ones. Now we have to test our deployment locally.

Testing Deployment Locally

Because the application is cloud-based, you might think that we need to deploy to the cloud to test it. With the Azure cloud service, this is not the case—we can use the Azure Compute Emulator that is available from Microsoft.

To test locally, set the GroupBrush.Cloud project as the StartUp project. Once this is set, we can run/debug the project using the Emulator by pressing F5. When the application is running, we see output similar to Figure 10-10 by right-clicking the Azure Emulator in the task notification area and then clicking Show Compute Emulator UI.

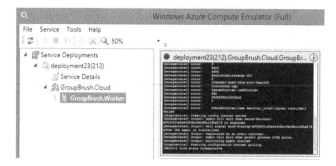

Figure 10-10. *Azure Compute Emulator*

With our application running locally, we now have to deploy it to the cloud.

Deploying an Application to the Cloud

We are finally ready to deploy our application to the cloud. We have implemented the code that will run the server, created the cloud service that will host the server, created the SQL database to persist the data for the server, configured the server environments, and tested the server locally. The deployment is very straightforward and simple to do. The deployment will generally take minutes to complete, so expect to wait when you need to deploy.

It is possible to deploy your service to a staging environment first and then move it to a "production" environment once you have validated that it works on staging. We will show how to directly deploy to "production," which is the same as staging (it just requires selecting a different environment in the publishing steps). To deploy to "production," follow these steps:

1. Right-click the GroupBrush.Cloud project and click Publish, as shown in Figure 10-11.

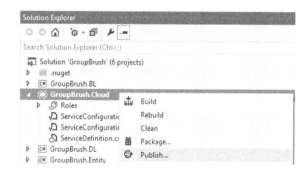

Figure 10-11. *Cloud Service context menu*

2. Sign in to the Azure account and click Next.

3. In the Publish Settings section shown in Figure 10-12, do the following:

    a. Choose the cloud service that was set up earlier.

    b. Change the environment to **Production**.

    c. Click Next.

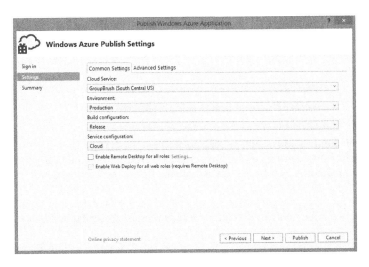

***Figure 10-12.** Publish Settings dialog box*

4. Validate settings in the Publish Summary dialog box similar to Figure 10-13.

***Figure 10-13.** Publish summary dialog box*

5. Click Publish.

Now that we have successfully published, our application should be live in the cloud. But what if it is very popular and needs to scale? Scaling the application is discussed next.

Scaling the Server

To scale our application beyond the one instance, we need to be able to address the following areas:

- Communication between instances

- In-memory storage

- Different authentication between machines

Once we have addressed these areas, the application should be able to scale up well.

The first issue to address is the communication between instances, which is critical to ensure that a message from a user on one instance is available on all other instances. To address this, we can use one of the many scaleout solutions that SignalR supports.

For this application, in which there are a lot of messages, and delay is very noticeable, the Redis scaleout solution is the best fit. The solution requires a dedicated server, but it is far better than the SQL or MessageBus solution for our application.

Azure recently added Redis Cache as a PaaS, which works well and is very easy to set up. To support scaling for our application, add the Redis Cache to Azure with the following steps:

1. Log in to http://portal.azure.com.

2. Click the New(+) button in the bottom left.

3. Click on Redis Cache.

4. Enter a name for the cache.

5. Choose the resource group of the existing application objects.

6. Choose the same location as the existing application.

7. Click Create.

We now have a Redis cache that is ready to use.

Moving on to the in-memory storage, which worked well when there was one instance, but does not work now because the data would be in memory on different instances. Because we are using Redis as our scaleout solution, we can also use it as shared memory between the instances.

To do this, we need to create a class that implements IMemStorage for Redis. So we create the RedisStorage class that derives from IMemStorage, as shown in Listing 10-79.

Listing 10-79. RedisStorage Class Definition

```
public class RedisStorage : IMemStorage
```

The RedisStorage constructor in Listing 10-80 has one dependency that is injected. The injected item is RedisConfiguration, defined in Listing 10-81, that provides the configuration for Redis.

Listing 10-80. RedisStorage Constructor

```
public RedisStorage(RedisConfiguration redisConfiguration)
{
    _redisConfiguration = redisConfiguration;
    _userNames = new Dictionary<int, string>();
}
```

Listing 10-81. RedisConfiguration Entity Class

```
public class RedisConfiguration
{
    public string HostName { get; set; }
    public string Password { get; set; }
    public int Port { get; set; }
    public bool UseRedis { get; set; }
    public string EventKey { get; set; }
    public RedisConfiguration(string hostName, string password, bool useRedis)
    {
        HostName = hostName;
        Password = password;
        UseRedis = useRedis;
        Port = 6379;
        EventKey = "GroupBrush";
    }
}
```

Listing 10-82 shows the private variables for RedisStorage. There are four prefixes that are used to keep the keys unique between the types of objects. There is also an in-memory dictionary to store the username to prevent numerous lookups to the Redis server for username.

Listing 10-82. RedisStorage Private Variables

```
private const string TRANSACTION_PREFIX = "CanvasTransaction:";
private const string ACTION_PREFIX = "CanvasBrushAction:";
private const string USERS_PREFIX = "CanvasUsers:";
private const string USERNAMES_PREFIX = "CanvasUsernames:";
private readonly RedisConfiguration _redisConfiguration;
Dictionary<int, string> _userNames;
```

The first method is the AddBrushAction method, which connects to the Redis server to get the next transaction number for the canvas and uses it as the sequence for the CanvasBrushAction that is passed in. Next, it takes the CanvasBrushAction and serializes it into JSON and adds it to the canvas list on the Redis server. Finally, it returns the CanvasBrushAction object.

Listing 10-83. AddBrushAction Method

```
public CanvasBrushAction AddBrushAction(string canvasId, CanvasBrushAction brushData)
{
    int transactionNumber = 0;
    using (var conn = new RedisConnection(_redisConfiguration.HostName,_redisConfiguration.
    Port,password: _redisConfiguration.Password))
    {
        conn.Open();
        var incrTask = conn.Hashes.Increment(0, TRANSACTION_PREFIX + canvasId, "transaction");
        transactionNumber = (int)incrTask.Result;
    }
    brushData.Sequence = transactionNumber;
    string serializedData = JsonConvert.SerializeObject(brushData);
    using (var conn = new RedisConnection(_redisConfiguration.HostName,_redisConfiguration.
    Port,password: _redisConfiguration.Password))
```

```
    {
        conn.Open();
        conn.Lists.AddLast(0, ACTION_PREFIX + canvasId, serializedData);
    }
    return brushData;
}
```

The GetBrushActions method shown in Listing 10-84 contacts the Redis server and asks for all CanvasBrushActions that have been stored from the current position to the latest entry. If there are results returned from Redis, it deserializes each JSON object and adds it to the list of actions to return. These actions are then sorted by sequence number. Finally these actions are returned.

Listing 10-84. GetBrushActions Method

```
public List<CanvasBrushAction> GetBrushActions(string canvasId, int currentPosition)
{
    List<CanvasBrushAction> actions = new List<CanvasBrushAction>();
    string[] storedActions = null;
    using (var conn = new RedisConnection(_redisConfiguration.HostName,_redisConfiguration.
    Port,password: _redisConfiguration.Password))
    {
        conn.Open();
        var rangeTask = conn.Lists.RangeString(0, ACTION_PREFIX + canvasId, currentPosition,
        Int32.MaxValue);
        storedActions = rangeTask.Result;
    }
    if (storedActions != null)
    {
        foreach (string storedAction in storedActions)
        {
            actions.Add(JsonConvert.DeserializeObject<CanvasBrushAction>(storedAction));
        }
        actions.Sort(new Comparison<CanvasBrushAction>((a, b) => {
        return a.Sequence.CompareTo(b.Sequence); }));
    }

        return actions;
}
```

The GetCanvasUser method in Listing 10-85 is very simple: it connects to the Redis server to get a list of users that have connected to that canvas. The method then puts all the users through a HashSet to get unique users, which it returns.

Listing 10-85. GetCanvasUsers Method

```
public List<string> GetCanvasUsers(string canvasId)
{

    List<string> returnValue = new List<string>();
    HashSet<string> uniqueList = new HashSet<string>();
    using (var conn = new RedisConnection(_redisConfiguration.HostName,_redisConfiguration.
    Port,password: _redisConfiguration.Password))
```

```
{
    conn.Open();
    var getAllTask = conn.Sets.GetAllString(0, USERS_PREFIX + canvasId);
    uniqueList = new HashSet<string>(getAllTask.Result.ToList());
}
returnValue = uniqueList.ToList<string>();
return returnValue;
}
```

The AddUserToCanvas method in Listing 10-86 is another simple method that adds the passed-in ID to the list of users on the Redis server for the specified canvas ID.

Listing 10-86. AddUserToCanvas Method

```
public void AddUserToCanvas(string canvasId, string id)
{
    using (var conn = new RedisConnection(_redisConfiguration.HostName,_redisConfiguration.
    Port,password: _redisConfiguration.Password))
    {
        conn.Open();
        conn.Sets.Add(0, USERS_PREFIX + canvasId, id);
    }
}
```

The RemoveUserFromCanvas method in Listing 10-87 is similar to the previous method, but it removes the user instead of adding it.

Listing 10-87. RemoveUserFromCanvas Method

```
public void RemoveUserFromCanvas(string canvasId, string id)
{
    using (var conn = new RedisConnection(_redisConfiguration.HostName,_redisConfiguration.
    Port,password: _redisConfiguration.Password))
    {
        conn.Open();
        conn.Sets.Remove(0, USERS_PREFIX + canvasId, id);
    }
}
```

The GetUserName and StoreUserName methods shown in Listing 10-88 use a combination of in-memory and RedisStorage to store the data. To prevent a lot of out-of-process lookups for username in the GetUserName method, the method looks at its internal username structure first to see whether it exists. If it does not, it connects to the Redis server to retrieve it. The StoreUserName method first stores the data on the Redis server and then stores it in memory.

Listing 10-88. GetUserName and StoreUserName Methods

```
public string GetUserName(int id)
{
    string userName = null;
    if (_userNames.ContainsKey(id))
    {
        userName = _userNames[id];
    }
```

```
    else
    {
        using (var conn = new RedisConnection(_redisConfiguration.HostName,_redisConfiguration.
        Port,password: _redisConfiguration.Password))
        {
            conn.Open();
            var getTask = conn.Strings.GetString(0, USERNAMES_PREFIX + id.ToString());
            userName = getTask.Result;
            _userNames[id] = userName;
        }
    }
    return userName;
}
public void StoreUserName(int id, string userName)
{
    using (var conn = new RedisConnection(_redisConfiguration.HostName, _redisConfiguration.
    Port,password: _redisConfiguration.Password))
    {
        conn.Open();
        conn.Strings.Set(0, USERNAMES_PREFIX + id.ToString(), userName).Wait();
    }
    _userNames[id] = userName;
}
```

Once all the parts of the RedisStorage class are put together, we see the complete class (see Listing 10-89).

Listing 10-89. Complete RedisStorage Class

```
public class RedisStorage : IMemStorage
    {
        private const string TRANSACTION_PREFIX = "CanvasTransaction:";
        private const string ACTION_PREFIX = "CanvasBrushAction:";
        private const string USERS_PREFIX = "CanvasUsers:";
        private const string USERNAMES_PREFIX = "CanvasUsernames:";
        private readonly RedisConfiguration _redisConfiguration;
        Dictionary<int, string> _userNames;
        public RedisStorage(RedisConfiguration redisConfiguration)
        {
            _redisConfiguration = redisConfiguration;
            _userNames = new Dictionary<int, string>();
        }
        public CanvasBrushAction AddBrushAction(string canvasId, CanvasBrushAction brushData)
        {
            int transactionNumber = 0;
            using (var conn = new RedisConnection(_redisConfiguration.HostName,_redisConfiguration.
            Port,password: _redisConfiguration.Password))
            {
                conn.Open();
                var incrTask = conn.Hashes.Increment(0, TRANSACTION_PREFIX + canvasId,
                "transaction");
                transactionNumber = (int)incrTask.Result;
            }
```

```csharp
    brushData.Sequence = transactionNumber;
    string serializedData = JsonConvert.SerializeObject(brushData);
    using (var conn = new RedisConnection(_redisConfiguration.HostName,_redisConfiguration.
    Port,password: _redisConfiguration.Password))
    {
        conn.Open();
        conn.Lists.AddLast(0, ACTION_PREFIX + canvasId, serializedData);
    }
    return brushData;
}
public List<CanvasBrushAction> GetBrushActions(string canvasId, int currentPosition)
{
    List<CanvasBrushAction> actions = new List<CanvasBrushAction>();
    string[] storedActions = null;
    using (var conn = new RedisConnection(_redisConfiguration.HostName,_redisConfiguration.
    Port,password: _redisConfiguration.Password))
    {
        conn.Open();
        var rangeTask = conn.Lists.RangeString(0, ACTION_PREFIX + canvasId, currentPosition,
        Int32.MaxValue);
        storedActions = rangeTask.Result;
    }
    if (storedActions != null)
    {
        foreach (string storedAction in storedActions)
        {
            actions.Add(JsonConvert.DeserializeObject<CanvasBrushAction>(storedAction));
        }
        actions.Sort(new Comparison<CanvasBrushAction>((a, b) => { return a.Sequence.
        CompareTo(b.Sequence); }));
    }
    return actions;
}
public List<string> GetCanvasUsers(string canvasId)
{

    List<string> returnValue = new List<string>();
    HashSet<string> uniqueList = new HashSet<string>();
    using (var conn = new RedisConnection(_redisConfiguration.HostName,_redisConfiguration.
    Port,password: _redisConfiguration.Password))
    {
        conn.Open();
        var getAllTask = conn.Sets.GetAllString(0, USERS_PREFIX + canvasId);
        uniqueList = new HashSet<string>(getAllTask.Result.ToList());
    }
    returnValue = uniqueList.ToList<string>();
    return returnValue;
}
public void AddUserToCanvas(string canvasId, string id)
{
    using (var conn = new RedisConnection(_redisConfiguration.HostName,_redisConfiguration.
    Port,password: _redisConfiguration.Password))
```

```
            {
                conn.Open();
                conn.Sets.Add(0, USERS_PREFIX + canvasId, id);
            }
        }

        public void RemoveUserFromCanvas(string canvasId, string id)
        {
            using (var conn = new RedisConnection(_redisConfiguration.HostName,_redisConfiguration.
            Port,password: _redisConfiguration.Password))
            {
                conn.Open();
                conn.Sets.Remove(0, USERS_PREFIX + canvasId, id);
            }
        }
        public string GetUserName(int id)
        {
            string userName = null;
            if (_userNames.ContainsKey(id))
            {
                userName = _userNames[id];
            }
            else
            {
                using (var conn = new RedisConnection(_redisConfiguration.HostName,_
                redisConfiguration.Port,password: _redisConfiguration.Password))
                {
                    conn.Open();
                    var getTask = conn.Strings.GetString(0, USERNAMES_PREFIX + id.ToString());
                    userName = getTask.Result;
                    _userNames[id] = userName;
                }
            }
            return userName;
        }
        public void StoreUserName(int id, string userName)
        {
            using (var conn = new RedisConnection(_redisConfiguration.HostName,_redisConfiguration.
            Port,password: _redisConfiguration.Password))
            {
                conn.Open();
                conn.Strings.Set(0, USERNAMES_PREFIX + id.ToString(), userName).Wait();
            }
            _userNames[id] = userName;
        }
    }
```

With RedisStorage complete, we have taken care of the second issue about in-memory. So the final issue to address is different authentication between machines.

Whenever you deploy an application instance, it is created with a unique key. So if you are deploying more than one instance, each instance has its own unique key. Each time a cookie is encrypted on the server, it will be encrypted with a key that other instances cannot decrypt.

To correct this, we can create a class that will encrypt and decrypt the keys the same way on every instance. The AesDataProtector class implements IDataProtector (see Listing 10-90). For this class, we inject in the constructor the password and salt that we want it to use. The constructor then uses a built-in function to return bytes we can use as the key and initial vector (IV).

Listing 10-90. AesDataProtector Class

```
public class AesDataProtector : IDataProtector
    {
        private byte [] _IV;
        private byte [] _key;
        public AesDataProtector(string password, string salt)
        {
            Rfc2898DeriveBytes key = new Rfc2898DeriveBytes(password, Encoding.ASCII.GetBytes(salt));
            _key = key.GetBytes(256 / 8);
            _IV = key.GetBytes(128 / 8);
        }

        public byte[] Protect(byte[] userData)
        {
            byte[] encrypted;
            using (AesCryptoServiceProvider aesAlg = new AesCryptoServiceProvider() )
            {
                aesAlg.Key = _key;
                aesAlg.IV = _IV;
                ICryptoTransform encryptor = aesAlg.CreateEncryptor(aesAlg.Key, aesAlg.IV);
                using (MemoryStream msEncrypt = new MemoryStream())
                {
                    using (CryptoStream csEncrypt = new CryptoStream(msEncrypt, encryptor,
                    CryptoStreamMode.Write))
                    {
                        csEncrypt.Write(userData, 0, userData.Length);
                        csEncrypt.FlushFinalBlock();
                        encrypted = msEncrypt.ToArray();
                    }
                }
            }
            return encrypted;
        }

        public byte[] Unprotect(byte[] protectedData)
        {
            byte[] output = null;
            using (AesCryptoServiceProvider aesAlg = new AesCryptoServiceProvider())
            {
                aesAlg.Key = _key;
                aesAlg.IV = _IV;
```

```
        ICryptoTransform decryptor = aesAlg.CreateDecryptor(aesAlg.Key, aesAlg.IV);

        using (MemoryStream msDecrypt = new MemoryStream(protectedData))
        {
            using (CryptoStream csDecrypt = new CryptoStream(msDecrypt, decryptor,
            CryptoStreamMode.Read))
            {
                byte[] buffer = new byte[8];
                using (MemoryStream msOutput = new MemoryStream())
                {
                    int read;
                    while ((read = csDecrypt.Read(buffer, 0, buffer.Length)) > 0)
                    {
                        msOutput.Write(buffer, 0, read);
                    }
                    output = msOutput.ToArray();
                }
            }
        }
    }
    return output;
    }
}
```

There are two functions, Protect and Unprotect, which are very simple and do an encryption on the data in the Protect function and a decryption on the data in the Unprotect function.

To use the new AesDataProtector class, we must provide a provider class that implements the IDataProtectionProvider interface (see Listing 10-91). The class is constructed so that an AesDataProtector is to be injected in the constructor when the Create method is called to return this AesDataProtector.

Listing 10-91. AesDataProtectionProvider Class

```
public class AesDataProtectionProvider : IDataProtectionProvider
{
    AesDataProtector _dataProtector;
    public AesDataProtectionProvider(AesDataProtector dataProtector)
    {
        _dataProtector = dataProtector;
    }
    public IDataProtector Create(params string[] purposes)
    {
        return _dataProtector;
    }
}
```

With the scaling limitations addressed, let's add the scaling to our project with the following steps:

1. Run the following command from the Package Manager Console for the Default package of GroupBrush.Worker and GroupBrush.Web:

   ```
   Install-Package Microsoft.AspNet.SignalR.Redis
   ```

2. Run the following command from the Package Manager Console for the Default package of GroupBrush.BL:

    ```
    Install-Package BookSleeve -version x.y.z
    ```

    a. Make sure the installed version is the same as the other projects.

    ```
    Install-Package Newtonsoft.Json  -version x.y.z
    ```

    b. Make sure the installed version is the same as the other projects.

3. Add the RedisConfiguration class with the contents of Listing 10-81 in the GroupBrush.Entity project.

4. Add the RedisStorage class with the contents of Listing 10-89 under the Storage folder in the GroupBrush.BL project.

5. Add a DataProtectors solution folder to the GroupBrush.BL project.

6. Add the AesDataProtector class with the contents of Listing 10-90 under the DataProtectors folder in the GroupBrush.BL project.

7. Add the AesDataProtectionProvider class with the contents of Listing 10-91 under the DataProtectors folder in the GroupBrush.BL project.

8. Add configuration settings to the GroupBrush.Worker role:

    a. Add a setting named GroupBrushRedisHostname with the value of the host name of the Redis server (the host name under the properties menu for Azure Redis Cache).

    b. Add a setting named GroupBrushRedisPassword with the value of the password of the Redis server (the primary under the keys menu for Azure Redis Cache).

    c. Add a setting named UseRedis with the value of true for cloud configuration and false for local configuration.

9. Add the contents of Listing 10-92 to the top of the WireUp method in the UnityWireupConfiguration class.

Listing 10-92. Redis Configuration Settings

```
string groupBrushRedisHostname = CloudConfigurationManager.GetSetting("GroupBrushRedisHostname");
string groupBrushRedisPassword = CloudConfigurationManager.GetSetting("GroupBrushRedisPassword");
string strUseRedis = CloudConfigurationManager.GetSetting("UseRedis") ?? "false";
bool useRedis = bool.Parse(strUseRedis);
RedisConfiguration redisConfiguration =
new RedisConfiguration(groupBrushRedisHostname,groupBrushRedisPassword,useRedis);
dependencyResolver.RegisterInstance<RedisConfiguration>(redisConfiguration);
```

    10.   Replace the line from Listing 10-93 with Listing 10-94 in the `UnityWireupConfiguration` class.

Listing 10-93. IMemStorage Setting to Replace

```
dependencyResolver.RegisterType<IMemStorage,
MemoryStorage>(new ContainerControlledLifetimeManager());
```

Listing 10-94. IMemStorage Replacement Setting

```
if (useRedis)
{
    dependencyResolver.RegisterType<IMemStorage, RedisStorage>(new
    ContainerControlledLifetimeManager(), new InjectionConstructor(redisConfiguration));
}
else
{
    dependencyResolver.RegisterType<IMemStorage, MemoryStorage>(new
    ContainerControlledLifetimeManager());
}
```

    11.   Add the logic in Listing 10-95 at the top of the `Configuration` method in `StartUp.cs`.

Listing 10-95. Redis Configuration Logic for StartUp.cs

```
string strUseRedis = CloudConfigurationManager.GetSetting("UseRedis") ?? "false";
bool useRedis = bool.Parse(strUseRedis);
```

    12.   Add the logic in Listing 10-96 between the `UseWebApi` and `MapSignalR` functions of the `Configuration` method in StartUp.cs.

Listing 10-96. Redis Configuration for SignalR in StartUp.cs

```
RedisConfiguration redisConfiguration = dependencyResolver.Resolve<RedisConfiguration>();
if (redisConfiguration.UseRedis)
{
    GlobalHost.DependencyResolver.UseRedis(redisConfiguration.HostName, redisConfiguration.Port,
    redisConfiguration.Password, redisConfiguration.EventKey);
}
```

    13.   Update the instance count in the `GroupBrush.Worker` Configuration tab to increase the number of instances.

There is now a fully functioning server, so the next step is to create the clients that can connect to it.

Developing the Clients

To connect to the server, we will create a JavaScript client. Even though the clients will run on their own machines, we have to host the content for them on the server. To do this, we will use the OWIN Static Files middleware to serve up the content in the form of URLs that a normal web site would have. The content is stored in a specific structure, and the OWIN middleware needs to be added, so we complete the following steps before moving on:

1. Run the following command from the Package Manager Console for the Default package of GroupBrush.Web and GroupBrush.Worker.

   ```
   Install-Package Microsoft.AspNet.SignalR.JS
   Install-Package Microsoft.Owin.StaticFiles
   ```

2. Add a solution folder named Content to the GroupBrush.Web project.

3. Add a solution folder named Content to the Public folder in the GroupBrush.Web project.

4. Add a solution folder named Scripts to the Public folder in the GroupBrush.Web project.

5. Add a solution folder named Styles to the Public folder in the GroupBrush.Web project.

6. Add a solution folder named Styles to the GroupBrush.Web project.

7. Add the content in Listing 10-97 to the end of the Configuration method in the StartUp.cs file.

Listing 10-97. Options to Set Up the OWIN Static Files Middleware

```
var sharedOptions = new SharedOptions() { RequestPath = new PathString(string.Empty), FileSystem =
new PhysicalFileSystem(".//public//content") };
app.UseDefaultFiles(new Microsoft.Owin.StaticFiles.DefaultFilesOptions(sharedOptions) {
DefaultFileNames = new List<string>() { "index.html" } });
app.UseStaticFiles("/public");
app.UseStaticFiles("/content");
app.UseStaticFiles("/scripts");
app.UseStaticFiles("/styles");
app.UseStaticFiles(new StaticFileOptions(sharedOptions));
```

In Listing 10-97, the first line sets the option to redirect any request for the root document to the Public content folder. The next line sets the default document of index.html if the requested path does not contain a file. The remaining lines set up their respective paths to respond to requests for those paths.

Developing the Client Homepage

For our client, there are three views that the user will see: homepage signed out, homepage signed in, and canvas room page.

The first page users see is homepage signed out, as shown in Figure 10-14, which presents a page for visitors to create an account or sign in. Once users log in, they see a screen similar to Figure 10-15, which gives them the ability to sign out, create canvases, or join canvases. Both these views are the same index.html page in Listing 10-98, but with different .css classes applied. The last view is the canvas page that can be seen later in the chapter in Figure 10-16. In this view, the user can have real-time drawings and chat.

Figure 10-14. *Signed-out index page*

Figure 10-15. *Signed-in index page*

Listing 10-98. Index.html

```
<!DOCTYPE html>
<html xmlns="http://www.w3.org/1999/xhtml">
<head>
    <title>Group Brush</title>
    <link rel="stylesheet" type="text/css" href="/public/styles/Index.css" />
    <script src="/public/scripts/jquery-1.6.4.min.js"></script>
    <script src="/public/scripts/Index.js"></script>
</head>
<body>
    <div id="mainContent">
        <div id="mainMessage">
            <h1>Group Brush</h1>
            <div id="loadingMessage">Loading...</div>
        </div>
        <div id="actionContent">
            <div class="loggedOut" id="createAccountContent">
```

```
          <div>
              <span>Welcome to Group Brush</span><br />
              <span>This site is for friends to draw together.
              Please Sign-In or Create an account.</span>
          </div>
          <div id="createAccount">
              <span class="sectionTitle">Create account</span><br />
              <span>User name:</span><input name="username" id="username" type="text" /><br />
              <span>Password:</span><input name="password" id="password" type="password" /><br />
              <span>Verify Password:</span><span id="passwordNotEqual" class="error">Passwords
              do not match</span><input name="verifyPassword" id="verifyPassword"
              type="password" />
              <span id="createAccountError" class="error">Could not create account</span>
              <button id="btnCreateAccount">Create Account</button>
          </div>
      </div>
      <div class="loggedIn" id="canvasActionContent">
          <div id="createCanvasContainer">
              <span class="sectionTitle">Create shared canvas</span>
              <span>Canvas name:</span><input name="canvasname" id="canvasname"
              type="text" /><br />
              <span>Canvas Description:</span><input name="canvasdescription"
              id="canvasdescription" type="text" /><br />
              <span id="createCanvasError" class="error">Could not create canvas</span>
              <button id="btnCreateCanvas">Create Canvas</button>
          </div>
          <div id="joinCanvasContainer">
              <span class="sectionTitle">Join shared canvas</span>
              <span>Canvas name:</span><input name="canvasname" id="canvasname"
              type="text" /><br />
              <span id="joinCanvasError" class="error">Could not join canvas</span>
              <button id="btnJoinCanvas">Join Canvas</button>
          </div>
      </div>
  </div>
</div>
<div id="userContent">
    <div class="loggedOut">
        <div id="loginWidget">
            <div id="LogIn">
                <form id="loginForm">
                    <span id="signIn">Sign In</span><br />
                    <span>User name:</span><input name="username" id="username" type="text" />
                    <span>Password:</span><input name="password" id="password" type="password" />
                </form>
                <span id="loginError" class="error">Could not login</span>
                <button id="btnLogin">Login</button>
            </div>
        </div>
    </div>
```

```
            <div class="loggedIn">
                <div id="LogOut">
                    <button id="btnLogout">Logout</button>
                </div>
            </div>
        </div>
    </body>
</html>
```

The HTML in Listing 10-98 shows the divs that are for the loggedIn and loggedOut states. The HTML and styling demonstrated in this chapter are simplified and not best practices, so we do not go into much detail for them.

Moving on to look at the .css classes in Listing 10-99, most of the styling is to set up the div containers for the various page functions. Both the loggedOut and loggedIn .css are set to display: none; this is done because a server-side loggedIn check in the JavaScript will set the correct state when the page loads.

Listing 10-99. Index.css

```css
div.loggedOut{
    display: none;
}
div.loggedIn{
    display: none;
}
div#mainContent{
    float: left;
}
div#userContent{
    float: left;
}
div#mainMessage h1{
    font-size: 72px;
}
span.error{
    color:red;
    display:none;
}
div#actionContent>div{
    border: 1px solid black;
    float:left;
}
div#actionContent div.loggedIn div{
    height: 220px;
}
div#actionContent div.loggedOut div{
    height: 300px;
}
div#actionContent div div{
    width: 200px;
    float: left;
    border-left: 1px solid black;
    border-right: 1px solid black;
}
```

```css
div#actionContent div div span{
    padding: 4px;
}
div#actionContent div div input{
    display: block;
    margin-left: 4px;
    margin-top: 4px;
}
div#actionContent div div button{
    display: block;
    margin-left: 4px;
    margin-top: 4px;
}
span.sectionTitle{
    font-size:larger;
}
```

For our client to work, there is a lot of JavaScript that has to be in place. Even for a simple page like the homepage, it will have many helper functions, JavaScript events, and Ajax calls.

The homepage JavaScript has three helper functions in Listing 10-100: showAsLoggedIn, showAsLoggedOut, and openCanvas. The first two methods change the .css to show the loggedIn or loggedOut view. The third method is called once a canvas ID has been returned from the server so that the canvas page can be loaded. To support mobile devices that don't allow pop-ups, we'll check the window width and height. If both the measurements are below the threshold, the script will redirect the page; otherwise, it will open a new window to the new canvas.

Listing 10-100. Index.JS Helper Functions

```javascript
function showAsLoggedIn() {
    $('div.loggedIn').show();
    $('div.loggedOut').hide();
}
function showAsLoggedOut() {
    $('div.loggedOut').show();
    $('div.loggedIn').hide();
}
function openCanvas(id) {
    var canvasURL = "/Content/Canvas.html?canvasId=" + id;
    if (window.innerWidth <= 800 && window.innerHeight <= 600) {
        window.location.href = canvasURL;
    }
    else {
        window.open(canvasURL, "_blank");
    }
}
```

The rest of the JavaScript logic for the homepage occurs once we determine the page is fully loaded by the $(document).ready handler being called, which lets us know it is safe to bind to the events. The only event that we are interested in is the click event, to which we'll add a handler for all the buttons on the page.

The buttons on the page are for logging in, creating an account, creating a canvas, and joining a canvas. There is an additional click handler added to every button to reset the error text .css in case it was displayed. Besides binding events in the ready method, we also do an Ajax call to determine whether the user is logged in, which occurs at the end of the ready function and can be seen at the end of Listing 10-106.

The first binding we'll look at is the login button in Listing 10-101. Whenever the login button is clicked, the values for the username and password input fields are added to a JSON object as UserName and Password, respectively. Next, an Ajax call is made to the server to try to log in with the values from the JSON object. If the Ajax call is successful and returns with "success", the logged-in status is shown. If the call is successful and does not have "success" or the call fails, the logged-out page will be shown.

Listing 10-101. Login Button Logic

```
$('#btnLogin').click(function () {
    var dataObject = { "UserName": $('form#loginForm input#username').val(), "Password":
    $('form#loginForm input#password').val() };
    $.ajax({
        url: '/public/api/login',
        type: 'post',
        contentType: "application/json",
        data: JSON.stringify(dataObject),
        success: function (data, status) {
            if (status == "success" && data == "Success") {
                showAsLoggedIn();
            }
            else {
                $('span#loginError').show();
            }
        },
        error: function (data) {
            $('span#loginError').show();
            showAsLoggedOut();
        }
    });
});
```

The next binding is the create account button in Listing 10-102. Whenever the button is clicked, the values for password and password verify input fields are compared. If they are not equal, and an error message is shown, the event is ended. If they are equal, the username and password input fields are added to a JSON object as UserName and Password, respectively. Next, an Ajax call is made to the server to create an account with the values from the JSON object. If the Ajax call is successful and returns with "success", the account creation was successful and the logged-in status is shown. If the call is successful and does not have "success" or the call fails, the logged-out page will be shown with an error message.

Listing 10-102. Create Account Button Logic

```
$('#btnCreateAccount').click(function () {
    $('span#passwordNotEqual').hide();
    if ($('div#createAccount input#password').val()
    != $('div#createAccount input#verifyPassword').val())
    {
        $('span#passwordNotEqual').show();
        return;
    }
    var dataObject = {
        "UserName": $('div#createAccount input#username').val(),
        "Password": $('div#createAccount input#password').val()
    };
```

```
$.ajax({
    url: '/public/api/user',
    type: 'post',
    contentType: "application/json",
    data: JSON.stringify(dataObject),
    success: function (data, status) {
        if (status == "success" && data == "Success") {
            showAsLoggedIn();
        }
        else
        {
            $('span#createAccountError').show();
        }
    },
    error: function (data) {
        showAsLoggedOut();
        $('span#createAccountError').show();
    }
});
});
```

Now for the create canvas button binding in Listing 10-103. Whenever the button is clicked, the canvas name and canvas description input fields are added to a JSON object as Name and Description, respectively. Next an Ajax call is made to the server to create a canvas with the values from the JSON object. If the Ajax call is successful and returns with "success", the canvas creation was successful and the openCanvas function is called to open the canvas room page. If the call is successful and does not have "success" or the call fails, an error message is shown.

Listing 10-103. Create Canvas Button Logic

```
$('#btnCreateCanvas').click(function () {
    var dataObject = {
        "Name": $('div#createCanvasContainer input#canvasname').val(),
        "Description": $('div#createCanvasContainer input#canvasdescription').val()
    };
    $.ajax({
        url: '/api/canvas',
        type: 'post',
        contentType: "application/json",
        data: JSON.stringify(dataObject),
        dataType: "Json",
        success: function (data, status) {
            if (status == "success" && data != undefined) {
                openCanvas(data)
            }
            else {
                $('span#createCanvasError').show();
            }
        },
        error: function (data) {
            $('span#createCanvasError').show();
        }
    });
});
```

Next is the join canvas button binding in Listing 10-104. Whenever the button is clicked, the canvas name input field is added to a JSON object as Name. Then an Ajax call is made to the server to join a canvas with the values from the JSON object. If the Ajax call is successful and returns with "success", joining the canvas was successful and the openCanvas function is called to open the canvas room page. If the call is successful and does not have "success" or the call fails, an error message is shown.

Listing 10-104. Join Canvas Button Logic

```
$('#btnJoinCanvas').click(function () {
    var dataObject = {
        "Name": $('div#joinCanvasContainer input#canvasname').val()
    };
    $.ajax({
        url: '/api/canvas',
        type: 'put',
        contentType: "application/json",
        data: JSON.stringify(dataObject),
        dataType: "Json",
        success: function (data, status) {
            if (status == "success" && data != undefined) {
                openCanvas(data)
            }
            else {
                $('span#joinCanvasError').show();
            }
        },
        error: function (data) {
            $('span#joinCanvasError').show();
        }
    });
});
```

The last button binding on the homepage is the logout button in Listing 10-105. Whenever the button is clicked, an Ajax call is made to the server to log out. If the Ajax call is successful, the logout page will be shown. Otherwise, there is no feedback if the call was unsuccessful.

Listing 10-105. Logout Button Logic

```
$('#btnLogout').click(function () {
    $.ajax({
        url: '/public/api/logout',
        type: 'post',
        success: function (data) {
            showAsLoggedOut();
        }
    });
});
```

Listing 10-106. Complete Index.JS File

```
function showAsLoggedIn() {
$('div.loggedIn').show();
    $('div.loggedOut').hide();
}
function showAsLoggedOut() {
    $('div.loggedOut').show();
    $('div.loggedIn').hide();
}
function openCanvas(id) {
    var canvasURL = "/Content/Canvas.html?canvasId=" + id;
    if (window.innerWidth <= 800 && window.innerHeight <= 600) {
        window.location.href = canvasURL;
    }
    else {
        window.open(canvasURL, "_blank");
    }
}
$(document).ready(function () {
    $('div#mainContent button').bind('click', function () { $('span.error').hide();})
    $('#btnLogin').click(function () {
        var dataObject = { "UserName": $('form#loginForm input#username').val(), "Password":
        $('form#loginForm input#password').val() };
        $.ajax({
            url: '/public/api/login',
            type: 'post',
            contentType: "application/json",
            data: JSON.stringify(dataObject),
            success: function (data, status) {
                if (status == "success" && data == "Success") {
                    showAsLoggedIn();
                }
                else {
                    $('span#loginError').show();
                }
            },
            error: function (data) {
                $('span#loginError').show();
                showAsLoggedOut();
            }
        });
    });
    $('#btnCreateAccount').click(function () {
        $('span#passwordNotEqual').hide();
        if ($('div#createAccount input#password').val()
        != $('div#createAccount input#verifyPassword').val())
```

```
            {
                $('span#passwordNotEqual').show();
                return;
            }
            var dataObject = {
                "UserName": $('div#createAccount input#username').val(),
                "Password": $('div#createAccount input#password').val()
            };
            $.ajax({
                url: '/public/api/user',
                type: 'post',
                contentType: "application/json",
                data: JSON.stringify(dataObject),
                success: function (data, status) {
                    if (status == "success" && data == "Success") {
                        showAsLoggedIn();
                    }
                    else
                    {
                        $('span#createAccountError').show();
                    }
                },
                error: function (data) {
                    showAsLoggedOut();
                    $('span#createAccountError').show();
                }
            });
        });
        $('#btnCreateCanvas').click(function () {
            var dataObject = {
                "Name": $('div#createCanvasContainer input#canvasname').val(),
                "Description": $('div#createCanvasContainer input#canvasdescription').val()
            };
            $.ajax({
                url: '/api/canvas',
                type: 'post',
                contentType: "application/json",
                data: JSON.stringify(dataObject),
                dataType: "Json",
                success: function (data, status) {
                    if (status == "success" && data != undefined) {
                        openCanvas(data)
                    }
                    else {
                        $('span#createCanvasError').show();
                    }
                },
                error: function (data) {
                    $('span#createCanvasError').show();
                }
            });
        });
```

```javascript
$('#btnJoinCanvas').click(function () {
    var dataObject = {
        "Name": $('div#joinCanvasContainer input#canvasname').val()
    };
    $.ajax({
        url: '/api/canvas',
        type: 'put',
        contentType: "application/json",
        data: JSON.stringify(dataObject),
        dataType: "Json",
        success: function (data, status) {
            if (status == "success" && data != undefined) {
                openCanvas(data)
            }
            else {
                $('span#joinCanvasError').show();
            }
        },
        error: function (data) {
            $('span#joinCanvasError').show();
        }
    });
});
$('#btnLogout').click(function () {
    $.ajax({
        url: '/public/api/logout',
        type: 'post',
        success: function (data) {
            showAsLoggedOut();
        }
    });
});
$.ajax({
    url: '/public/api/loginStatus',
    type: 'get',
    success: function (data,status,x) {
        if (status == "success" && data == "loggedIn") {
            showAsLoggedIn();
        }
        else {
            showAsLoggedOut();
        }
    },
    error: function (data) {
        $('div.loggedOut').show();
    },
    complete: function () {
        $('#loadingMessage').hide();
    }
});
});
```

Now that have gone over the homepage section, let's add the files to our project with the following steps:

1. Create an HTML page named index.html with the content of Listing 10-98 in the Content folder under the Public folder.

    a. Update the version numbers for the scripts to be the same as the version in the Scripts folder.

    b. Update the Copy To Output Directory property to Copy Always.

2. Create a .css page named index.css with the content of Listing 10-99 in the Styles folder under the Public folder.

    a. Update the Copy To Output Directory property to Copy Always.

3. Create a JavaScript page named index.js with the content of Listing 10-106 in the Scripts folder under the Public folder.

    a. Update the Copy To Output Directory property to Copy Always.

Next we will create the canvas room, in which real-time drawing and chat happens.

Developing the Client Canvas Room

The HTML for the canvas room is basically just the structure for demonstration purposes. Figure 10-16 shows that there is not much HTML in the room.

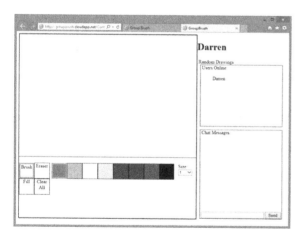

Figure 10-16. *Canvas page*

There are a couple of things to point out in the HTML, however: the stacked canvases, the status messaging, and data attributes on the brushes and colors. Listing 10-107 shows three canvases of the same size and position that have different z-indexes. We stack the canvases this way so that we can temporarily draw to these canvases and erase what is there without having to worry about redrawing what was on the canvas before. The other thing to look at in the bottom of the HTML in Listing 10-107 is the status messages that we display, depending on the connection state. The data attributes on the brushes and colors are used by the JavaScript to determine what brush to use and what color the brush should be.

Listing 10-107. Canvas.html

```html
<!DOCTYPE html>
<html xmlns="http://www.w3.org/1999/xhtml">
<head>
    <title>GroupBrush</title>
    <link rel="stylesheet" type="text/css" href="/styles/Canvas.css" />
    <script src="/public/scripts/jquery-1.6.4.min.js"></script>
    <script src="/public/scripts/jquery.signalr-2.0.3.min.js"></script>
    <script src="/signalr/hubs"></script>
    <script src="/scripts/canvas.js"></script>
</head>
<body>
    <div id="canvasContent" class="connectionContent">
        <div id="mainContent">
            <div id="canvasContainer">
                <div style="position:relative; width: 600px;height: 400px;">
                    <canvas width="600" height="400" id="scratchCanvas"
                    style="position:absolute; z-index: 3;"></canvas>
                    <canvas width="600" height="400" id="drawingCanvas"
                    style="position:absolute; z-index: 2;"></canvas>
                    <canvas width="600" height="400" id="cursorCanvas"
                    style="position: absolute; z-index: 1;"></canvas>
                </div>
            </div>
            <div id="toolboxContainer">
                <div class="brushes">
                    <div class="brush tool selected" data-brushtype="1">Brush</div>
                    <div class="brush tool" data-brushtype="2">Eraser</div>
                    <div class="brush tool" data-brushtype="3">Fill</div>
                    <div class="brush tool" data-brushtype="4">Clear All</div>
                </div>
                <div class="colors">
                    <div class="color tool selected" data-colorvalue="#FF0000" id="Red"> </div>
                    <div class="color tool" data-colorvalue="#FFA500" id="Orange"> </div>
                    <div class="color tool" data-colorvalue="#FFFF00" id="Yellow"> </div>
                    <div class="color tool" data-colorvalue="#00FF00" id="Green"> </div>
                    <div class="color tool" data-colorvalue="#0000FF" id="Blue"> </div>
                    <div class="color tool" data-colorvalue="#800080" id="Purple"> </div>
                    <div class="color tool" data-colorvalue="#A52A2A" id="Brown"> </div>
                    <div class="color tool" data-colorvalue="#000000" id="Black"> </div>
                </div>
                <div class="sizeContainer">
                    <span>Size:</span>
                    <select id="sizes">
                        <option value="1">1</option>
                        <option value="2">2</option>
                        <option value="4">4</option>
                        <option value="8">8</option>
                        <option value="16">16</option>
                        <option value="32">32</option>
                        <option value="64">64</option>
```

```
                            <option value="128">128</option>
                        </select>
                    </div>
                </div>
            </div>
            <div id="sideContent">
                <h1 id="CanvasName"></h1>
                <span id="CanvasDescription"></span>
                <div id="onlineUsersContainer">
                    <span>Users Online:</span>
                    <ul id="userList"></ul>
                </div>
                <div id="chatContainer">
                    <span>Chat Messages:</span>
                    <div id="chatMessagesContainer">
                        <ul id="chatMessages"></ul>
                    </div>
                    <div id="chatInputContainer">
                        <input type="text" id="chatInput" />
                        <button id="btnSendMessage">Send</button>
                    </div>
                </div>
            </div>
        </div>
        <div id="loadingCanvasContent" class="connectionContent">
            <span>Connecting...</span>
        </div>
        <div id="syncingCanvasContent" class="connectionContent">
            <span>Syncing...</span>
        </div>
        <div id="reloadCanvasContent" class="connectionContent">
            <span>Connection problems </span>
            <button id="btnReload">Reload</button>
        </div>

</body>
</html>
```

Once again, the `.css` for this project is very basic, and there really isn't much to the content in Listing 10-108 other than setting up the flow and containers of the page, brush colors, and status message display.

Listing 10-108. Canvas.css

```
div#mainContent{
    float: left;
    width: 600px;
    height: 600px;
    border: solid 2px black;
}
```

```css
div#sideContent{
    float: left;
    width: 300px;
    height: 600px;
}
div#canvasContainer{
    border-bottom: 1px solid black;
}
div#toolboxContainer{
    width: 600px;
    height: 100px;
    margin-top: 20px;
}
div#toolboxContainer{
    width: 600px;
    height: 100px;
}
div#toolboxContainer div.brushes {
    width: 110px;
    float: left;
}
div#toolboxContainer div.colors {
    width: 430px;
    float: left;
}
div#toolboxContainer div.colors div#Red {
    background-color: #FF0000;
}
div#toolboxContainer div.colors div#Orange {
    background-color: #FFA500;
}
div#toolboxContainer div.colors div#Yellow {
    background-color: #FFFF00;
}
div#toolboxContainer div.colors div#Green {
    background-color: #00FF00;
}
div#toolboxContainer div.colors div#Blue {
    background-color: #0000FF;
}
div#toolboxContainer div.colors div#Purple {
    background-color: #800080;
}
div#toolboxContainer div.colors div#Brown {
    background-color: #A52A2A;
}
div#toolboxContainer div.colors div#Black {
    background-color: #000000;
}
```

```css
div#toolboxContainer div.actions {
    width: 50px;
    float: left;
}
div#toolboxContainer div.tool {
    width: 50px;
    height: 50px;
    float: left;
    border: 1px solid black;
    text-align: center;
}
div#toolboxContainer div.selected {
    border: 5px solid #AAAAAA;
    width: 42px;
    height: 42px;
}
div#onlineUsersContainer{
    border: 1px solid black;
    margin: 0px 10px 10px 10px;
    height: 200px;
}
div#chatContainer{
    border: 1px solid black;
    margin: 10px;
    height: 290px;
    position: relative;
}
div#chatInputContainer{
    position:absolute;
    bottom: 0px;
}
div#sideContent ul li {
    list-style: none;
}
div#sideContent span{
    margin-left: 4px;
}
div#sideContent input{
    margin-left: 4px;
    width: 210px;
}
div#canvasContent{
    display:none;
}
div#syncingCanvasContent{
    display:none;
}
div#reloadCanvasContent{
    display:none;
}
```

```
body{
    touch-action:none;
}
canvas#scratchCanvas{
    -ms-user-select:none;
}
```

The code for the client is very complex, so we will break it down into smaller related functions. As with the HTML, the JavaScript is for example purposes only and may not be using best practices.

Listing 10-109 shows the variables for the canvas room. The first variable, hubProxy, is used to store the proxy to the SignalR hub. The next variable, userList, is an array that is used to store the users displayed in the user list. The lastCursorPositionTime variable marks the last time the current user's cursor was sent to the server. The lastDrawTime variable was the last time the draw positions were sent to the server. The lastSequence variable stores the latest draw sequence that has been received. The isBrushown and firstTouch variables keep track of whether a drag event is occurring. The brushPositions array stores the positions that need to be sent to the server. The otherBrushCursors array stores the username, position, and last update time of the other canvas room users' cursors. The isDrawingContinued variable is for the Canvas object to know whether it needs to move the position context before it should draw. Finally, the cleanUpCursorCanvasTimer variable stores the setTimeout handle so that it can be cancelled.

Listing 10-109. Canvas.js Variables

```
var hubProxy = null;
var userList = [];
var lastCursorPositionTime = 0;
var lastDrawTime = 0;
var lastSequence = 0;
var isBrushDown = false;
var firstTouch = null;
var brushPositions = [];
var otherBrushCursors = [];
var isDrawingContinued = false;
var cleanUpCursorCanvasTimer = null;
```

Besides variables for the canvas room, there are also "objects" that can be passed around the script. The first object shown in Listing 10-110 is the Position object, which stores the x and y coordinates of a position. The next object, OtherBrush, stores the brush (cursor) name, position, and last update time. The last object, CurrentBrushData, retrieves the current selected color, size, and type from the HTML DOM and is returned as an "object" that can be sent to the server.

Listing 10-110. Canvas.js Objects

```
function Position(x, y) {
    this.x = x;
    this.y = y;
}
function OtherBrush(userName, x, y) {
    this.UserName = userName;
    this.x = x;
    this.y = y;
    this.updateTime = Date.now();
}
```

```
function CurrentBrushData() {
    this.Color = $('div.color.tool.selected').data('colorvalue') || 1;
    this.Size = $('select#sizes').val() || 1;
    this.Type = $('div.brush.tool.selected').data('brushtype') || 1;
}
```

The next similar sets of logic are the helper methods shown in Listing 10-111. The getCanvasId method looks into the query string to find the canvas ID by looking for a query string key of 'canvasId'. If the canvas ID cannot be found in the query string, this function redirects the page back to the site root.

Listing 10-111. Canvas.js Helper Methods

```
function getCanvasId() {
    var canvasId = null;
    var queryString = window.location.search.substring(1);
    var queryStringArray = queryString.split('&');
    for (var x = 0; x < queryStringArray.length; x++) {
        var keyValue = queryStringArray[x].split('=');
        if (keyValue.length > 1) {
            var queryKey = keyValue[0];
            var queryValue = keyValue[1];
            if (queryKey == 'canvasId') {
                canvasId = queryStringArray[x];
            }
        }
    }
    if (canvasId == undefined || canvasId.length != 45) {
        window.location('/');
    }
    return canvasId;
}

function connectionChange(contentToShow) {
    $('div.connectionContent').hide();
    if (contentToShow != undefined)
        $(contentToShow).show();
}
$(document).ready(function () {
    $('div.color.tool').click(function () {
        $('div.color.tool').removeClass('selected');
        $(this).addClass('selected');
    });
    $('div.brush.tool').click(function () {
        $('div.brush.tool').removeClass('selected');
        $(this).addClass('selected');
    });
    $('div#reloadCanvasContent button#btnReload').click(function () {
        connect();
    });
    connect();
});
```

The connectionChange helper method is used whenever the viewing state of the canvas room needs to change. It hides all the major content div sections with a class name of 'connectionContent'. If it can find the content of the passed-in .css selector, it shows that content.

The last helper method is the ready function provided by JQuery when the document is fully loaded. We use this helper function to add a click binding for the color and brushes div containers that will change the selected color or brush. The helper also adds a click binding for the reload button that is displayed when the connection cannot connect. Finally, this function calls the connect method that connects the SignalR hub (discussed next).

The connect method is one of the most important methods of the canvas room script (see Listing 10-112). This method is responsible for connecting to the SignalR hub and binding all its events. If the hub connection is successful, this method binds the mouse and touch events for the canvas and synchronizes the canvas to the latest on the server.

Listing 10-112. Connect Method

```
function connect() {
    connectionChange('div#loadingCanvasContent');
    var canvasId = getCanvasId();
    var connection = $.hubConnection('/signalr', { qs: canvasId });
    hubProxy = connection.createHubProxy('CanvasHub');
    hubProxy.on('MoveOtherCursor', function (userName, x, y) {
        drawOtherBrush(userName, x, y)
    });
    hubProxy.on('UserChatMessage', function (message) {
        $('#chatMessages').append('<li>' + message + '</li>')
    });
    hubProxy.on('UserConnected', function (userName) {
        userConnected(userName);
    });
    hubProxy.on('UserDisconnected', function (userName) {
        userDisconnected(userName);
    });
    hubProxy.on('DrawCanvasBrushAction', function (canvasBrushAction) {
        drawCanvasBrushAction(canvasBrushAction);
    });
    connection.reconnecting(function () {
        connectionChange('div#loadingCanvasContent');
    });
    connection.reconnected(function () {
        syncRoom();
    });
    connection.disconnected(function () {
        connectionChange('div#reloadCanvasContent');
    });
    connection.start().done(function () {
        $('#btnSendMessage').click(function () {
            hubProxy.invoke('SendChatMessage', $('#chatInput').val()).done(function()
            {$('#chatInput').val('');});
        });
    });

    var canvasTouch = document.getElementById('scratchCanvas');
    canvasTouch.addEventListener('touchstart', touchStart, false);
    canvasTouch.addEventListener('touchmove', touchMove, false);
```

```
canvasTouch.addEventListener('touchend', touchEnd, false);
canvasTouch.addEventListener('touchleave', touchEnd, false);
canvasTouch.addEventListener('touchcancel', touchEnd, false);

if (window.navigator.msPointerEnabled) {
    canvasTouch.addEventListener('MSPointerDown', msTouchStart, false);
    canvasTouch.addEventListener('MSPointerMove', msTouchMove, false);
    canvasTouch.addEventListener('MSPointerUp', msTouchEnd, false);
}
else
{
    var canvas = $('#scratchCanvas');
    canvas.bind('mousemove', mouseMove);
    canvas.bind('mousedown', mouseDown);
    canvas.bind('mouseup', mouseUp);
}
syncRoom();
    });
}
```

For our application, there are two types of drawing that occur based on other users' events: drawing the other users' cursor and drawing their brush actions.

Drawing the other users' cursors occurs when the server calls the drawOtherBrush method. This method stores the brush (cursor) position in an array based on username. The event then calls the drawAllBrushes method, which cancels any pending cleanup timers.

The method clears the canvas that the cursors are drawn on to and then loops through the array of users' cursors, drawing any that been updated within the last second. If any cursors were drawn, this method creates a timer that will fire in one-half second to call the drawAllBrushes methods to repeat the process.

The second event is to draw the other users' brush actions (see Listing 10-133). This event is also triggered by the server when it calls the drawCanvasBrushAction method, which stores the latest drawing sequence and draws the passed-in canvasBrushAction. If the canvasBrushAction type is 1 or 2, it draws or erases, respectively, at the positions defined. If the canvasBrushAction type is 3 or 4, it fills or clears the whole canvas, respectively.

Listing 10-113. Drawing Other Brushes Methods

```
function drawOtherBrush(userName, x, y) {
    otherBrushCursors[userName] = new OtherBrush(userName, x, y);
    drawAllBrushes();
}
function drawAllBrushes()
{
    if (cleanUpCursorCanvasTimer != null) clearTimeout(cleanUpCursorCanvasTimer);
    var dirtyCanvas = false;
    var c = document.getElementById("cursorCanvas");
    var ctx = c.getContext("2d");
    ctx.fillStyle = "#000000";
    ctx.clearRect(0, 0, 600, 400);
    for (var key in otherBrushCursors) {
        var currentBrush = otherBrushCursors[key];
```

```
        if (Date.now() - currentBrush.updateTime < 1000) {
            dirtyCanvas = true;
            ctx.fillRect(currentBrush.x - 5, currentBrush.y - 5, 10, 10);
            ctx.fillText(currentBrush.UserName, currentBrush.x + 10, currentBrush.y);
        }
    }
    if(dirtyCanvas) cleanUpCursorCanvasTimer = setTimeout(function () { drawAllBrushes(); }, 500);
}
function drawCanvasBrushAction(canvasBrushAction) {
    var c = document.getElementById('drawingCanvas');
    var ctx = c.getContext("2d");
    ctx.beginPath();
    lastSequence = canvasBrushAction.Sequence;
    if (canvasBrushAction.Type == 1 || canvasBrushAction.Type == 2) {
        var brushActionSize = canvasBrushAction.Size;
        ctx.strokeStyle = canvasBrushAction.Color;
        ctx.lineWidth = brushActionSize;
        if (canvasBrushAction.BrushPositions.length > 0) {
            ctx.moveTo(canvasBrushAction.BrushPositions[0].X, canvasBrushAction.BrushPositions[0].Y);
        }
        for (var x = 0; x < canvasBrushAction.BrushPositions.length; x++) {
            var position = canvasBrushAction.BrushPositions[x];
            ctx.lineTo(position.X, position.Y);
            if (canvasBrushAction.Type == 1)
                ctx.stroke();
            else if(canvasBrushAction.Type == 2)
                ctx.clearRect(position.X, position.Y, brushActionSize, brushActionSize)
        }
    }
    else if (canvasBrushAction.Type == 3) {
        ctx.fillStyle = canvasBrushAction.Color;
        ctx.fillRect(0, 0, 600, 400);
    }
    else if (canvasBrushAction.Type == 4) {
        ctx.clearRect(0, 0, 600, 400);
    }
    ctx.closePath();
}
```

The userConnected and userDisconnected methods in Listing 10-114 are called from the SignalR hub whenever a user is connected or disconnected. When this occurs, the user is added or removed from the in-memory list of users. This list of users is then redrawn with the drawUserList method.

Listing 10-114. User Connection Methods

```
function userConnected(userName) {
    var alreadyExists = false;
    for (var x = 0; x < userList.length; x++) {
        if (userList[x] == userName) {
            alreadyExists = true;
            break;
        }
    }
    if(!alreadyExists)   userList.push(userName);
    drawUserList();
}
function userDisconnected(userName) {
    for (var x = userList.length - 1; x > -1; x--) {
        if (userList[x] == userName) {
            userList.splice(x, 1);
        }
    }
    drawUserList();
}
function drawUserList() {
    var userListHTML = [];
    for (var x = 0; x < userList.length; x++) {
        userListHTML.push('<li>');
        userListHTML.push(userList[x]);
        userListHTML.push('</li>');
    }
    $('#userList').html(userListHTML.join(''));
}
```

For the canvas room, one of the critical functions is to be able to draw. The drawing methods shown in Listing 10-115 handle the generic input, logging of the drawing, and actual drawing to the canvas objects.

Listing 10-115. Drawing Methods

```
function canvasBrushMove(position) {
    if (isBrushDown) {
        storeDrawCoordinates(position);
    }
    if (Date.now() - lastCursorPositionTime > 100) {
        lastCursorPositionTime = Date.now()
        hubProxy.invoke('MoveCursor', position.x, position.y);
    }
}
function canvasBrushDown(position) {
    isBrushDown = true;
    storeDrawCoordinates(position);
    return true;
}
function canvasBrushUp(position) {
    isBrushDown = false;
    storeDrawCoordinates(position);
```

```
        sendBrushData(brushPositions);
        brushPositions = [];
        isDrawingContinued = false;
        var c = document.getElementById("scratchCanvas");
        var ctx = c.getContext("2d");
        ctx.closePath();
        ctx.clearRect(0, 0, 600, 400);
}
function sendBrushData(brushPositionsData)
{
        var currentBrushData = new CurrentBrushData();
        var brushData = {
            BrushPositions: brushPositionsData,
            ClientSequenceId: Date.now(),
            Color: currentBrushData.Color,
            Size: currentBrushData.Size,
            Type: currentBrushData.Type
        }
        hubProxy.invoke('SendDrawCommand', brushData).fail(function (error) {
        });
}
function storeDrawCoordinates(position) {
        var c = document.getElementById("scratchCanvas");
        var ctx = c.getContext("2d");
        var allowChange = false;
        if (brushPositions.length > 0)
        {
            var lastPosition = brushPositions[brushPositions.length - 1];
            if (Math.abs(lastPosition.x - position.x) >= 1 || Math.abs(lastPosition.y - position.y)
             >= 1) allowChange = true;
        }
        else {
            allowChange = true;
        }
        if (!isDrawingContinued) {
            ctx.beginPath();
            isDrawingContinued = true;
            ctx.moveTo(position.x, position.y);
        }
        var currentBrushData = new CurrentBrushData();
        ctx.strokeStyle = currentBrushData.Color;
        ctx.lineWidth = currentBrushData.Size;
        ctx.lineTo(position.x, position.y);
        ctx.stroke();
        brushPositions.push(position);
        if (Date.now() - lastDrawTime > 50) {
            lastDrawTime = Date.now();
            var tempPositions = brushPositions.splice(0);
            brushPositions.push(position);
            sendBrushData(tempPositions);
        }
```

For the drawing to occur, we need to handle the input when the brush is brought down, is moved, or is brought up. When the brush is brought down, it triggers the canvasBrushDown method. We set a variable that a drag is occurring and store the position of the brush.

The next input is triggered when the brush is moved, which calls the canvasBrushMove method. If the brush is part of a drag, the coordinates are stored. If the time since the last brush positions sent to the server is more than 50 milliseconds, the unsent brush positions are then sent to the server.

The last input is when the brush is brought up, which triggers the canvasBrushUp method. This method stops the drag, stores the brush's position, sends the brush data to the server, clears the brush positions array, and clears the canvas surface that was recording the brush's position.

In the various input methods, the brush position was being stored by the storeDrawCoordinates method. In this method, the position of the brush is drawn to a canvas. The brush positions are then stored in an array. Every so often, these positions are cleared from the array and sent to the server using the sendBrushData method.

The sendBrushData method is the method that gets the current brush size, color, and type. It combines them with the passed-in brush positions and the current time in a numeric format. It then takes this data and sends it to the hub by calling the SendDrawCommand server-side method.

Because the application is critically dependent on the input methods for it to work, we support both mouse and touch movements. As shown previously, there are generic methods for brush down, move, and up. Listing 10-116 shows three methods for mouse, touch for Microsoft-based browsers, and touch for non-Microsoft-based browsers.

Listing 10-116. User Input Capture Methods

```
function getDrawPosition(e) {
    var canvasRect = document.getElementById('scratchCanvas').getBoundingClientRect();
    var xPos = e.clientX - canvasRect.left;
    var yPos = e.clientY - canvasRect.top;
    return new Position(xPos, yPos);
}
function mouseMove(e) {
    canvasBrushMove(getDrawPosition(e));
}
function mouseDown(e) {
    canvasBrushDown(getDrawPosition(e));
}
function mouseUp(e) {
    canvasBrushUp(getDrawPosition(e));
}
function msTouchStart(e) {
    e.preventDefault();
    if (firstTouch == null && e.buttons == 1) {
        firstTouch = e.pointerId;
        canvasBrushDown(new Position(e.clientX, e.clientY));
    }
}
function msTouchMove(e) {
    e.preventDefault();
    if (firstTouch == e.pointerId) {
        canvasBrushMove(new Position(e.clientX, e.clientY));
    }
}
function msTouchEnd(e) {
    e.preventDefault();
```

```
        if(e.buttons == 0 && firstTouch == e.pointerId){
            canvasBrushUp(new Position(e.clientX, e.clientY));
            firstTouch = null;
        }
    }
}
function touchStart(e) {
    e.preventDefault();
    if (firstTouch == null && e.changedTouches.length > 0) {
        var touchData = e.changedTouches[0];
        firstTouch = touchData.identifier;
        canvasBrushDown(new Position(touchData.pageX, touchData.pageY));
    }
}
function touchMove(e) {
    e.preventDefault();
    for (var t = 0; t < e.changedTouches.length; t++) {
        if (e.changedTouches[t].identifier == firstTouch) {
            var touchData = e.changedTouches[t];
            canvasBrushMove(new Position(touchData.pageX, touchData.pageY));
        }
    }
}
function touchEnd(e) {
    e.preventDefault();
    for (var t = 0; t < e.changedTouches.length; t++) {
        if (e.changedTouches[t].identifier == firstTouch) {
            firstTouch = null;
            var touchData = e.changedTouches[t];
            canvasBrushUp(new Position(touchData.pageX, touchData.pageY));
        }
    }
}
```

The methods are pretty self-explanatory, but note that the mouse methods determine the position in reference to the canvas, and the touch methods are set up to handle the touch pointer one at a time.

Whenever a canvas is first connected or reconnected, the code calls the syncRoom function to synchronize the canvas to what is latest on the server. It can synchronize by calling the SyncToRoom server-side hub method with the last known canvas sequence (see Listing 10-117). If this method returns successfully, it updates the users list and completes any brush actions. If the method fails, it changes the page state to the reload content.

Listing 10-117. Canvas Sync Method

```
function syncRoom() {
    connectionChange('div#syncingCanvasContent');
    hubProxy.invoke('SyncToRoom', lastSequence).done(function (canvasSnapShot) {
        userList = [];
        $.each(canvasSnapShot.Users, function () {
            userConnected(this);
        });
        $.each(canvasSnapShot.Actions, function () {
            drawCanvasBrushAction(this);
        });
```

```
        $('h1#CanvasName').html(canvasSnapShot.CanvasName);
        $('span#CanvasDescription').html(canvasSnapShot.CanvasDescription);
        connectionChange('div#canvasContent');
    }).fail(function () {
        connectionChange('div#reloadCanvasContent');
    });
}
```

Listing 10-118 gives the complete code for Canvas.js.

Listing 10-118. Complete Canvas.js

```
var hubProxy = null;
var userList = [];
var lastCursorPositionTime = 0;
var lastDrawTime = 0;
var lastSequence = 0;
var isBrushDown = false;
var firstTouch = null;
var brushPositions = [];
var otherBrushCursors = [];
var isDrawingContinued = false;
var cleanUpCursorCanvasTimer = null;

function Position(x, y) {
    this.x = x;
    this.y = y;
}
function OtherBrush(userName, x, y) {
    this.UserName = userName;
    this.x = x;
    this.y = y;
    this.updateTime = Date.now();
}
function CurrentBrushData() {
    this.Color = $('div.color.tool.selected').data('colorvalue') || 1;
    this.Size = $('select#sizes').val() || 1;
    this.Type = $('div.brush.tool.selected').data('brushtype') || 1;
}

function getCanvasId() {
    var canvasId = null;
    var queryString = window.location.search.substring(1);
    var queryStringArray = queryString.split('&');
    for (var x = 0; x < queryStringArray.length; x++) {
        var keyValue = queryStringArray[x].split('=');
        if (keyValue.length > 1) {
            var queryKey = keyValue[0];
            var queryValue = keyValue[1];
            if (queryKey == 'canvasId') {
                canvasId = queryStringArray[x];
            }
```

```
        }
    }
    if (canvasId == undefined || canvasId.length != 45) {
        window.location('/');
    }
    return canvasId;
}
function connectionChange(contentToShow) {

    $('div.connectionContent').hide();
    if (contentToShow != undefined)
        $(contentToShow).show();
}
$(document).ready(function () {
    $('div.color.tool').click(function () {
        $('div.color.tool').removeClass('selected');
        $(this).addClass('selected');
    });
    $('div.brush.tool').click(function () {
        $('div.brush.tool').removeClass('selected');
        $(this).addClass('selected');
    });
    $('div#reloadCanvasContent button#btnReload').click(function () {
        connect();
    });
    connect();
});

function connect() {
    connectionChange('div#loadingCanvasContent');
    var canvasId = getCanvasId();
    var connection = $.hubConnection('/signalr', { qs: canvasId });
    hubProxy = connection.createHubProxy('CanvasHub');
    hubProxy.on('MoveOtherCursor', function (userName, x, y) {
        drawOtherBrush(userName, x, y)
    });
    hubProxy.on('UserChatMessage', function (message) {
        $('#chatMessages').append('<li>' + message + '</li>')
    });
    hubProxy.on('UserConnected', function (userName) {
        userConnected(userName);
    });
    hubProxy.on('UserDisconnected', function (userName) {
        userDisconnected(userName);
    });
    hubProxy.on('DrawCanvasBrushAction', function (canvasBrushAction) {
        drawCanvasBrushAction(canvasBrushAction);
    });
    connection.reconnecting(function () {
        connectionChange('div#loadingCanvasContent');
    });
```

```
        connection.reconnected(function () {
            syncRoom();
        });
        connection.disconnected(function () {
            connectionChange('div#reloadCanvasContent');
        });
        connection.start().done(function () {
            $('#btnSendMessage').click(function () {
                hubProxy.invoke('SendChatMessage', $('#chatInput').val()).done(function()
                {$('#chatInput').val('');});
            });

            var canvasTouch = document.getElementById('scratchCanvas');
            canvasTouch.addEventListener('touchstart', touchStart, false);
            canvasTouch.addEventListener('touchmove', touchMove, false);
            canvasTouch.addEventListener('touchend', touchEnd, false);
            canvasTouch.addEventListener('touchleave', touchEnd, false);
            canvasTouch.addEventListener('touchcancel', touchEnd, false);

            if (window.navigator.msPointerEnabled) {
                canvasTouch.addEventListener('MSPointerDown', msTouchStart, false);
                canvasTouch.addEventListener('MSPointerMove', msTouchMove, false);
                canvasTouch.addEventListener('MSPointerUp', msTouchEnd, false);
            }
            else
            {
                var canvas = $('#scratchCanvas');
                canvas.bind('mousemove', mouseMove);
                canvas.bind('mousedown', mouseDown);
                canvas.bind('mouseup', mouseUp);
            }
            syncRoom();
        });
}

function syncRoom() {
    connectionChange('div#syncingCanvasContent');
    hubProxy.invoke('SyncToRoom', lastSequence).done(function (canvasSnapShot) {
        userList = [];
        $.each(canvasSnapShot.Users, function () {
            userConnected(this);
        });
        $.each(canvasSnapShot.Actions, function () {
            drawCanvasBrushAction(this);
        });
        $('h1#CanvasName').html(canvasSnapShot.CanvasName);
        $('span#CanvasDescription').html(canvasSnapShot.CanvasDescription);
        connectionChange('div#canvasContent');
    }).fail(function () {
        connectionChange('div#reloadCanvasContent');
    });
}
```

```
function drawOtherBrush(userName, x, y) {
    otherBrushCursors[userName] = new OtherBrush(userName, x, y);
    drawAllBrushes();
}
function drawAllBrushes()
{
    if (cleanUpCursorCanvasTimer != null) clearTimeout(cleanUpCursorCanvasTimer);
    var dirtyCanvas = false;
    var c = document.getElementById("cursorCanvas");
    var ctx = c.getContext("2d");
    ctx.fillStyle = "#000000";
    ctx.clearRect(0, 0, 600, 400);
    for (var key in otherBrushCursors) {
        var currentBrush = otherBrushCursors[key];
        if (Date.now() - currentBrush.updateTime < 1000) {
            dirtyCanvas = true;
            ctx.fillRect(currentBrush.x - 5, currentBrush.y - 5, 10, 10);
            ctx.fillText(currentBrush.UserName, currentBrush.x + 10, currentBrush.y);
        }
    }
    if(dirtyCanvas) cleanUpCursorCanvasTimer = setTimeout(function () { drawAllBrushes(); }, 500);
}
function drawCanvasBrushAction(canvasBrushAction) {
    var c = document.getElementById('drawingCanvas');
    var ctx = c.getContext("2d");
    ctx.beginPath();
    lastSequence = canvasBrushAction.Sequence;
    if (canvasBrushAction.Type == 1 || canvasBrushAction.Type == 2) {
        var brushActionSize = canvasBrushAction.Size;
        ctx.strokeStyle = canvasBrushAction.Color;
        ctx.lineWidth = brushActionSize;
        if (canvasBrushAction.BrushPositions.length > 0) {
            ctx.moveTo(canvasBrushAction.BrushPositions[0].X, canvasBrushAction.
            BrushPositions[0].Y);
        }
        for (var x = 0; x < canvasBrushAction.BrushPositions.length; x++) {
            var position = canvasBrushAction.BrushPositions[x];
            ctx.lineTo(position.X, position.Y);
            if (canvasBrushAction.Type == 1)
                ctx.stroke();
            else if(canvasBrushAction.Type == 2)
                ctx.clearRect(position.X, position.Y, brushActionSize, brushActionSize)
        }
    }
    else if (canvasBrushAction.Type == 3) {
        ctx.fillStyle = canvasBrushAction.Color;
        ctx.fillRect(0, 0, 600, 400);
    }
    else if (canvasBrushAction.Type == 4) {
        ctx.clearRect(0, 0, 600, 400);
    }
    ctx.closePath();
}
```

```
function getDrawPosition(e) {
    var canvasRect = document.getElementById('scratchCanvas').getBoundingClientRect();
    var xPos = e.clientX - canvasRect.left;
    var yPos = e.clientY - canvasRect.top;
    return new Position(xPos, yPos);
}
function mouseMove(e) {
    canvasBrushMove(getDrawPosition(e));
}
function mouseDown(e) {
    canvasBrushDown(getDrawPosition(e));
}
function mouseUp(e) {
    canvasBrushUp(getDrawPosition(e));
}
function msTouchStart(e) {
    e.preventDefault();
    if (firstTouch == null && e.buttons == 1) {
        firstTouch = e.pointerId;
        canvasBrushDown(new Position(e.clientX, e.clientY));
    }
}
function msTouchMove(e) {
    e.preventDefault();
    if (firstTouch == e.pointerId) {
        canvasBrushMove(new Position(e.clientX, e.clientY));
    }
}
function msTouchEnd(e) {
    e.preventDefault();
    if(e.buttons == 0 && firstTouch == e.pointerId){
        canvasBrushUp(new Position(e.clientX, e.clientY));
        firstTouch = null;
    }
}
function touchStart(e) {
    e.preventDefault();
    if (firstTouch == null && e.changedTouches.length > 0) {
        var touchData = e.changedTouches[0];
        firstTouch = touchData.identifier;
        canvasBrushDown(new Position(touchData.pageX, touchData.pageY));
    }
}
function touchMove(e) {
    e.preventDefault();
    for (var t = 0; t < e.changedTouches.length; t++) {
        if (e.changedTouches[t].identifier == firstTouch) {
            var touchData = e.changedTouches[t];
            canvasBrushMove(new Position(touchData.pageX, touchData.pageY));
        }
    }
}
```

```javascript
function touchEnd(e) {
    e.preventDefault();
    for (var t = 0; t < e.changedTouches.length; t++) {
        if (e.changedTouches[t].identifier == firstTouch) {
            firstTouch = null;
            var touchData = e.changedTouches[t];
            canvasBrushUp(new Position(touchData.pageX, touchData.pageY));
        }
    }
}
function canvasBrushMove(position) {
    if (isBrushDown) {
        storeDrawCoordinates(position);
    }
    if (Date.now() - lastCursorPositionTime > 100) {
        lastCursorPositionTime = Date.now()
        hubProxy.invoke('MoveCursor', position.x, position.y);
    }
}
function canvasBrushDown(position) {
    isBrushDown = true;
    storeDrawCoordinates(position);
    return true;
}
function canvasBrushUp(position) {
    isBrushDown = false;
    storeDrawCoordinates(position);

    sendBrushData(brushPositions);
    brushPositions = [];
    isDrawingContinued = false;
    var c = document.getElementById("scratchCanvas");
    var ctx = c.getContext("2d");
    ctx.closePath();
    ctx.clearRect(0, 0, 600, 400);
}
function sendBrushData(brushPositionsData)
{
    var currentBrushData = new CurrentBrushData();
    var brushData = {
        BrushPositions: brushPositionsData,
        ClientSequenceId: Date.now(),
        Color: currentBrushData.Color,
        Size: currentBrushData.Size,
        Type: currentBrushData.Type
    }
    hubProxy.invoke('SendDrawCommand', brushData).fail(function (error) {
    });
}
```

```javascript
function storeDrawCoordinates(position) {
    var c = document.getElementById("scratchCanvas");
    var ctx = c.getContext("2d");
    var allowChange = false;
    if (brushPositions.length > 0)
    {
        var lastPosition = brushPositions[brushPositions.length - 1];
        if (Math.abs(lastPosition.x - position.x) >= 1 || Math.abs(lastPosition.y - position.y)
        >= 1) allowChange = true;
    }
    else {
        allowChange = true;
    }
    if (!isDrawingContinued) {
        ctx.beginPath();
        isDrawingContinued = true;
        ctx.moveTo(position.x, position.y);
    }
    var currentBrushData = new CurrentBrushData();
    ctx.strokeStyle = currentBrushData.Color;
    ctx.lineWidth = currentBrushData.Size;
    ctx.lineTo(position.x, position.y);
    ctx.stroke();
    brushPositions.push(position);
    if (Date.now() - lastDrawTime > 50) {
        lastDrawTime = Date.now();
        var tempPositions = brushPositions.splice(0);
        brushPositions.push(position);
        sendBrushData(tempPositions);
    }

}
function userConnected(userName) {
    var alreadyExists = false;
    for (var x = 0; x < userList.length; x++) {
        if (userList[x] == userName) {
            alreadyExists = true;
            break;
        }
    }
    if(!alreadyExists)    userList.push(userName);
    drawUserList();
}
function userDisconnected(userName) {
    for (var x = userList.length - 1; x > -1; x--) {
        if (userList[x] == userName) {
            userList.splice(x, 1);
        }
    }
    drawUserList();
}
```

```
function drawUserList() {
    var userListHTML = [];
    for (var x = 0; x < userList.length; x++) {
        userListHTML.push('<li>');
        userListHTML.push(userList[x]);
        userListHTML.push('</li>');
    }
    $('#userList').html(userListHTML.join(''));
}
```

Now that we have gone over all the canvas room logic, let's add it to the project with the following steps:

1. Add an HTML file called Canvas.html with the contents of Listing 10-107 in the Content folder of the GroupBrush.Web project.

    a. Update the version numbers for the scripts to be the same as the version in the Scripts folder.

    b. Update the Copy To Output Directory property to Copy Always.

2. Add a .css file called Canvas.css with the contents of Listing 10-108 in the Styles folder of the GroupBrush.Web project.

    a. Update the Copy To Output Directory property to Copy Always.

3. Add a JavaScript file called Canvas.js with the contents of Listing 10-118 in the Scripts folder of the GroupBrush.Web project.

    a. Update the Copy To Output Directory property to Copy Always.

4. Move all jQuery files in the Scripts directory to the Scripts directory in the Public directory.

    a. Update the Copy To Output Directory property to Copy Always.

6. Right-click the GroupBrush.Cloud project and click Publish (see Figure 10-17).

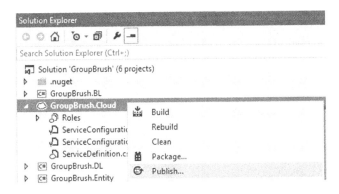

Figure 10-17. *Cloud Service context menu*

7. Validate the settings in the Publish summary dialog box (similar to Figure 10-18).

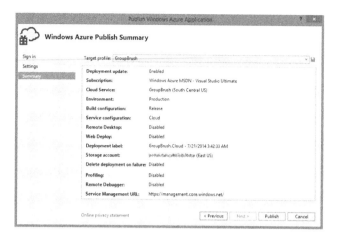

Figure 10-18. *Publish summary dialog box*

8. Click Publish.

We have now successfully deployed the completed project. Try it out! Figure 10-19 shows an example of the application in action.

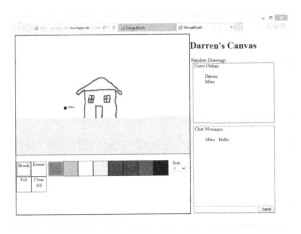

Figure 10-19. *Canvas page*

This example shows only one client, the JavaScript client. There are many more clients that are possible to add using the existing server structure that we have already created.

Summary

We have created an application that allows us to draw and message collaboratively in real time. The application is also secured with authentication. The application has the capability to scale as needed without much work after we add the needed code to scale. Finally, we can support a variety of clients with the server we created.

We hope you have enjoyed reading the book and now have a solid understanding of SignalR. We wish you the best of luck in your future SignalR projects.

Index

C

Get the eBook for only $10!

Now you can take the weightless companion with you anywhere, anytime. Your purchase of this book entitles you to 3 electronic versions for only $10.

This Apress title will prove so indispensible that you'll want to carry it with you everywhere, which is why we are offering the eBook in 3 formats for only $10 if you have already purchased the print book.

Convenient and fully searchable, the PDF version enables you to easily find and copy code—or perform examples by quickly toggling between instructions and applications. The MOBI format is ideal for your Kindle, while the ePUB can be utilized on a variety of mobile devices.

Go to www.apress.com/promo/tendollars to purchase your companion eBook.